Skills for Preschool Teachers

Third Edition

Janice J. Beaty

Elmira College

MERRILL PUBLISHING COMPANY
A Bell & Howell Information Company
Columbus   Toronto   London   Melbourne

Cover Photo: © Merrill/Lloyd Lemmermann

Published by Merrill Publishing Company
A Bell & Howell Information Company
Columbus, Ohio 43216

This book was set in Serifa Light

Administrative Editor: Jeff Johnston
Production Editor: Linda Hillis Bayma
Cover Designer: Cathy Watterson
Text Designer: Cynthia Brunk

Photo Credits: Janice Beaty, pp. 45, 77, 146, 188, 220, 224, 236, 250, 268, 280; Paul Conklin,
p. 172; Janet Gagnon, p. 193; Merrill Publishing, pp. 42, 56, 212, Ben Chandler, pp. 33, 108,
177, Bruce Johnson, pp. 84, 92, 121, Lloyd Lemmermann, pp. 26, 130, and Charles Wolfgang,
p. 204.

Library of Congress Catalog Card Number: 87-61081
International Standard Book Number: 0-675-20803-3
Printed in the United States of America
1 2 3 4 5 6 7 8 9—93 92 91 90 89 88

In memory of a special teacher and friend
Kathryn L. Jenkins

Janice J. Beaty, associate professor in Human Services at Elmira College, Elmira, New York, is director of the Human Services Program as well as project manager of the Head Start CDA Training Program. Dr. Beaty teaches undergraduate and graduate courses in early childhood education and children's literature. She is an author of children's books (*Nufu and the Turkeyfish; Plants in His Pack; Seeker of Seaways; Guam Today and Yesterday*) as well as teacher-training textbooks (*Observing Development of the Young Child; The Computer as a Paintbrush*). Dr. Beaty has developed training materials and films for the Child Development Associate program and has traveled around the country to make presentations at CDA Training Institutes and workshops. Her interest in people of other cultures has lured her to such diverse locations as the island of Guam in the western Pacific and San Salvador Island in the Bahamas. Her present studies focus on young children's learning through self-discovery with materials in their environment.

PREFACE

This introductory text presents and discusses basic classroom skills for preschool teachers. It is designed for use by college students preparing to be teachers in nursery schools, day care centers, Head Start, prekindergarten, and kindergarten programs. It is also useful for inservice teachers and aides who are updating their skills or preparing for the national Child Development Associate (CDA) assessment.

The skills for working with three- to five-year-old children in a classroom setting are presented in thirteen chapters. Each chapter is a self-contained learning module with objectives, text, learning activities, question sheets, lists of supplementary texts and film resources, and an evaluation sheet. Students may progress through each chapter at their own pace. To gain the greatest value from this program, the student should be in a position to apply the ideas in the text in an early childhood classroom. Many college programs place their students in a nursery school setting for several mornings a week so they may accomplish the prescribed learning activities with young children.

College programs that use this text as background material for a practicum experience often expect students to complete three to four of the chapters in one semester. To determine which chapters a student should work on, some programs perform an initial assessment as the student works in an early childhood classroom; the instructor uses the Teacher Skills Checklist as an observation tool.

The student is also asked to complete a self-evaluation with the Checklist, as described in "Initial Assessment." The observer and the student then meet to compare Checklist results and decide on which of the thirteen areas the student needs to concentrate.

The other checklists—The Activity Area Checklist, Large Motor Checklist, Small Motor Checklist, Language Assessment Checklist, Book Selection Checklist, Self-Concept Checklist, and Child Involvement Checklist—are useful inservice observation tools.

The thirteen chapters of the text are arranged in the same order as the skills in the Teacher Skills Checklist. Each chapter provides theoretical background on the particular skill as well as ideas for practical application in working with young children and their families.

New Features in the Third Edition

The Teacher Skills Checklist has been expanded to include a page for each of the thirteen skill areas with space provided for recording documentation of the skill indicators, as well as space to record the strengths and needs of the student. Use of this teacher observation tool is discussed in detail in "Initial Assessment."

Each chapter now includes information and activities for supporting children with special needs. Other new or expanded topics include personal safety, abused children, using the Activity Area Checklist, using a computer, making plans for individual children, parents as classroom volunteers, respecting parents' views when they differ from yours, and an expanded discussion of what it means to be an early childhood professional. Each chapter concludes with a summary of the information presented, thus giving the reader an overview of its contents.

Suggested Readings at the end of each chapter feature the most recent early childhood publications on each topic.

Use as a Companion Text

This third edition of *Skills for Preschool Teachers* is designed to be used as a companion volume with the author's text *Observing Development of the Young Child* (Merrill, 1986). While *Skills for Preschool Teachers* is intended as a teacher development textbook, the companion volume *Observing Development of the Young Child* is a child development book, focusing on six major areas of development: emotional, social, motor, cognitive, language, and creative.

Like this text, *Observing Development of the Young Child* is based on an observational checklist, the Child Skills Checklist, with each major item of the Checklist represented by a chapter in the book: Self-Identity; Emotional Development; Social Play; Prosocial Behavior; Large Motor Development; Small Motor Development; Cognitive Development: Classification and Seriation; Cognitive Development: Number, Time, Space, Memory; Spoken Language; Written Language; Art Skills; and Imagination.

Ideas and activities are presented to promote child development in each of the child skill areas. Important features of the text include methods for observing child development, planning for individual children based on Checklist results, descriptions of children's books to promote development in each of the areas, new information on the development of human emotions, a discussion of moral development, and a chapter on "emergent writing" in young children.

Students and teachers are encouraged to obtain a copy of *Observing Development of the Young Child* to be used in conjunction with the third edition of *Skills for Preschool Teachers*.

Acknowledgments

Many thanks to Bonny Helm, Elmira College CDA Field Supervisor, who read the manuscript and suggested appropriate changes and additions; to Mary Maples, Elmira College CDA Field Supervisor, who also gave valuable suggestions; and to the many trainers, students, education coordinators, college instructors, and people in the field who have used the text and offered their constructive criticism for this revised edition.

      I also wish to thank the reviewers for their helpful comments and suggestions—Kathleen Buss, University of Wisconsin at Stevens Point; Clifford C. Brooks, Bowling Green State University; Mary L. Patrick, Yakima Valley Community College; and Deborah J. Smith, University of Southern Mississippi.

Janice J. Beaty

CONTENTS

CHECKLISTS

Introduction

THE SELF-TAUGHT MODULE APPROACH

The book introduces a new approach to training teachers and aides in early childhood classroom skills: the self-taught module training program. It is based on the premise that students learn more effectively when they become deeply involved in their own instruction. The self-taught module approach allows the student to help determine his or her own needs, to participate in selecting a trainer, to assist in setting up a training prescription, to work at his or her own pace in an early childhood setting, and finally, to help determine when the objectives have been accomplished and the training finished.

Children in the preschool classroom also strive to become independent and self-directed in their learning. Thus it is appropriate that their teachers and aides develop classroom skills to assist the children toward this end through the teachers' own self-taught training.

The self-taught approach is also based on the premise that training in classroom skills, to be effective, should be individualized. The program contains thirteen module chapters that can be prescribed separately, or in any combination or sequence, to meet the individual's training needs.

Each chapter in the program is self-contained and can be used independently to upgrade particular skills during inservice training. For college students in preservice training, all the chapters can be used to provide them with the basic skills necessary for successful preschool teaching.

The skills derive from the six general areas designated in 1973 and revised in 1983 by the Administration for Children, Youth, and Families and the Child Development Associate National Credentialing Program as basic competencies for persons with primary classroom responsibility for groups of young children three to five years of age:

    I.   To establish and maintain a safe, healthy learning environment.
    II.   To advance physical and intellectual competence.
    III. To support social and emotional development and provide positive guidance.
    IV. To establish positive and productive relationships with families.
    V.   To insure a well-run, purposeful program responsive to participant needs.
    VI. To maintain a commitment to professionalism.

From each of these competency areas (also known as Competency Goals), key words have been extracted to serve as the focus for teacher training. These key words, known as Functional Areas, are as follows:

1. Safe
2. Healthy
3. Learning Environment
4. Physical
5. Cognitive
6. Communication
7. Creative
8. Self
9. Social

10. Guidance
11. Families
12. Program Management
13. Professionalism

Each of these thirteen Child Development Associate (CDA) Functional Areas is discussed in a separate chapter of this text.

True learning occurs when students have opportunities to make practical applications of theoretical ideas. Therefore, the classroom skills acquired through this self-taught approach should be performed in actual preschool settings. If the student already serves as a teacher, aide, or volunteer in a Head Start classroom, day care center, nursery school, parent cooperative, or prekindergarten program, he or she may use the classroom as the location for completing the prescribed chapters. If enrolled in a college early childhood program, the student will need to volunteer at least three mornings a week in a nearby preschool classroom.

Students will also need a trainer to assist with their progression through the training program. The trainer will help with each student's initial assessment, review answers to question sheets, observe the student in the early childhood classroom, and meet regularly with the student to provide support and assistance as the learning activities are completed.

The trainer, in other words, serves as a support person who responds to the student's work and activities. The primary responsibility for progress through the self-taught module training program belongs to the student. Activities each student will be involved in include:

1. Initial assessment of present skills in an early childhood classroom based on observations by the trainer, using the Teacher Skills Checklist.
2. Self-assessment of present skills by the student, using the Teacher Skills Checklist.
3. Assessment conference with the trainer to discuss and compare results of the two checklists.
4. Training prescription of chapters based on the results of the assessment conference.
5. Step-by-step, self-directed progression through each of the assigned chapters.
6. Observation of the student by the trainer in the preschool classroom.
7. Regular meetings with the trainer to discuss assigned learning activities.

The intent of the self-taught module training program is to assist the student in acquiring classroom skills through a wide variety of learning techniques. Viewing a Mediapak, reading from the text, writing answers to questions, responding orally to a trainer's questions, performing focused observations of individual children, making file cards of classroom activities, creating special games and activities to meet children's needs, demonstrating evidence of competence through classroom performance—all of these learning activities are a part of each chapter. The Mediapaks listed at the end of most chapters can be obtained from McGraw Bookstore, Elmira College, Elmira, New York 14901.

The third edition of *Skills for Preschool Teachers* is a comprehensive multimedia program for training primary caregivers in early childhood programs. For those already employed in programs, it will help them assess their areas of need and strengthen their skills. For those preparing to work in such programs, it will help them develop entry-level skills in a classroom setting. And for anyone who qualifies, it will prepare him or her to stand for the final assessment for the Child Development Associate credential.

Initial
Assessment

Those who have chosen to work with young children know only too well the truth of the maxim that the beginning is the most important part of the work. They are dedicated to providing a happy and successful beginning for the child's first group learning experience away from home, with the hope that such a beginning will have a lasting effect on the child's future development.

So it is with beginners of any kind. If you have been one, you have undoubtedly realized how important it is for your future success to know at the outset where you stand, what will be expected of you, how you will be judged, and what support or encouragement you can expect.

Students in the self-taught module training program will begin with an initial assessment to help them determine what classroom skills they presently possess and what skills they need to strengthen.

The initial assessment is a threefold process involving both student and trainer. It consists of (1) a classroom observation of you by your trainer, using the Teacher Skills Checklist (see pages 11–24); (2) a self-evaluation using the same checklist; and (3) a conference between you and the trainer, to compare checklist results and arrange your personalized training prescription.

In a self-taught program, the student is always the initiator of any activity. Therefore, it is up to you, as the student, to begin the process.

SELECTING THE TRAINER

First, you will need to arrange for a trainer to make the initial assessment. If you are a college student, your early childhood instructor or supervising teacher may automatically become your trainer. In other instances, someone in the early childhood program where you will be volunteering may serve as the trainer.

If you are employed in an early childhood program, it is possible for a master teacher, educational coordinator, or director to be your trainer. Or, your program may wish to contract for the services of an outside field trainer through a local college or Head Start office.

It is important that the trainer be someone you have confidence in . . . someone who has had experience in an early childhood classroom . . . someone who can evaluate your classroom skills objectively . . . someone who will help and support you throughout your training program.

TEACHER SKILLS CHECKLIST

This checklist was developed and field-tested by the author to be used as an initial assessment instrument and training tool by both college students and CDA trainers and candidates. It is based on the previously mentioned Competency Goals and Functional Areas developed by the CDA National Credentialing Program.

Each page of the checklist represents one Functional Area and contains three indicators developed by the author to demonstrate competence in the particular area. Each chapter of the text then discusses one of these Functional Areas, with the three "indicators" serving as Specific Objectives for the chapter. Thus the

Teacher Skills Checklist serves not only as an initial assessment tool, but also as an outline for the text. For example:

> Chapter 1, "Maintaining a Safe Classroom"
> Functional Area: **Safe**
> Indicators: Promotes common safety practices within each activity area.
> Encourages children to follow common safety practices.
> Stops or redirects unsafe child behavior.

It is important for the student to refer to the text as he or she uses the Teacher Skills Checklist as an initial assessment tool.

ASSESSMENT BY THE TRAINER

Again, it is up to you to arrange for initial assessment by the trainer. The assessment should take place as soon as you are comfortably involved with the children and their activities. If you are a volunteer, you may want to wait for a week or so until you feel perfectly at ease in the classroom. Then your trainer can be invited to make the observation, checking off indicators on the Teacher Skills Checklist which he or she sees you performing. After each indicator, the trainer will make a brief explanation of the evidence of your performance under "Documentation." For example, after the **Safe** indicator "Promotes common safety practices within each activity area," the trainer might write: "Exposed pipes are covered with insulation which student asked to have done." Then the date of the observation is recorded.

Some observers wish to stay most of the day. Others prefer to observe for only an hour at a time on more than one day. I have found three one-hour observations on three days to be ideal.

SELF-ASSESSMENT

Next, you should go through the Teacher Skills Checklist yourself, checking off the items you see in the room or those you are performing. Be honest. Check only those items you have actually performed. A self-assessment is often a difficult one. If you are not sure about some of the items, put down a question mark instead of a checkmark. Your responses on the checklist are just as important as the trainer's in determining your training prescription. After each indicator you should also write an explanation of your performance under "Documentation." For example, after the **Safe** indicator "Encourages children to follow common safety practices," you could briefly describe an activity you had directed, such as: "Played a stoplight game with children before going on field trip down the street."

ASSESSMENT CONFERENCE

When both you and the trainer have finished the Teacher Skills Checklist, arrange a meeting to discuss the results. At this time you should go over your checklists together, discussing indicators that were checked as well as those that were not. A blank on the trainer's checklist may result from the trainer's not having had an opportunity to see you perform that particular skill. You will need to point this out. A blank on your checklist that corresponds to a checkmark by the trainer may be an area of confusion for you, which should be noted.

Indicators that are blank on both checklists need to be noted also. These may serve as a focal point for your training prescription. The chapters from sections that have the most unexplained blanks on both checklists will need to be included in the training prescription.

When you and your trainer have finished discussing the checklist in one functional area, then together you should decide on the strengths you have in that area as well as the needs. These should be recorded on your checklist and your trainer's in the spaces provided. For example, in Functional Area **Safe,** you might record:

STRENGTHS: Knows how to lead children in safety games that teach them common safety practices.

NEEDS: Needs to be aware of emergency procedures and practice them; for example, fire drills.

TRAINING PRESCRIPTION

The training prescription put together by you and your trainer is an outline of the training program you will follow, based on the checklist results. The prescription should note your areas of strength and point out your areas of need. A training prescription form can be found following the Teacher Skills Checklist.

The learning activities you will be working on are listed at the end of each chapter. Follow them in order.

TEACHER SKILLS CHECKLIST: INITIAL ASSESSMENT

Teacher's

Name: _____

Observer: _____ *(if observer assessment)*

TEACHER SKILLS CHECKLIST: INITIAL ASSESSMENT

COMPETENCY GOAL
I. To establish and maintain a safe, healthy learning environment.

FUNCTIONAL AREA AND DEFINITION
1. **SAFE**: Student helps to provide a safe environment and to prevent and reduce injuries.

STRENGTHS:

NEEDS:

Indicators	Documentation	Date		
___ Promotes common safety practices within each activity area.				
___ Encourages children to follow common safety practices.				
___ Stops or redirects unsafe child behavior.				

TEACHER SKILLS CHECKLIST: INITIAL ASSESSMENT (continued)

FUNCTIONAL AREA AND DEFINITION

2. **HEALTHY**: Student promotes good health and nutrition and helps to provide an environment that contributes to the prevention of illness.

STRENGTHS:

NEEDS:

Indicators	Documentation		Date
___ Encourages children to follow common health and nutrition practices.			
___ Provides and uses materials to insure children's health and cleanliness.			
___ Recognizes unusual behavior or symptoms of children who may be ill and provides for them.			

TEACHER SKILLS CHECKLIST: INITIAL ASSESSMENT (continued)

FUNCTIONAL AREA AND DEFINITION ~~(author)~~

3. **LEARNING ENVIRONMENT**: Student uses space, materials, and routines as resources for constructing an interesting and enjoyable environment that encourages exploration and learning.

STRENGTHS:

NEEDS:

Indicators	Documentation	Date
___ Determines what activity areas can and should be included in the classroom on the basis of program goals, space available, and number of children		
___ Separates activity areas and places them in appropriate spaces.		
___ Arranges equipment and materials so that children can make choices easily and independently.		

14

TEACHER SKILLS CHECKLIST: INITIAL ASSESSMENT (continued)

COMPETENCY GOAL
II. To advance physical and intellectual competence.

FUNCTIONAL AREA AND DEFINITION
4. **PHYSICAL**: Student provides a variety of equipment, activities, and opportunities to promote the physical development of children.

STRENGTHS:

NEEDS:

Indicators	Documentation	Date
___ Assesses physical needs of individual children and makes appropriate plans to promote their development.		
___ Provides equipment and activities to promote large and small motor skills in and out of the classroom.		
___ Provides opportunities for children to move their bodies in a variety of ways.		

TEACHER SKILLS CHECKLIST: INITIAL ASSESSMENT (continued)

FUNCTIONAL AREA AND DEFINITION

5. **COGNITIVE**: ~~Student~~ *Year* provides activities and experiences that develop questioning, probing, creativity, exploration, and problem solving appropriate to the developmental levels and learning styles of children.

STRENGTHS:

NEEDS:

Indicators	Documentation	Date
____ Helps children use all of their senses to explore their world.		
____ Helps children develop such concepts as shape, color, size, classification, seriation, number.		
____ Interacts with children in ways that encourage them to think and solve problems.		
— Actively listens to children evaluatheir thinking		

TEACHER SKILLS CHECKLIST: INITIAL ASSESSMENT (continued)

FUNCTIONAL AREA AND DEFINITION

6. **COMMUNICATION:** Student provides opportunities for children to understand, acquire, and use verbal and nonverbal means of communicating thoughts and feelings.

STRENGTHS:

NEERS:

Encourage children to communicate their feelings verbally

Indicators	**Documentation**	**Date**
Interacts with children in ways that encourage them to communicate their thoughts and feelings verbally.		
Provides materials and activities to promote language development.		
Uses books and stories with children to motivate listening and speaking.		

17

TEACHER SKILLS CHECKLIST: INITIAL ASSESSMENT (continued)

FUNCTIONAL AREA AND DEFINITION

CREATIVE: Student provides experiences that stimulate children to explore and express their creative abilities.

STRENGTHS:

NEEDS:

Indicators	Documentation	Date
___ Arranges a variety of art materials for children to explore on their own.		
___ Accepts children's creative products without placing a value judgment on them.		
___ Gives children the opportunity to have fun with music.		

TEACHER SKILLS CHECKLIST: INITIAL ASSESSMENT (continued)

COMPETENCY GOAL

III. To support social and emotional development and provide positive guidance.

FUNCTIONAL AREA AND DEFINITION

SELF: Student helps each child to know, accept, and take pride in himself or herself and to develop a sense of independence.

STRENGTHS:

NEEDS:

Reinforce children positive
behaviour verbally nonverbally.
Provide opportunities for children to
feel good about themselves & to develop a positive
self concept

Indicators	Documentation	Date
—— Accepts every child as a worthy human being and lets him or her know with nonverbal cues.		
—— Helps children to accept and appreciate themselves and each other.		
—— Provides many activities and opportunities for individual children to experience success.		

19

TEACHER SKILLS CHECKLIST: INITIAL ASSESSMENT (continued)

FUNCTIONAL AREA AND DEFINITION

6. SOCIAL: ~~Student~~ helps children learn to get along with others and encourages feelings of empathy and mutual respect among children and adults.

STRENGTHS:

NEEDS:

Indicators	Documentation	Date
___ Provides opportunities for children to work and play cooperatively.		
___ Helps, but does not pressure, the shy child to interact with others.		
___ Provides experiences that help children respect the rights and understand the feelings of others.		

teacher

teachspro

Approaches victim first in situations of conflict between two children.

TEACHER SKILLS CHECKLIST: INITIAL ASSESSMENT (continued)

FUNCTIONAL AREA AND DEFINITION

10. GUANCE: ~~Student~~ provides an environment in which children can learn and practice behaviors that are appropriate and acceptable individually and in a group.

Teacher

STRENGTHS:

NEEDS:

, Displays a consistent approach to
dealing with negative behaviour

, Does not make verbal contact or eye contact c
disruptive children during "time-out" period.

Indicators	Documentation	Date
___ Uses a variety of positive guidance methods to ~~help children control their negative behavior.~~ Reinforces positive behaviour after a negative episode		
___ Helps children establish limits for their behavior.		
Teacher displays a calm, firm, consistent approach		
___ Helps children handle negative feelings through acceptable outlets.		

21

TEACHER SKILLS CHECKLIST: INITIAL ASSESSMENT (continued)

COMPETENCY GOAL
IV. To establish positive and productive relationships with families.

FUNCTIONAL AREA AND DEFINITION
12. FAMILIES: ~~Student~~ _teacher_ maintains an open, friendly, and informative relationship with each child's family and encourages family involvement in the program.

STRENGTHS:

NEEDS: Emphasize strengths not needs with parents from a developmental point of view

Indicators _for growth_	Documentation	Date
___ Involves parents in planning and participating in children's programs.		
___ Communicates frequently with parents.		
___ Respects parents' views when program goals differ from parents' goals. _+ incorporate parents ideas_		

22

TEACHER SKILLS CHECKLIST: INITIAL ASSESSMENT (continued)

COMPETENCY GOAL

V. To ensure a well-run purposeful program responsive to participant needs.

FUNCTIONAL AREA AND DEFINITION Teacher

12. **PROGRAM MANAGEMENT**: Student is a manager who uses all available resources to ensure an effective operation. The student is a competent organizer, planner, and record keeper.

STRENGTHS:

NEEDS:

Should an aide nor other teacher be present? Is a team approach used with respect to program planning. Is there open communication?

Indicators	Documentation	Date
___ Uses a team approach to plan a flexible classroom schedule.		
___ Uses transitions and small group activities to accomplish the goals of the program.		
___ Plans for individual needs based on child observation and the interpretation of data obtained.		
___ Document objective measures one kept as needed		

TEACHER SKILLS CHECKLIST: INITIAL ASSESSMENT (continued)

COMPETENCY GOAL
VI. To maintain a commitment to professionalism.

FUNCTIONAL AREA AND DEFINITION
13 / **PROFESSIONALISM**: Student seeks out and takes advantage of opportunities to improve her or his competence, both for professional growth and for the benefit of children and families.

STRENGTHS:

NEEDS:

Indicators	Documentation		Date
___ Puts children and families first.			
___ Treats information about children and families confidentially.			
___ Takes every opportunity to improve professional growth.			

TRAINING PRESCRIPTION

Student _____ Date _____

Trainer _____

Strengths

1. _____   5. _____

2. _____   6. _____

3. _____   7. _____

4. _____   8. _____

Training Needs

1. _____   5. _____

2. _____   6. _____

3. _____   7. _____

4. _____   8. _____

Comments:

1 Maintaining a Safe Classroom

General Objective

To be able to set up and maintain a safe classroom environment and to reduce and prevent injuries.

Specific Objectives

- ☐ Promotes common safety practices within each activity area.
- ☐ Encourages children to follow common safety practices.
- ☐ Stops or redirects unsafe child behavior.

T he area of safety is of basic importance for all teachers of preschool children. Before we can offer developmental activities for the children who come to center-based programs, we must first guarantee them a safe environment. Their parents assume this to be the case. You as a child caregiver make the same assumption. But it is your responsibility to see that your classroom is truly safe. You must inspect each activity area in the room before the children's daily arrival, and again when children are busily playing with the equipment, to be sure the safety hazards sometimes found in particular areas are not present in yours.

PROMOTES COMMON SAFETY PRACTICES WITHIN EACH ACTIVITY AREA

Block Building Area

The principal safety feature of block building areas is the height of constructions. Some teachers permit children to build with wooden unit blocks or large hollow blocks only as high as a child's own height. Others allow children to climb on chairs to build towers and buildings as high as they can reach. The danger is that the tall buildings can fall on another child, or the climbing child can himself fall and be injured. You must decide if this situation poses a problem in your particular classroom. If this is a safety priority with you, you will want to establish block building rules with the children at the outset.

Since preliterate children will not be able to read the written rules you post, why not make illustrated rules for them? You could draw an outline of a block building next to the outline of a child to show the allowable height. Then repeat the drawing with a too-tall building and a line drawn through it to indicate "not allowed." Written rules should still be posted for classroom staff and volunteers.

A second common mishap in block building areas is that fingers can get stepped on. The builders often sit on the floor with their hands flat and their fingers exposed while other children walk through the area to get blocks from the shelves. You can prevent this kind of accident quite simply by not allowing children to build too close to the shelves. If your space is limited, you may want to section off building lots with masking tape on the floor.

Some teachers store large riding toys in the block building area. This tends to encourage children to ride in the area where others are building and can result in more treading on fingers or crashing into buildings. You may need to find a different area for riding trucks.

Book Area

Your library or reading corner should be a comfortable place for children to stretch out on the floor or curl up on a pillow to read. Make sure the floor is covered with a rug to keep it warm enough in cold weather, and that the particular location is free from drafts. If you use pillows, make sure there are no heat vents in the area that might be accidentally covered by the pillows. If you have a rocking chair, help children learn to control it. They tend to get carried away with child-size rockers and may tip over or rock on someone's fingers.

Dramatic Play Area

A possibly serious safety hazard in the housekeeping area is the height of clothes hooks for dress-up materials. Be sure your hooks are not at the children's eye level, so they cannot stumble against them and injure an eye.

If you use plastic dishes, knives, or spoons, make sure they are not broken. Sharp knives should not, of course, be used for play. Young children love to dress up with real jewelry. Be sure earrings are large, and that strings of beads are not broken. Tiny objects often find their way into young children's noses or ears.

Large Motor Area

Climbing equipment should be cushioned with pads or other material thick enough to prevent injuries in case a child falls. Establishing safety rules for climbers at the outset is important, but in addition, an adult should supervise the area when it is in use. If you have wheeled riding vehicles, establish safety rules, such as "no bumping," with traffic signs and safety games.

The teeter-totter is one of the more dangerous pieces of large motor equipment. A child can be thrown off even a small indoor teeter-totter when the child at the lower end jumps off unexpectedly. The safe use of a teeter-totter is a complex concept for threes and fours to learn; most teachers prefer not to use them.

Physically handicapped children should be involved in all of the activity areas of the classroom, including this one. Find ways to give them access to large motor experiences. Children in wheelchairs can throw and catch large, soft balls. True "mainstreaming" means that all children are included in classroom activities wherever possible. Use your ingenuity to accommodate everyone. In a catch and toss game, have everyone sit in chairs just as a physically handicapped child might.

A staff member needs to supervise large motor climbing, swinging, and sliding equipment both indoors and out.

Manipulative Area

If you have three-year-olds in your program, stringing beads should be large. Three-year-olds often put small objects into their mouths, noses, and ears.

Art Area

Strange as it may seem, sharp scissors are less dangerous for young children than dull ones. Dull scissors are so difficult to use that children can slip and cut themselves. Small, sharp scissors are therefore more useful in helping young children develop manipulative skills safely. An adult must keep a watchful eye on things when the scissors are out, however, and put them away when not in use.

Water spills can cause slipping in the art area. Have a sponge or mop handy for you and the children to use to keep the floors dry.

Music Area

If you have tape recorders or record players in the music area, be sure there are no extension cords to trip over. Children should not be allowed to plug or unplug the equipment. Battery-operated players are safer.

Science/Math Area

Small counting and sorting items, such as buttons, seeds, or beans, pose a problem for the youngest children, who tend to put such things in their mouths or up their noses. Certain houseplants are highly poisonous and thus pose a serious hazard to young children, who may be tempted to eat a leaf or berry. If you have plants in your classroom, keep them out of reach. Treatment for poisoning from ingesting plants is described in *A Sigh of Relief,* a first-aid handbook.

Sand/Water Area

Spilled water and sand are slippery and must be cleaned up when spills occur. Keep in the area a regular mop and broom with the handles cut down to child-size, so children can help with cleanup. They feel quite grown-up when allowed to participate in such an adult chore. To prevent spills in the first place, keep water and sand at low levels in the play tables. Children playing at the sand table can wear safety goggles to keep sand out of their eyes.

Be sure the toys and implements for sand and water play are not broken, rusty, or sharp-edged. Glass containers, such as baby food jars or eye droppers, should not be used because they are too easily broken. Replace them instead with plastic cups, containers, bottles, droppers, and meat-basters.

Woodworking Area

As with scissors, adult-size woodworking tools should also be used. Child-size hammers, saws, pliers, and screwdrivers are toys and are not meant to be used with real wood and nails. Children can learn the safe use of real tools in your woodworking area. By limiting the number of children in the area to two at a time, you can also control the safety hazards.

The woodworking area is of great interest to both boys and girls. They should be encouraged to learn the skills of pounding and sawing, with an adult supervising. Roofing nails and ceiling tiles are easier for beginners to manipulate than nails with small heads and regular wood. To cut down on noise, put rug squares under the pounding materials.

Another safety practice young children love to follow is the wearing of safety goggles. Keep two pairs of them in the woodworking corner and see how popular this area becomes.

Cooking Area

You will have to learn the local code governing hot food preparation in your community. Some schools and localities do not allow hot plates, electric frying pans, or other heating implements in the classroom. Some programs use only special kitchen areas for hot cooking; others allow hot cooking in the classroom. Whatever the case, an adult should always be in the area when food preparation is going on.

As with the woodworking area, the fewer children you allow to participate at one time, the greater safety control you have when dangerous appliances or implements are in use. Children can learn the rules about using electric appliances or sharp implements, but an adult must supervise nevertheless.

General Room Conditions

Check the heating system in your room. Exposed pipes should not be allowed, unless they are thoroughly protected with insulation. Radiators and space heaters should be sectioned off from children's direct contact. Portable electric or kerosene heaters are usually prohibited by fire codes or insurance regulations.

Electric cords and wires should not be accessible to children. Aquariums, incubators, and the like should be located near electrical outlets that are inaccessible to little hands.

Check your walls, furniture, and cupboards for peeling paint. Children love to pick it off and put it in their mouths. Be sure the paint is sanded down and refinished. Broken toys and furniture should be repaired or removed. Wooden equipment and room dividers should be checked for splintery surfaces and refinished if necessary. What about the corners of the room dividers? If children should stumble against them, will they be hurt? You may need to tape padding onto sharp edges.

Check the physical environment of your classroom in case you need to modify it for children with handicapping conditions. What about emergency exiting? Will you need a special ramp or other device? Should railings or handholds be attached to walls or stairways? Should one of the classroom staff assist the child in moving safely in and out of the building? It is important for the adults in the classroom to avoid overprotectiveness, so the child can develop his independence. On the other hand, it may occasionally be necessary to insist on adult help if the situation calls for it.

Stairs/Exits

What about stairs into or out of the building? Can children reach the railings? Are steps sturdy and unbroken? If covered with carpeting, is the carpeting in good condition? As a teacher of young children, you are accountable for all aspects of safety in their environment. Although others may be responsible for repairs and replacements, it is up to you to see that these are attended to.

Entrances and exits should be clearly marked. If you have bilingual children, all emergency signs and labels should be written in two languages. Pictorial signs should also be used here.

Bathroom

Here again, slippery floors may be the most common cause of injuries. Make it a practice to check bathroom floors from time to time during the day. Where are the bathroom cleaning and disinfecting materials stored? They should never be left within children's reach.

First-aid kits must also be stored away from children but be easily accessible to adults.

Outdoor Playground

Is the equipment on your playground in safe condition? Check it for loose parts, sharp edges, and cushioning under climbers and slides. A cushioning of sand, wood chips, or pebbles is preferable to grass or blacktop.

Swings with hard seats cause many accidents. Belt or tire swings are preferable. Your playground should also be sectioned off from roads, driveways, or parking lots. Check daily to make sure there are no broken bottles or other dangerous debris on the grounds.

ENCOURAGES CHILDREN TO FOLLOW COMMON SAFETY PRACTICES

Modeling Behavior

You are the model of safety behavior for your children. When they see you taking precautions with saws, hammers, knives, or electrical equipment, they will imitate you. Your behavior is much more effective than your trying to tell or "teach" them the proper rules. As you practice normal adult safety behavior, you should express it verbally to the children: "When I cook things like this in the deep-fry pan, I am very careful not to touch the sides or it would burn me," or "See how I cut the pumpkin. I move the knife away from me so I don't get cut. Now you try it."

You and your staff (plus volunteers) should discuss safety practices in the classroom so that all of you agree on the limits you will set for children and enforce them consistently. Young children do not necessarily understand rules by being told. They learn by doing, by being involved in the situation. For instance, you could demonstrate at the workbench how to hold the saw and make it work or have a carpenter come in and demonstrate. Then let the children try. When a child has learned to use the saw, let him show the next child how to use it.

Safety Rules

Let the children be involved in helping to decide on the safety rules for each classroom area. All of you should agree on the rules. How many children should be allowed in the woodworking area at one time? How high can a block building be? Should a child be allowed to stand on a chair to make it higher than he can reach from the floor? If not, the children need to know this. If they help make the rules, they will be more willing to follow them.

Do you have safety rules for various areas? Posting rules is helpful not only for the children and the staff, but also for volunteers and parents in the classroom. If there is an indoor climber, an adult should always be nearby to supervise. Taking turns and waiting for turns should be worked out ahead of time so there is no dangerous pushing and shoving on climbing equipment.

Do not overburden your children with rules. Make simple ones that everyone understands and that can be enforced easily. Children should be concerned with basics, such as not hurting themselves or others. We are sometimes overly concerned with rules and regulations—if there are too many, young children will simply not respond. Keep them simple, basic, and few in number.

Supervision

The classroom staff must work out a way to supervise potentially dangerous activities without nagging at children. Certain less dangerous things children need to learn for themselves without overprotectiveness from adults. Other activities should be more closely supervised. You and your staff need to work out this balance. If we want children to become independent, we should allow them to try things out for themselves. But if some of those things are indeed dangerous, we need to intervene.

Emergency Exiting

Certain situations demand rules and order. Emergency exiting from the building is one of them. Children should practice this over and over so that everyone understands how to do it without panic. Do not wait for your community fire inspector to make this happen. It is your responsibility to yourself, the children, and their families to see that fire drills are accomplished with ease. If any children have physical handicaps, you may need to make special arrangements for their safe exiting.

You should practice emergency exiting so that everyone knows how to do it without panic.

Field Trips

Field trips require special regulations. Children need to learn how to walk in groups, how to cross busy thoroughfares, how to wait for the teacher before they go forward. The adults as well as the children need to understand such procedures ahead of time. If children are transported in cars, buses, or subways, they and their parents must be aware of safe and unsafe child behavior in a vehicle.

In order to anticipate the safety problems inherent in any field trip, you should make a preliminary visit yourself to the site, if possible using the same mode of transportation your children will be using. Then you can make notes about safety situations in order to prepare the staff and the children for the trip. Talk to the people at the site as well, in case they have safety rules or advice you will need to know ahead of time. As you look at the field trip site, try to anticipate the kinds of exploring or trying-out activities your active children will attempt to do. Would any of these things be dangerous? What about children becoming separated from the group or going off by themselves? One of your staff members could be assigned to check on this.

Car Safety

Most states have enacted legislation governing car safety for young children. In New York and Ohio, for example, all children under four years of age must sit in state-approved car seats when riding in private cars. As a teacher, you can encourage them to follow this practice through classroom activities. Bring in a car seat and let them practice using it during dramatic play. Fasten a seat belt to a chair and let them pretend to be riding in a car.

Safety Signs

Children can learn about safety signs and signals through field trips outside the classroom and dramatic play props within. Through games and songs and stories, they can learn that red means "stop" and green means "go." Make a traffic light from a half-gallon milk carton. Cover it with dark contact paper and cut three holes in a vertical row through one side. Cover each with red, yellow and green cellophane or tissue paper or clear food wrap colored with felt tip pens. Make three small holes on the opposite side large enough to shine a pen flashlight through. Let the children play a "Red Light-Green Light" game by marching in a circle while someone shines the flashlight through the hole to signal "stop," "wait," or "go."

You can also make cardboard stop signs and other traffic signals for the children to use in block play. Follow this up with a visit by a police officer or school crossing guard, who will demonstrate safety rules. Although films are available for children, young preschoolers do not learn concepts as well from films as they do from active involvement with learning. Sitting still and listening to a teacher or film is not as effective a learning device as the other activities mentioned.

Once a concept is clear, books serve as a good follow-up, as long as they are read to individuals or small groups. Trying to teach a concept to a large group by reading a book is much less effective. Children need to be close enough to the reader to see the illustrations. They need to be able to respond individually to the teacher's questions, such as, "Can you find the traffic light in the picture? What color is it?" and to ask their own questions.

Two excellent books for reinforcing traffic safety concepts are the classic picture book *Red Light Green Light* by Golden McDonald and the wordless picture book *Truck* by Donald Crews. Let the children make up their own story as they watch Crews's eighteen-wheeler following traffic signs through the city and onto the highway. Let them make their own traffic signs for the classroom. Be sure to have a selection of toy cars and trucks in the block area after reading these books. Watch and listen to the children's dramatic play, and you will soon learn whether the children really understand these safety concepts.

Accidents

Emergency telephone numbers for police, fire department, doctors, and ambulance should be posted near your phone. All adults in the classroom should be familiar with them. Directions for handling such emergencies should also be posted there, in two languages if necessary. A list of children's home phone numbers as well as whom to contact if no one is home should be available near your phone.

A first-aid kit should be available, and at least one, and preferably all, of the classroom staff should know how to use it. Your program should consider devoting a staff meeting once a year to emergency procedures and first aid.

An excellent book on child safety and emergency measures is *A Sigh of Relief: The First-Aid Handbook for Childhood Emergencies*. It has simple directions for home safety, toy safety, school safety, car safety, playground safety, first-aid supplies, and over 100 pages of illustrated emergency instructions for accidents and injuries listed alphabetically from bites to sunstroke.

Personal Safety

The personal safety of the children in your care involves protecting them from harm or victimization by predatory adults. Sexual abuse of children by adults seems to be the primary danger involved. Although this is a very real threat to certain young children, many professionals feel that the child care community has overreacted to this threat in ways that are potentially harmful to children.

Not only have young children in centers been alerted to "stranger-danger" with films, diagrams, games, and exhortations by their teachers, but children have also been made to feel that it is their responsibility to protect themselves from such adults. We delude ourselves if we believe that three-, four-, or five-year-old children can successfully ward off the advances of an adult who intends to abuse them. When young children who are being abused find that they can't control the situation, then they become even more psychologically damaged because of guilt feelings. After all, they have been taught what to do. If they can't prevent this abuse, then they believe it must be their fault.

As a result of this kind of overreaction, we find many children in child care centers who are afraid of the other adults in their building, who run from friendly college students, who will not let health professionals examine them, or who may even show fear when their fathers undress them for bed or a bath.

In addition, many child care professionals themselves are afraid to enter the bathroom area with the children in their care and may refuse to help children clean themselves after accidents because the children could report them to their parents for touching them. Male child care workers are especially vulnerable to such charges, which thus drives out of the child care profession much-needed role models for young children.

We need to step back and think about what it is we are doing to young children when we instill in them this kind of fear. Not only does fear inhibit learning, but this kind of fear makes children all the more vulnerable to victimization. We also need to realize that most child sexual abuse occurs in the home and that 85 percent of such abuse is perpetrated by someone the child knows (Hull, 1986, p. 18).

What, then, should be our role in protecting the children in our charge? We should use our common sense in helping children learn not to go with strangers or accept rides from people they do not know. Scare tactics are out of place; so is the constant bombardment of children with "stranger-danger" films and lessons.

Who really needs to be educated in this matter is we, ourselves. We should look carefully at the message we want to get across to children. It should not be one of "overkill"—that there is danger in every stranger. It should not be one of "good touches" and "bad touches"—how is a preschooler to distinguish between the two? Otherwise we may be producing a generation of paranoid children who will keep their distance from one another as adults. Do we want to live in a society where caring, touching, and loving are perceived as threatening acts?

Instead, what we should do is encourage children to talk to a trusted adult when they feel uncomfortable, to go only with a trusted adult on the street or in a car, and to ask a trusted adult when they are unsure of what to do.

The child care staff and parents need to be involved in sensitve discussions of this issue and how it is to be handled in the center and at home. You may want to invite a psychologist or a health professional to contribute his or her expertise. A positive approach in which children learn to feel good about themselves and the people around them should be your goal for the children's personal safety.

STOPS OR REDIRECTS UNSAFE CHILD BEHAVIOR

Anticipating Unsafe Behavior

Unsafe child behavior can take many forms. It may consist of running in the classroom or halls, pushing or hitting other children, climbing too high, playing too roughly, or using materials in unsafe ways. You may be able to eliminate much unsafe behavior by anticipating it ahead of time. Arrange the physical environment so children do not have room for uncontrolled running. Have children walk with partners in the halls or on city streets. Carefully supervise potentially dangerous situations. For example, if you know ahead of time that young children are more adept at blowing out of straws than sucking up through them, you will be able to demonstrate this skill at the water table when suds and straws are used, and thus prevent children from sucking up and swallowing soapy water.

Children love to play with water. If they squirt it on the floor in the classroom or in the bathroom, they have created a slippery condition for others. You need to stop them firmly, not harshly, and redirect them by involving them in helping you to clean it up. Make it interesting, not a punishment.

Redirecting Unsafe Behavior

Telling a child to stop climbing so high or to stop building such a tall block building will not resolve your safety problems. Commands like these only encourage children to climb and build higher. A sensitive teacher knows that the best way to deal with such situations often requires redirecting unwanted behavior.

Go to the child personally (don't shout across a room), and ask him or her to show you how he can climb horizontally or swing hand over hand, or to show you how a very wide building would look. Giving a child another challenge will often redirect potentially dangerous behavior into something constructive.

Demonstrating Safe Behavior

An adult must be nearby to supervise the use of hammers, saws, paring knives, and pointed scissors. Children can and should learn to handle these implements safely. If you stop their unsafe use, you should then demonstrate the proper method and let the user try again.

If all the adults in the classroom demonstrate safety regulations consistently, children will not only learn to model such behavior, but also help you by showing others the safe way to live in their environment.

SUMMARY

Information from this chapter should help you set up and maintain a safe classroom environment and to reduce and prevent injuries. You should be able to assess the activity areas in the room for possible safety hazards such as electrical cords, exposed heating pipes or vents, slippery conditions, rugs that do not lie flat and could cause children to trip, as well as rough edges and sharp corners on room dividers. You should understand how to promote safety in each area with illustrated signs, simple basic rules, supervision where necessary, anticipation and redirection of unsafe child behavior, as well as role-playing and demonstration of safe behavior.

Children can learn the safety precautions they must practice on stairs and exits, in the bathroom, on field trips, and in cars. You can be involved in workshops or discussions of first aid, emergency situations, and children's personal safety. As a role model for safe behavior in the classroom, you will be taking the first step to assure children and their families that your program is making a serious commitment to each child's well-being.

LEARNING ACTIVITIES

1. Read Chapter 1, "Maintaining a Safe Classroom," and answer Question Sheet 1-A.
2. View Mediapak H, "Outdoor Play Equipment," and answer Question Sheet 1-B.
3. Read one or more of the books listed under Suggested Readings. Begin a card file with ten file cards that describe ideas for promoting safety in your classroom. Include the reference source on each card.
4. Have one of your staff members hold a fire drill or emergency exiting drill. Observe and record what happens. Write up the results and make recommendations for improvement.
5. Help a small group of children learn a particular safety concept, using ideas and techniques from this chapter. (Your trainer can visit and observe.)
6. List the contents of your classroom first-aid kit and describe a use for each item.
7. Arrange and conduct a field trip for some or all of the children, during which you make appropriate use of safety measures. Write up the results and suggestions for improvement. (Your trainer can go along.)
8. Begin a Portfolio of evidence of your skills. Add one piece of evidence for each of the following Teacher Skills Checklist items:
   a. Promotes common safety practices within each activity area.
   b. Encourages children to follow common safety practices.
   c. Stops or redirects unsafe child behavior.
   Evidence should reflect what you, not another staff member, have done. Ideas for kinds of evidence are listed under Suggested Evidence for Portfolio.
9. Complete the Chapter 1 Evaluation Sheet and return it and your answers to Question Sheets 1-A and 1-B to the appropriate college or program official.

QUESTION SHEET 1-A

(Based on Chapter 1, "Maintaining a Safe Classroom")

1. Who is responsible for providing and maintaining a safe classroom environment?
2. With what safety factors should classroom caregivers be concerned?
3. What are some of the dangerous materials a classroom might contain?
4. What dangers to young children are posed by their entering and exiting a building?
5. How can these dangers be overcome?
6. How can you, as a teacher, model specific safety practices for your children?
7. How do children best learn safety rules?
8. What are the safety aspects of field trips with which you should be concerned?
9. How would you handle an emergency situation such as a child's falling and being injured?
10. What unsafe child behavior might occur in your classroom, and how could you redirect it?

QUESTION SHEET 1-B

(Based on Medipak H, "Outdoor Play Equipment")

1. What should be your main concerns when equipping your playground?
2. What is the most dangerous aspect of climbers?
3. How can you minimize this danger?
4. How should you prepare playground cable spools to eliminate safety hazards?
5. How can the dangerous aspects of slides be overcome?
6. What materials can be used for cushioning under equipment?
7. What is the most dangerous aspect of swings?
8. How can this danger be minimized?
9. How can you overcome the dangerous aspect of teeter-totters?
10. How can blacktop surfaces be used with a minimum of danger?

SUGGESTED EVIDENCE FOR PORTFOLIO

Select a piece of equipment, an activity, or a safety idea you have had something to do with, to show your skill in this area. Some suggestions are:

1. A "before" and "after" photo of your playground or building exit with a written explanation of how you changed the unsafe element in the photo and how it has worked out.
2. A list of the contents of your first-aid kit and an explanation of how you would use each item.
3. A detailed description (with photos, if possible) of a safety activity or game you have performed with the children.
4. A list of all cleaning fluids, sprays, poisons, and potentially dangerous materials your center owns and a description of how each is stored safely away from children, and how this is checked on.
5. A description of a child with a behavior problem or handicapping condition that has implications for the child's safety, with an explanation of how you have handled it to prevent harm to the child or others.

Each piece of evidence should be accompanied by a write-up explaining how this shows your competence in the area of **Safe,** and how the activity is developmentally appropriate for your children.

SUGGESTED READINGS

Alberta Recreation and Parks. *Play Space Safety.* Ypsilanti, Mich.: High/Scope Press, 1986.

Comer, Diana E. *Developing Safety Skills with the Young Child.* Albany, N.Y.: Delmar, 1987.

Endsley, Richard C., and Marilyn R. Bradbard. *Quality Day Care: A Handbook of Choices for Parents and Caregivers.* Englewood Cliffs, N.J.: Prentice-Hall, 1981.

Freeman, Lory. *A Kid's Guide to First Aid.* Seattle, Wash.: Parenting Press, 1983.

Froschi, Merle, et al. *Including All of Us: An Early Childhood Curriculum About Disability.* New York: Education Equity Concepts, 1984.

Green, Martin. *A Sigh of Relief: The First-Aid Handbook for Childhood Emergencies.* New York: Bantam, 1977.

Hull, Karla. *Safe Passages: A Guide for Teaching Children Personal Safety.* Dawn Sign Press, 1986.

Marotz, Lynn, et al. *Health, Safety, and Nutrition for the Young Child.* Albany, N.Y.: Delmar, 1985.

CHILDREN'S BOOKS

Bridwell, Norman. *What Do They Do When It Rains?* New York: Scholastic, 1969.

Buckley, Richard, and Eric Carle. *The Foolish Tortoise.* Natick, Mass.: Picture Book Studio USA, 1985.

Crews, Donald. *Truck.* New York: Greenwillow, 1980.

Hines, Anna Grossnickle. *Maybe a Band-Aid Will Help.* New York: E. P. Dutton, 1984.

McDonald, Golden. *Red Light Green Light.* Garden City, N.Y.: Doubleday, 1944.

McPhail, David. *Pig Pig Goes to Camp.* New York: E. P. Dutton, 1983.

Siebert, Diane. *Truck Song.* New York: Harper & Row, 1984.

Wells, Rosemary. *A Lion for Lewis.* New York: Dial Press, 1982.

Zion, Gene. *Harry By the Sea.* New York: Harper & Row, 1965.

SOUND FILMSTRIPS

Beaty, Janice J. "Outdoor Play Equipment." Mediapak H, *Skills for Preschool Teachers.* Elmira, N.Y.: McGraw Bookstore, Elmira College, 1979.

CHAPTER 1 EVALUATION SHEET
MAINTAINING A SAFE CLASSROOM

1. Student_____

2. Trainer_____

3. Center where training occurred_____

4. Beginning date_____ Ending date_____

5. Describe what student did to accomplish General Objective

   _____

   _____

6. Describe what student did to accomplish Specific Objectives

   Objective 1_____

   _____

   Objective 2_____

   _____

   Objective 3_____

   _____

7. Evaluation of student's Learning Activities
   (Trainer Check One)   (Student Check One)

   _____ Highly superior performance   _____

   _____ Superior performance   _____

   _____ Good performance   _____

   _____ Less than adequate performance   _____

Signature of Trainer: Signature of Student:

_____   _____

Comments:

2 Maintaining a Healthy Classroom

General Objective

To be able to set up and maintain a healthy classroom that promotes good child health and nutrition and is free from factors contributing to illness.

Specific Objectives

☐ Encourages children to follow common health and nutrition practices.
☐ Provides and uses materials to insure children's health and cleanliness.
☐ Recognizes unusual behavior or symptoms of children who may be ill and provides for them.

H ealth practices, like those of safety, are best taught to young children through behavior modeling on the part of the classroom adults, as well as through games, stories, and real experiences in which children can become involved.

Nutrition facts, for example, become meaningful for young children not by memorizing basic food groups, but through classroom experiences with real food. Children learn to wash their hands before meals not because they know it kills germs, but because they see the teacher doing it.

ENCOURAGES CHILDREN TO FOLLOW COMMON HEALTH AND NUTRITION PRACTICES

Exercising

While large motor equipment provides children the opportunity to exercise their large muscles, you should also plan a time for strenuous running and movement in a gymnasium or on an outdoor playground. If neither is available, you can take your children for a follow-the-leader run around the building instead. Let children who cannot run play catch with a beanbag, or provide some other activity that encourages them to move. For programs that do not have indoor or outdoor space large enough for running, encourage children to run or jump in place to one of the body action chants in Chapter 4. Such exercise improves muscle tone, increases appetite, and makes resting easier.

Resting

Healthy young children seem to be perpetual motion machines, never stopping to take a breath. Yet they do need to practice a balance of active and quiet activities. It is up to the classroom staff to make sure a rest time is part of the daily program.

This does not mean the teacher should make the children put their heads down on the table for fifteen minutes every morning at ten o'clock, whether they need a rest or not. Rest time should come as a natural follow-up to exertion rather than as a formal period at a certain time of day. If there has been no strenuous activity during the morning, a group rest time is unnecessary. If you schedule one anyway, you will probably spend most of it trying to keep the children quiet. On the other hand, when children are truly tired, they welcome a quiet period.

Children with physical handicaps may tire more quickly than others. It is up to you to recognize the situation, provide a quiet place for the children, and make sure they stop to rest when they need one.

Some programs have a quiet period just before lunch when the children put mats on the floor and pursue quiet activities by themselves. Solitary activity is a refreshing change if a child has been with a large and active group all morning.

If yours is an all-day program, you should provide a formal nap period in the afternoon. Use cots or mats wherever you have spare space. If you are using the regular classroom space, try to section off an area for children who no longer take afternoon naps. Dim the lights in the room, but after the nappers have fallen asleep, you can whisper to the nonsleepers that they may go to this special area and play quietly. Individual mats help make this a quiet time for nonsleepers.

To encourage resting, you may want to read a story at the beginning of the quiet period. *Goodnight Moon* is a quiet story in which a little bunny is encouraged to go to sleep as the room grows progressively darker on every page. *Close Your Eyes* is a warm story about a father getting his little girl ready for bed and encouraging her to use her imagination when her eyes are closed. *Flocks of Birds* follows a similar theme; it is about a girl who is not sleepy, whose mother encourages her to imagine flocks of birds moving as the girl lies in bed.

Washing

Children must learn to wash their hands before meals and after using the bathroom. Do you serve as their model? They will do it because you ask them to and because it is an interesting sort of task, but you should model the same behavior—they should see you washing your hands, too.

The practice of cleanliness through washing can be stimulated in other ways. Once a week it is a good idea to bathe the "babies" in the doll corner. If your center does not have a toy sink, bring in a plastic tub. Both boys and girls can have an enjoyable time with water, as well as practice cleanliness. Let them wash the doll's clothes as well. This is the time to talk about cleanliness and how it keeps us healthy.

Children love to play with water, so approach these activities with a sense of pleasure rather than drudgery.

Nutrition

Children learn very quickly what foods we consider important, not by what we say, but by observing the kinds of food we serve in the classroom. Do you serve cookies and milk for snack? Do you serve cake or cupcakes for birthdays? If you want children to become acquainted with delicious fruits and interesting vegetables as well, plan some exciting food activities with them.

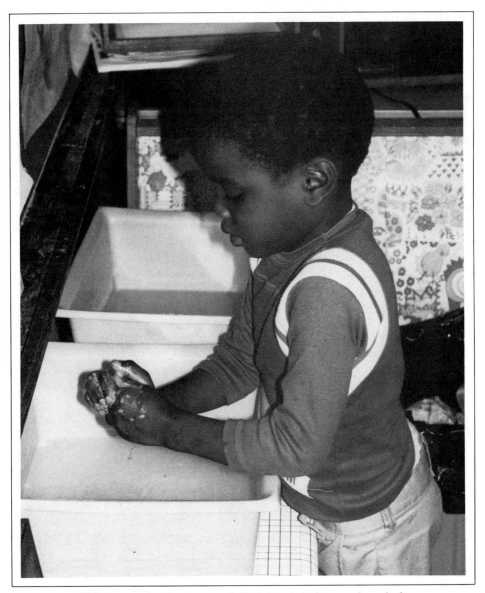

Children need to learn to wash their hands before meals and after using the bathroom.

How about "Banana Surprise" or "Frozen Fruit Slush" or "Hairy Harrys" (from the book *More Than Graham Crackers*) for a birthday celebration? The children can have the fun of making their own party refreshments as well as eating them. "Banana Surprise" uses bananas, graham cracker crumbs, and peanut butter and gives children practice with the small motor skills of peeling, cutting, spreading, and rolling.

"Frozen Fruit Slush" uses orange and lemon juice, mashed bananas, honey, and milk. A refrigerator and ice cube trays are necessary. This activity can also teach the science concept of freezing. "Hairy Harrys" consist of apple slices spread with peanut butter and topped with alfalfa sprouts and raisins. The children can even make their own peanut butter.

Let the children also make their own daily snacks, such as "Stuffed Celery" from the book *Good Times with Good Foods*. Besides scrubbing and cutting the celery, they can make a variety of fillings—cottage cheese, cream cheese, or peanut butter. This book contains an excellent collection of nutritious recipes, each illustrated with simple step-by-step picture directions that you can copy onto a recipe chart for the children to follow as they prepare the food.

Once children have experiences with real foods, teachers can introduce other fun nutrition activities. "Food puppets" can visit the class to talk about their favorite foods. Besides recipes, *Cool Cooking for Kids* has many pages of ideas for puppets and food games. One is a "Shoe-box Train" with decorated shoe boxes representing each of the four basic food groups. The children have to sort and categorize cut-out pictures of the foods for the train to carry.

Picture books can also reinforce the nutrition ideas you are introducing. *The Very Hungry Caterpillar* is a favorite as he eats his way through the days of the week, one fruit at a time, until he nearly makes himself sick during his Saturday junk food orgy. *Bread and Jam for Frances* is another classic: the story of the badger named Frances who refuses to eat anything but bread and jam until she finds that is all she'll get. *Gregory the Terrible Eater* is the hilarious story of a little goat who wants human food and must learn to eat "correctly" by being served one piece of "goat food" at a time, for example, "spaghetti and a shoelace in tomato sauce."

Medical Tests and Examinations

Although a classroom teacher is not usually responsible for setting up medical tests and examinations for the children, you can certainly support the health specialist who does. You and the specialist need to work together to plan and carry out classroom activities to acquaint children with these examinations to make them less threatening.

Before an eye test, let the children practice holding a card over one eye and responding to an eye chart. Before an ear test, have the health specialist demonstrate or talk to the children about what will occur. The nurse in one Head Start program pasted together a three-dimensional model of an ear inside a shoe box. Through a hole in one end the children could shine a flashlight to see the parts of the "ear" just as the doctor would.

Be honest with children about what will happen. If their fingers will be pricked to draw blood, have a pretend demonstration with a nurse officiating. Invite a dental hygienist to demonstrate a dental checkup. Let the children play doctor or dentist in the doll corner with appropriate props.

Other Health Practices

Again, you are the model for the children to follow. Be sure your own health practices are worth following. If you want children to clean their plates at lunch, then you should set the example. If you smoke, do it in a private place away from the children. If you want children to stop biting their fingernails, be sure you don't bite yours.

Sometimes a story can help motivate the desired behavior. Although written for six- and seven-year olds, *The Quitting Deal* is a well-done, contemporary story about Jennifer, who wants to break her thumb-sucking habit, and her mother, who wants to quit smoking. It should stimulate discussion about breaking unhealthy habits.

PROVIDES AND USES MATERIALS TO INSURE CHILDREN'S HEALTH AND CLEANLINESS

The classroom and bathroom environments must be clean and sanitary. Even when a janitorial staff does the cleaning, it is your responsibility to make sure they have done it properly and that it remains in good condition during the day. Floors, tabletops, and food serving areas should be kept clean. Food should be stored properly and garbage disposed of promptly.

Light, heat, and ventilation should be kept at healthy levels. Children and their parents need to be informed about the type of clothing children should wear at the center. If an extra sweater is necessary and the parents cannot provide one, you may have to seek other sources. Keep a supply of extra clothing items on hand in case children have spills or accidents or lose clothing items such as mittens.

Your classroom also needs a basic supply of tissues, paper towels, paper cups, and soap. If you use sheets or blankets for napping, these must be individually labeled and washed periodically. Also make sure eating utensils are washed and stored properly.

Toothbrushing after meals is an important habit for young children to learn. Each child needs his or her own individual brush marked with a name or symbol that the child can recognize. The brush storage spot should also be marked. Some centers use upside down egg cartons, but a parent could also make a wooden toothbrush holder. Using only one tube of toothpaste increases the possibility of passing germs from one child to the next. You might want to consider having small individual tubes for each child. Some centers also turn small individual paper cups upside down and place a blob of toothpaste on each one. The child then swipes the paste off the bottom of the cup and onto his brush. Then he uses the cup to rinse with afterwards. However you prefer to do it, make sure children brush after each meal.

RECOGNIZES UNUSUAL BEHAVIOR OR SYMPTOMS OF CHILDREN WHO MAY BE ILL, AND PROVIDES FOR THEM

Sick days for the children in your program are inevitable, and you need to be prepared. Can you recognize when children are ill? Does your center have the space and staff to provide for them? If not, have you made arrangements with parents for alternate caregivers?

Policies about caring for sick children must be discussed with the staff and the children's parents so that everyone is familiar with the procedures.

The booklet *Sick Child Care for Parents and Child Care Providers* gives helpful hints on common childhood illnesses, when to call the doctor, and comfort measures for sick children. The leaflet "Parents' Guide for Calling a Doctor" asks simple questions about eight common childhood illnesses and gives advice about what to do, depending on the answers.

Child caregivers need to know general information about the seriousness of children's illnesses. For instance, children with a running nose, slight cough, slight headache, or slight stomachache may remain in the classroom. But children with a fever, vomiting, an earache, a congested cough, a bad headache, or a sore throat should be sent home or to the caregiver previously arranged for when parents are working. In the meantime the child needs to be isolated from the others. These arrangements should be set up ahead of time by the center and the parents.

You should be familiar with children's health needs. Are any of them on medication? Do any of them have allergies? What about physical limitations? Some children become fatigued more easily than others. Whether or not you are responsible for keeping the children's health records, you should familiarize yourself with them and be able to respond to individual needs.

Abused Children

Abused children are children whose parents or caregivers have mistreated or intentionally injured them. As a teacher or child-care worker, it is your responsibility to report suspected cases of child abuse. This type of mistreatment of children includes physical, emotional, and sexual abuse, as well as physical and emotional neglect. Physical abuse is easiest to recogize because of its visible signs, but it is possible to identify other forms of abuse as well.

Physically abused children may display repeated or unexplained injuries, burns, bruises, welts, or missing patches of hair. They may complain of harsh treatment or be unusually fearful of adults, including parents. Sometimes they may appear to be malnourished or dehydrated. They may also be withdrawn or sometimes disruptive. Physically neglected children are often unclean and may have bad odors from dirty clothing or hair. They may be dressed inappropriately for weather conditions or wear shoes and clothing of the wrong size. They may have untreated illnesses or injuries. They may be hungry or chronically tired and may spend much time alone.

Emotionally abused or neglected children are more difficult to identify, but they are generally unhappy and seldom smile. Sometimes they, too, are withdrawn or disruptive. Often they react without emotion to unpleasant statements or situations. They may appear apathetic and seldom participate in classroom activities.

Sexually abused children may have underclothing that is torn or stained. They may complain of pain or itching in the genital area or may have difficulty going to the bathroom. They may also be withdrawn or have trouble getting along with others.

Such children need help of two kinds. First you must accept them as worthy human beings in your classroom and let them know it. They will need to experience success and be praised for it. At the same time the abuse must be stopped.

The law requires that child caregivers report cases of child abuse. Most states have toll-free hot lines available twenty-four hours a day; the telephoned report must be followed by a written report within twenty-four hours. The state then contacts the local Department of Social Services, which sends caseworkers to investigate and take action with the family involved.

If you suspect a child is a victim of abuse or neglect, you should contact your center director or health specialist to evaluate the situation. Also ask to have your program conduct an inservice session to outline its policies for dealing with abuse and neglect.

Handicapped Children

Many handicapped children have special health needs. They may need special medication or a special diet. They may become fatigued more easily than other children and thus need fewer strenuous activities and more rest. Your center health specialist or family worker should help you determine this. Parent conferences should also be arranged to determine how best to serve the child with special needs. It is important to maintain close contact with parents of these children so they can let you know their expectations and concerns.

Be aware, however, that many parents may not have fully accepted their child's handicapping condition. You may need to sit down with the parents and a health or mental health specialist to discuss your concerns, and provide parents with information, resources, and referrals to help their child.

Can the child move freely, easily, and safely in the classroom? You may have to rearrange furniture, widen walkways, or make activity areas more accessible. What about special toys, equipment, and activities? Books such as *Mainstreaming in Early Childhood Education, A Step-by-Step Learning Guide for Retarded Infants and Children,* and *Young Children with Special Needs* offer many suggestions.

SUMMARY

You should be able to set up and maintain a healthy classroom that promotes good health and nutrition and is free from factors contributing to illness. You will be providing daily opportunities for your children to exercise both indoors and out whether or not a large space is available. The balance of active and quiet activities you set up will also include rest periods as a natural follow-up to exertion, although you will accommodate individual needs for children who no longer nap during the day.

Washing hands and brushing teeth will be an important part of your program, with care taken to prevent transfer of germs during toothbrushing. Nutritional needs for your children will be met through snacks and meals. In addition they will learn good food habits through their own fun experiences with nutritional foods.

Your children will be prepared to take medical tests and examinations through preliminary classroom activities set up by you or a health specialist. You will be able to recognize symptoms of illness in children and know how to deal with them. Characteristics of abused children will also be familiar to you, along with the response you and your center must make. The health needs of children with handicapping conditions will also be recognized and accommodated in your center.

LEARNING ACTIVITIES

1. Read Chapter 2, "Maintaining a Healthy Classroom," and answer Question Sheet 2-A.
2. View a health filmstrip and discuss its contents with your trainer.
3. Read one or more of the books listed under Suggested Readings. Add ten cards to your file with ideas for promoting health and nutrition in your classroom. Include the reference source on each card.
4. Make a card for each child in your class on which to record information about general health, approximate weight and height, energy level, napping habits, eating habits, any special health concerns, and, where necessary, suggestions for health improvement.
5. Use ideas from this chapter to help a small group of children learn a particular health or nutrition practice. (The trainer can observe.)
6. Celebrate a child's birthday with one of the nutritious food ideas described in this chapter. (The trainer can observe.)
7. Make a list of health facilities or human resources in your community that children and families can use for dealing with injuries, illness, dental health, mental health, abuse, and handicapping conditions.
8. Continue your Portfolio of evidence of your skills. Add one piece of evidence for each of the following Teacher Skills Checklist items:
   a. Encourages children to follow common health and nutrition practices.
   b. Provides and uses materials to insure children's health and cleanliness.
   c. Recognizes unusual behavior or symptoms of children who may be ill and provides for them.
   Evidence should reflect what you, not another staff member, have done.
9. Complete the Chapter 2 Evaluation Sheet and return it and the answers to Question Sheet 2-A to the appropriate college or program official.

QUESTION SHEET 2-A

(Based on Chapter 2, "Maintaining a Healthy Classroom")

1. How are good health practices best taught to young children?
2. How should you provide for large muscle exercise?
3. When should children have rest time in the classroom?
4. What can you do to encourage children to rest or nap?
5. How can children best be encouraged to keep clean?
6. How do children learn what foods the teacher considers most important?
7. What kinds of foods besides cookies and cake can you use for a birthday celebration?
8. How should you prepare children for an eye examination?
9. How can you help children break bad habits such as nail biting?
10. What should you do when a child becomes ill in your classroom?

SUGGESTED EVIDENCE FOR PORTFOLIO

1. A photo of a health activity the children perform, such as bathing dolls or cleaning the house, with a written explanation of how you used the activity to teach children about common health practices.
2. A list of the snacks you served in your classroom for one week, with a written explanation of how you and the children were involved in preparing them and learning about nutrition.
3. An explanation of your role in rest or nap periods, and how they contribute to the children's health.
4. Health records of one or more children (use pseudonyms to preserve confidentiality) with an explanation of how you have made individual plans to accommodate each child's health problems.
5. A description of any health referrals you have made or conferences you have had with parents, explaining the reason for initiating them and their outcome, and how this shows your competence in this area.

Each piece of evidence should be accompanied by a write-up explaining how this shows your competence in the area of **Healthy** and how the activity is developmentally appropriate for your children.

SUGGESTED READINGS

Allen, K. Eileen. *Mainstreaming in Early Childhood Education.* Albany, N.Y.: Delmar, 1980.

Bananas, Child Care Information & Referral. *Sick Child Care Book for Parents and Child Care Providers.* 6501 Telegraph Ave., Oakland, Calif. 94609, 1980.

Berger, Eugenia Hepworth. *Parents as Partners in Education: The School and Home Working Together,* 2nd ed. Columbus, Ohio: Merrill Publishing Co., 1987.

Braun, Samuel J., and Miriam G. Lasher. *Are You Ready to Mainstream?* Columbus, Ohio: Merrill Publishing Co., 1978.

Cherry, Clare. *Think of Something Quiet.* Belmont, Calif.: Pitman, 1981.

Cook, Ruth E., Annette Tessier, and Virginia B. Armbruster. *Adapting Early Childhood Curricula: Suggestions for Meeting Special Needs,* 2nd ed. Columbus, Ohio: Merrill Publishing Co., 1987.

Deiner, Penny Low. *Resources for Teaching Young Children with Special Needs.* New York: Harcourt Brace Jovanovich, 1983.

Endres, Jeannette Brakhane, and Robert E. Rockwell. *Food, Nutrition, and the Young Child,* 2nd ed. Columbus, Ohio: Merrill Publishing Co., 1986.

Fallen, Nancy H., and Warren Umansky. *Young Children with Special Needs.* 2nd ed. Columbus, Ohio: Merrill Publishing Co., 1985.

Fraser, Brian G. *The Educator and Child Abuse.* Chicago: National Committee for Prevention of Child Abuse, 1977.

Hart-Rossi, Janie. *Protect Your Child from Sexual Abuse: A Parent's Guide.* Seattle, Wash.: Parenting Press, 1984.

Johnson, Vicki M., and Roberta A. Werner. *A Step-by-Step-Learning Guide for Retarded Infants and Children.* Syracuse, N.Y.: Syracuse University Press, 1975.

Learning Institute of North Carolina. *Good Times with Good Foods.* Greensboro, N.C.: LINC, 1976.

Marotz, Lynn, Jeanettia Rush, and Marie Cross. *Health, Safety and Nutrition for the Young Child.* Albany, N.Y.: Delmar, 1985.

McClenahan, Pat, and Ida Jaqua. *Cool Cooking for Kids.* Belmont, Calif.: Fearon, 1976.

Murphy, Albert T. *Special Children, Special Parents: Personal Issues with Handicapped Children.* Englewood Cliffs, N.J.: Prentice-Hall, 1981.

O'Brien, Shirley. *Child Abuse: A Crying Shame.* Provo, Utah: Brigham Young University Press, 1980.

Paul, Aileen. *Kids Cooking Without a Stove.* Garden City, N.Y.: Doubleday & Company, 1975.

Pipes, Peggy L. *Nutrition in Infancy and Childhood.* St. Louis: C. V. Mosby, 1977.

Reinisch, Edith H., and Ralph E. Minear, Jr. *Health of the Preschool Child.* New York: John Wiley, 1978.

Smith, Tom E.C., Barrie Jo Price, and George E. Marsh II. *Mildly Handicapped Children and Adults.* St. Paul: West Publishing Co., 1986.

Wanamaker, Nancy, et al. *More Than Graham Crackers.* Washington, D.C.: National Association for the Education of Young Children, 1979.

CHILDREN'S BOOKS

Brighton, Catherine. *The Picture.* Boston: Faber & Faber, 1985.

Brown, Margaret Wise. *Goodnight Moon.* New York: Harper & Row, 1947.

Burningham, John. *Where's Julius?* New York: Crown Publishers, 1986.

Carle, Eric. *The Very Hungry Caterpillar.* New York: Crowell, 1971.

Hoban, Russell. *Bread and Jam for Frances.* New York: Scholastic, 1972.

Marzolla, Jean. *Close Your Eyes.* New York: Dial Press, 1978.

McPhail, David. *The Bear's Toothache.* Boston: Little, Brown, 1972.

Perez, Carla. *Your Turn, Doctor.* New York: Dial Books for Young Readers, 1982.

Sharmat, Mitchell. *Gregory, the Terrible Eater.* New York: Scholastic, 1980.

Showers, Paul. *No Measles, No Mumps for Me.* New York: Thomas Y. Crowell, 1980.

Stevens, Kathleen. *The Beast in the Bathtub.* New York: Harper & Row, 1978.

Tobia, Tobi. *The Quitting Deal.* New York: Penguin, 1975.

Wahl, Jan. *Jamie's Tiger.* New York: Harcourt Brace Jovanovich, 1978.

Zolotow, Charlotte. *Flocks of Birds.* New York: Thomas Y. Crowell, 1965.

SOUND FILMSTRIPS

Child Abuse and Neglect. Tuckahoe, N.Y.: Campus Film Distributors.

Health and Safety. Tuckahoe, N.Y.: Campus Film Distributors.

Nutrition. Tuckahoe, N.Y.: Campus Film Distributors.

Physical and Health Impairments. Tuckahoe, N.Y.: Campus Film Distributors.

CHAPTER 2 EVALUATION SHEET
MAINTAINING A HEALTHY CLASSROOM

1. Student _____

2. Trainer _____

3. Center where training occurred _____

4. Beginning date _____ Ending date _____

5. Describe what student did to accomplish General Objective

   _____

   _____

6. Describe what student did to accomplish Specific Objectives

   Objective 1 _____

   _____

   Objective 2 _____

   _____

   Objective 3 _____

   _____

7. Evaluation of student's Learning Activities
   (Trainer Check One)   (Student Check One)

   _____ Highly superior performance   _____

   _____ Superior performance   _____

   _____ Good performance   _____

   _____ Less than adequate performance   _____

Signature of Trainer: Signature of Student:

_____   _____

Comments:

3 Establishing a Learning Environment

General Objective

To be able to set up and arrange an early childhood classroom so that children will become self-directed in their learning.

Specific Objectives

☐ Determines what activity areas can and should be included in the classroom on the basis of program goals, space available, and number of children.
☐ Separates activity areas and places them in appropriate spaces.
☐ Arranges equipment and materials so children can make choices easily and independently.

I n early childhood classrooms, it is often the physical arrangement of equipment and materials that determines what will happen. The physical arrangement conveys a message to the children, telling them what they may or may not do, and what it is we expect of them.

Wide, open spaces tell them they may run and shout. Small, closed-in spaces indicate quiet and limited access for only a few children at a time. Carpeted areas invite children to sit on the floor. Pillows near bookshelves say, "Relax and look at a book."

Water containers full to the brim are asking to be spilled. An inch or two of water in the bottom gives children freedom to move it around.

Tall shelves stuffed with art materials say, "This is not for you to touch," to many children. To the adventurous, they say, "See if you can reach us!"

A table with four chairs invites four children to sit down. One puzzle on the table invites a squabble. Thus, how we arrange our classrooms helps decide what will take place in them.

GOALS

What do we want to happen? The primary goal of many early childhood programs is to promote a child's positive self-image. If that is your goal, you will want to arrange your classroom in a way that will help children develop confidence, help them feel good about themselves as people, and help them become self-directed in learning activities.

The physical arrangement of the classroom can do this if you keep the children in mind when you arrange the activity areas.

DETERMINES WHAT ACTIVITY AREAS CAN AND SHOULD BE INCLUDED IN THE CLASSROOM ON THE BASIS OF PROGRAM GOALS, SPACE AVAILABLE, AND NUMBER OF CHILDREN

Determining Activity Areas

Activity areas are called by a variety of terms in different programs or different parts of the country: *centers, stations, zones,* or *play units.* Whatever you call yours, it is the area in your classroom devoted to a particular activity.

The number and kinds of activity areas your classroom should contain depends upon program goals, space, and number of children. Many programs follow state or federal government regulations that require from thirty-five to fifty square feet of space per child.

Many early childhood programs follow the ratio of five children to one adult. That means if you employ a teacher, a teacher's aide, and a volunteer, you will be serving fifteen children. Three- and four-year-old children need such close adult support. However, two adults can often handle a classroom of twenty or more five- and six-year-olds.

A rule of thumb many programs follow allows four children in an activity area. Young children have difficulty working or playing on their own with larger groups. If you serve fifteen children, you will need a minimum of four activity areas. If you serve twenty children, you will need a minimum of five areas, more if possible. What will they be?

Ideally, you will be able to include a permanent block building area, book area, dramatic play area, manipulative area, art area, and science/math area. You may also be able to set up areas for large motor activities, music, sand or water play, woodworking, and cooking on a temporary basis (or permanent, whenever possible) in the space available.

Activity Area Checklist

Many teachers-in-training have profited by the use of a field-tested checklist to learn to arrange the physical environment of the classroom. The Activity Area Checklist has proved helpful to teachers in the field since its development by the author in 1974.

Activity area checklist

Student_____ Date_____

DIRECTIONS: Place a checkmark in the space before each item observed in the classroom.

1. Provide classroom areas for:
   _____ Block building
   _____ Books
   _____ Dramatic play
   _____ Large motor activities
   _____ Manipulative activities
   _____ Art
   _____ Music
   _____ Science/math
   _____ Sand/water play
   _____ Woodworking
   _____ Cooking
   _____ Child's private area

2. Organize block building area to contain:
   _____ Blocks in order on shelves
   _____ Enough blocks for several children to build large buildings
   _____ Room for children to build undisturbed
   _____ Large and small figures and trucks
3. Organize book area to contain:
   _____ Books appropriate for preschoolers
   _____ Multiethnic books
   _____ Books arranged at children's level
   _____ Books in good condition
   _____ Books arranged attractively
   _____ A comfortable place to enjoy books
   _____ A location away from noisy activities
4. Organize dramatic play area to contain:
   _____ Appropriate equipment, furniture and accessories
   _____ A full-length mirror
   _____ Men's and women's dress-up clothes
   _____ Clothes out where children can see them
   _____ Materials neatly arranged for easy selection and return
   _____ Dolls of different skin colors
   _____ Language props such as two telephones
5. Locate large motor activities and equipment:
   _____ To promote climbing, balancing, large movements
   _____ In an area where children can use them freely and safely
   _____ Away from quiet activities
6. Arrange manipulative materials:
   _____ Close to the area where they will be used
   _____ For easy selection and return by children
   _____ With enough materials for several children at once
   _____ With materials of varying levels of complexity
   _____ So that necessary parts and pieces are not missing
7. Have art materials for immediate use:
   _____ Located near tables or easels where they will be used
   _____ Usable with minimum adult direction
   _____ For easy selection and return by children
8. Arrange music equipment and activities to:
   _____ Include sound- and rhythm-producing materials
   _____ Include body movements
   _____ Include songs with children
   _____ Include record player and records

9. Include in science/math corner:
  _____ Children's displays or collections
  _____ Materials for sorting, counting
  _____ Changing materials or displays
  _____ Animal, fish, or insect pets
  _____ Plants
  _____ Appropriate books
  _____ A computer
10. Arrange sand and water activities:
  _____ With enough accessories for several to play with at once ·
  _____ To be used with minimum adult direction
  _____ Near source of water
  _____ For easy cleanup
11. Provide woodworking activities with:
  _____ Usable pounding, sawing equipment
  _____ Enough equipment for more than one child
  _____ Wood scraps, nails, etc.
  _____ Safety limits to protect children
  _____ Necessary adult supervision
  _____ Minimum adult direction
12. Include in cooking activities:
  _____ A variety of food preparation
  _____ Use of real facilities
  _____ Utensils such as knives, spoons, beaters
  _____ Necessary adult supervision
  _____ Minimum adult direction
13. Provide general room conditions with:
  _____ A cubby, shelf, or box for each child's possessions
  _____ Adequate storage space so room can be kept orderly
  _____ Noisy activities separated from quiet activities
  _____ Uncluttered space where children can move freely
  _____ Any special arrangements for handicapped children
  _____ Pictures, photos, displays at child's height
  _____ Appropriate preventive measures for safety hazards
  _____ Light, air, and heat conditions at best possible levels

Permission is granted by the publisher to reproduce this checklist for record keeping.

Using the Checklist

You can use the Activity Area Checklist as a guide to setting up your classroom from scratch or as an assessment tool to help evaluate your present physical arrangement. Looking at the twelve areas suggested by the checklist, you can determine how many of these can be accommodated in your own program according to the program's goals, the number of children, the space available, and your and the children's interests and needs.

After assessing your own classroom by checking off items on the Activity Area Checklist, you will need to take the next step in the evaluation of your learning environment. On a separate sheet of paper you should record what we call an "Evidence List" of how each item on the checklist serves your children. For instance, under area

> 1. Provide classroom areas for:
> _____ Block building

we ask our students to record on their Evidence List how their block building area serves their children. One student wrote: "Block building: Blocks are stored lengthwise on low shelves with cutout diagrams for each shape block so children can make choices and return them with ease." Another wrote: "Block building: Area is separated from dramatic play area by shelf dividers; has room for six children with building space marked on floor with masking tape."

It is important not only to set up these various areas, but also to know how to use them with children. Each of the twelve areas mentioned on the checklist is discussed in this chapter. Students who have difficulty knowing how an area is used may want to read about it first before making their Evidence List.

```
1. Provide classroom areas for:
   _____ Block building
   _____ Books
   _____ Dramatic play
   _____ Large motor activities
   _____ Manipulative activities
   _____ Art
   _____ Music
   _____ Science/math
   _____ Sand/water play
   _____ Woodworking
   _____ Cooking
   _____ Child's private area
```

Child's Private Area

The child's private area mentioned in the checklist is not an activity area, but should somehow be provided on a permanent basis if your goal is to promote a positive self-image. It is a place where a child can get away by himself when the need arises. If yours is an all-day program, such a location is a necessity. Three- and four-year-olds, especially, find large groups of children overpowering if they must be with them for any length of time.

An overstuffed chair in a comfortable corner away from noisy activities may be all that is needed. Some classrooms use a large cardboard carton with a cut-out door and window for a hut or store or playhouse. This can serve as the private area when dramatic play is finished. A packing crate serves the same purpose. So does a card table covered with a blanket for the child to crawl under. Some centers have a loft that can be used as well.

It is important that the private area be located in the classroom and not totally isolated in another part of the building. Children need to be by themselves, but at the same time, they like to know what others are doing. Being isolated in another room is too much like punishment.

Block Building

Wooden unit blocks have played an important role in early childhood programs since their introduction by Carolyn Pratt in her Greenwich Village Play School during the

---

2. Organize block building area to contain:
   _____ Blocks in order on shelves
   _____ Enough blocks for several children to build large buildings
   _____ Room for children to build undisturbed
   _____ Large and small figures and trucks

---

early years of the century.* Her units, half units, double units, arches, bridges, ramps, and so forth, have stimulated children's imagination and creativity in constructing buildings of all sizes and shapes. The blocks have helped develop children's perceptual skills, such as eye-hand coordination, as they match sizes or balance one block on another when building towers and skyscrapers. They have promoted counting and categorizing skills as children learn to sort shapes and sizes during pickup. They have helped reinforce ideas gained on field trips when children use them to reconstruct the fire station or farm they have just visited.

Many prepackaged nursery school sets of unit blocks contain too few blocks for children to construct even a small number of moderate-sized buildings at

---

* Frank Caplan and Theresa Caplan, *The Power of Play* (New York: Doubleday, 1974), pp. 267-73.

one time. It is better to order the blocks separately by size according to the amount of space available in the classroom.

Most teachers believe that unit blocks are well worth their rather high expense. But if you have no money to buy them, it is possible to make a set of "blocks" yourself, using cardboard milk cartons and masking tape or contact paper. Collect as many half gallons, quarts, pints, and half-pints as possible. Then cut and fold each top flat and cover the entire carton with masking tape or plain contact paper. Bring the parents together for a "block-making bee" and a get-acquainted session.

Hollow cardboard blocks are also available, but these should not be substituted for the wooden unit blocks. The hollow cardboard blocks are similar to the large, hollow wooden blocks and help develop large motor skills in children. Both the wooden and hollow cardboard blocks are popular with children for building child-size buildings they can climb on and into. You may want to store these on shelves in the same area as your unit blocks if you want them used there. On the other hand, because they involve large motor skills, you may want to keep them in the area where climbing, jumping, and balancing activities go on.

It is important to store block building accessories in the same area with the unit blocks, so children will know they are available and use them with the blocks. Small wooden figures of people and animals are popular if you want dramatic play to occur. Sometimes children want to play only with blocks, but often they want to pretend that people and animals are doing things in the block buildings. Small and large trucks are also appropriate accessories. String for electric wires and plastic aquarium tubing for water hoses are often effective if children have been looking at and talking about real wires and hoses after visits to a service station, a fire department, a construction site, or a street near the center.

Since the block building area is such a good one for follow-up activities after field trips, you should be alert during the trip for ways the experience can be duplicated in the block corner. A picture of the firehouse, post office, or farm you have just visited can be taped up in the block corner at the children's eye level to stimulate building. An added impetus to building is having the appropriate accessories located where children will see and use them. (For more information on block building, see Chapter 9.)

Book Area

Early childhood specialists tell parents that reading to their preschool children is one of the most important things they can do to help their development. Preschool programs must go even further. You should not only read to the children; you should also provide opportunities for children to get together with books on their own. If children are going to succeed in school, if they are going to develop the necessary verbal skills, they need to be introduced to books in a pleasurable way as early as possible.

In other words, the book area should be one of the most comfortable and inviting areas in your classroom. A soft throw rug, bright puffy pillows, and a rocking chair may be the items you will choose. You need not go to great expense. A parent will often volunteer to cover bed pillows for the book corner. Carpet stores may donate rug samples when they are finished with them. Children love to participate in carpeting their own book nook with multicolored rug squares.

Because the book area is a quiet one, it should be separated from noisy areas by room dividers or placed next to other quiet activities, such as art or science.

Books should be displayed in the most inviting way possible. If book covers are torn or missing, repair or replace them. A torn book is not inviting to a child, except perhaps to mutilate it further. Torn books, in fact, communicate several things to children. They tell them their teachers are not very concerned about keeping books in good condition. This must mean books are not important, or someone

---

3. Organize book area to contain:
   _____ Books appropriate for preschoolers
   _____ Multiethnic books
   _____ Books arranged at children's level
   _____ Books in good condition
   _____ Books arranged attractively
   _____ A comfortable place to enjoy books
   _____ A location away from noisy activities

---

would see that they were kept in shape. They also tell children that it must be all right to tear a book, since someone already has.

If you have a large book collection, you should display only part of it and change the books from time to time. Putting out all the books at once confuses the children. Be sure the books are displayed at their eye level. Bookshelves are often made for older children; scale them down to your children's height.

Where do the books come from? A bookmobile? A library? Private donations? No matter what their source, you should be the one to choose the books for your classroom. Preschool children do not yet know how to select the best books. You need to acquire that knowledge, if you do not have it, and put it to use. With the number of children's books presently being published, you must become familiar not only with the best books, but also with selection techniques, so you will be able to choose wisely from among the many books available.

Some should be multiethnic books. They should show children of different races and cultures as main characters. Whether or not you have black or Hispanic or Native American children in your classroom, you should still have books that portray this multiethnicity of American life. There are excellent picture books available today showing children of almost every race and culture. From Ezra Jack Keats's characters, Peter and Archie, the inner-city black boys, to Taro Yashima's Momo, the Japanese girl in New York City, modern children's books show boys and girls of every race doing interesting things in a setting any reader can understand and respond to. (For more information on children's books, see Chapter 6.)

Dramatic Play Area

Young children live in a world of pretending. To adults who view fantasy with misgivings, this may seem unhealthy. It is quite the contrary. Young children are not trying to escape from reality; they are trying to understand it. They are doing their best to deal with people and circumstances that sometimes confuse them. They are trying to bring some sense, order, and control into their world.

To assist them in their pretending, we provide a classroom area that encourages imaginative play. Some programs call it the *housekeeping corner, doll corner,* or *dress-up corner.* Others prefer the term *family corner* to eliminate sexist overtones.

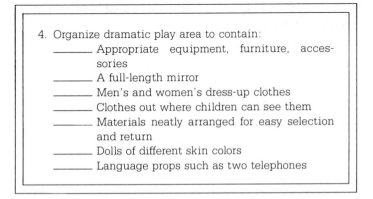

4. Organize dramatic play area to contain:
   _____ Appropriate equipment, furniture, accessories
   _____ A full-length mirror
   _____ Men's and women's dress-up clothes
   _____ Clothes out where children can see them
   _____ Materials neatly arranged for easy selection and return
   _____ Dolls of different skin colors
   _____ Language props such as two telephones

This area often contains kitchen furnishings, such as a stove, refrigerator, sink, cupboards, and table, scaled to child size. Some programs have a store with shelves and a counter in the dramatic play area. Some have a bedroom, with mirror, dresser, and doll beds.

All these arrangements are familiar to children, and encourage them to dress up and play a variety of roles without teacher involvement: mother, father, uncle, aunt, grandmother, grandfather, sister, brother, baby, storekeeper. Playing these roles helps children experience life from another point of view. It helps them understand these roles, and in many instances, helps them work out fears and frustrations in their own lives.

The little girl who dresses up as Mommy and then proceeds to beat the baby doll is not necessarily imitating a role she has seen enacted at home. She is more likely expressing her own frustration of being in a helpless, powerless role as a child. Dramatic play allows such frustrations to be expressed in acceptable and harmless ways. Fears of going to the doctor can be played out ahead of time through such pretending. Dramatic play experiences help a child gain a healthy and positive self-concept.

You should provide both men's and women's clothes, hats, and shoes. Teen-agers' clothes are just as appropriate and, in fact, fit the children even better than adult sizes.

Your dolls should be of different skin colors, whether or not your children are. Let us introduce children to the fascinating variety of Americans in a positive way as early as possible. Attitudes that last a lifetime develop in the early years.

Children learn much about themselves through dramatic play. They quickly learn how other children respond to them in the frank give-and-take of peer play. They should be able to look at themselves in the full-length mirror that should be a part of every dramatic play area. (For more information on play, see Chapter 9.)

Large Motor Area

If your program has a well-equipped outside playground, you may wonder why you should provide a large motor area inside. It is essential during the preschool years for children to practice large motor skills as often as possible every day, whether or not they go outside. Also, some skills, such as walking on a balance beam, can be practiced more easily inside.

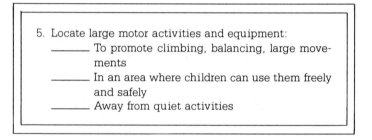

5. Locate large motor activities and equipment:
   _____ To promote climbing, balancing, large movements
   _____ In an area where children can use them freely and safely
   _____ Away from quiet activities

An indoor wooden climber is perhaps the best single piece of equipment if you have room for only one. A homemade substitute could be a packing crate and a ladder, or a loft with a ladder and slide. Cardboard cartons with low doors cut in both ends make fine tunnels to promote crawling skills. Even an ordinary chair can serve as a piece of climbing/jumping equipment when nothing else is available. Any teacher can make an obstacle course out of ordinary classroom furnishings, masking tape, and imagination.

As you become more aware of how closely intellectual development is tied to motor control, you will want to provide many opportunities for children to practice control of their bodies in the classroom. Plan to include movement activities in the daily program, and make sure that children have the opportunity to play outside whenever possible. (For more information on motor activities, see Chapter 4.)

Manipulative Area

Manipulative skill is the ability to use one's hands and fingers with dexterity. It is important for young children to develop such skill so they learn not only to button and zip clothes, tie shoes, and hold a pencil with ease, but also so they can later learn to read without difficulty. Eye-hand coordination is a prerequisite for developing the visual perception necessary to read from left to right.

Early childhood classrooms generally have many games and puzzles to promote small motor coordination. All puzzles provide this practice. Wooden commercial puzzles, of which each piece is a separate part of a person's or animal's body, are the best ones to start with for unskilled three-year-olds. You may need to try out your puzzles with your children in the beginning to make sure they are not too difficult. Children may need help at first to experience success. They may also need encouragement to stay with the puzzle until they finish it, and then praise for a job well done. As the children's skills increase, you can add more challenging puzzles or games to the manipulative area.

An almost unlimited supply of commercial material is available to fill your manipulative shelves: interlocking bricks, stacking toys, dominos, Tinkertoys, snapping beads, stringing beads, and table blocks. You may want to add teacher-made

6. Arrange manipulative materials:
   _____ Close to the area where they will be used
   _____ For easy selection and return by children
   _____ With enough materials for several children at once.
   _____ With materials of varying levels of complexity
   _____ So that necessary parts and pieces are not missing

games to the area. Not only will you save money with homemade materials, but you can also provide directly for the children's needs.

It is important to check the manipulative games frequently to see that parts and pieces are not missing. It is frustrating for a child to try to put together a puzzle with missing pieces. Either replace the pieces or discard the puzzle. Of course, it is equally trying for you to keep track of all the parts. Some classrooms use plastic margarine containers with an outline of a part traced on the tops to encourage children to put away pieces where they belong. Opening and closing these storage containers give children additional practice in developing small motor coordination.

Being able to hold a pencil is another small motor skill children will eventually need to accomplish. Some are ready now. You might try setting up a "writing table" in your manipulative area. It could contain primary size pencils, crayons and magic markers, and paper and pads of various sizes to encourage scribbling and eventually printing. (For more information on manipulative activities, see Chapter 4.)

Art Area

Most early childhood programs use art activities almost every day. But art activity seems to be controlled more frequently by adults in the classroom than almost any other activity. Teachers or aides usually get out the art supplies, pass out the paper, give instructions, then remain in the area to make sure their instructions are carried out.

If we truly want to help a child develop a positive self-image, we should allow the child to be as independent in art activities as in dramatic play or block building. Freedom to explore and experiment encourages and supports creativity. Direction and instruction are surely appropriate in certain art activities and at certain times, but we should also allow children the opportunity to try out paints of their own choosing with paper they select. This is possible when child-level shelves hold the art materials near the tables or easels where they will be used, when materials are arranged in order for easy selection and return by the children, and when children are allowed and encouraged to participate in setting up and cleaning up art activities. When children become independent in art, they will happily choose this activity on their own during the daily work/play period.

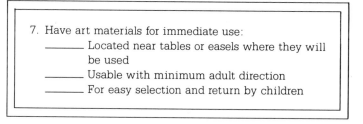

7. Have art materials for immediate use:
_____ Located near tables or easels where they will be used
_____ Usable with minimum adult direction
_____ For easy selection and return by children

The location of the art area, a quiet activity, should be removed from the more boisterous doings of the classroom. If you have a water source in the room, the art area should be nearby if at all possible. With minimum direction, children can become entirely independent in setup and cleanup when the materials are nearby. (For more information on art activities, see Chapter 7.)

Music Area

There is perhaps more controversy over this particular area of the early childhood classroom than any other. More than half the early childhood practitioners in the author's survey were strongly opposed to having a permanent music area with music-making devices freely available for the children during the daily work/play period. A lesser number of teachers believed just as strongly that record players and rhythm instruments should be left out and available for children during appropriate times.

Some teachers felt that musical devices used indiscriminately were too noisy, and had an adverse effect on the classroom atmosphere. Others felt that creative expression was inhibited when no musical devices at all were available for children's experimentation. They added that adults' discomfort with musical production was not a justifiable reason for denying it to children.

I have concluded that this must be a personal choice. Your classroom should reflect your own ideas, goals, and philosophy. If you feel uncomfortable with music, perhaps you can find someone to contribute to your program who is at ease

8. Arrange music equipment and activities to:
   _____ Include sound- and rhythm-producing materials
   _____ Include body movements
   _____ Include songs with children
   _____ Include record player and records

with singing and playing an instrument. Often, high school or college-age guitarists or senior citizen piano players are proud to lend their talents to an early childhood program.

Some music areas contain shelves to store rhythm instruments. Instruments can also be stored on hooks attached to a pegboard wall. Either way, it is a good idea to trace around each instrument with a magic marker to give children yet another opportunity to match shapes and return materials to their proper locations.

An inexpensive record player that children can learn to operate by themselves is a wise investment. Rules directing and restricting its use are not difficult for children to learn and are satisfying for young children to follow. Records, however, should not be the extent of your classroom music, for they tend to be a passive listening form. Children also need opportunities to make their own music—singing, humming, whistling, or playing a harmonica, a drum, or an autoharp. (For more information on music, see Chapter 7.)

Science/Math Area

In some programs, science and math activities are relegated to a side cupboard or window ledge. Teachers and aides who realize that such an area can be the most exciting spot in the classroom often reserve much more space: a cozy corner with a table for the daily "science object," shelves for children's collections, and space for the tools of science and math—magnifying glasses of different sizes, magnets of different sizes, tweezers, a tape measure or wind-up ruler, a balance, and a box of Cuisenaire rods, for starters.

9. Include in science/math corner:
   _____ Children's displays or collections
   _____ Materials for sorting, counting
   _____ Changing materials or displays
   _____ Animal, fish, or insect pets
   _____ Plants
   _____ Appropriate books
   _____ A computer

There is space for a terrarium full of ferns and moss and wintergreen gathered on a trip to the woods. There is an aquarium for goldfish or tropicals and a book nearby for identifying them. There is often a cage with a gerbil or guinea pig in residence. Shelves closest to the window contain bean sprouts in paper cups.

There will be something going on in the science corner every day in such a classroom. An egg carton full of a bean-seed-button mixture encourages children to sort and classify, or perhaps weigh the items with the balance. A chart to record how many inches each child's beans have grown invites all kinds of measuring with the wind-up ruler. A sealed box in the middle of the table with the sign, "Guess what's inside. Tell your guess to the tape recorder," has the curious ones asking what the sign says, shaking the box, listening closely, and cautiously recording their guesses. Another sign, "Bring something green tomorrow," sets off a babble of ideas.

Children in such a classroom expect to be challenged to find something out. They know they must use their five senses plus the available science tools to discover "how much" or "what kind" or "how many." What's more, these children have learned to do it on their own because of the arrangement of the materials and the stimulating manner in which science objects are displayed.

Such children will welcome the addition of a personal computer to their science area. More and more early childhood educators have come to realize that these powerful interactive learning tools can be used with great success by preschoolers. The exploring-through-play and trial-and-error style used by young children to investigate new objects is exactly the way the computer is set up to teach. Teachers must choose good preschool software programs and then integrate them into the curriculum by providing parallel activities for each program. Children learn concepts such as symbolization, cause-and-effect, matching, and numbers, as well as skills such as learning to take turns, participating in conversation, and being creative with art programs. *The Computer as a Paintbrush* (Beaty and Tucker, 1987) tells how to set up and use a computer in an early childhood classroom. (For more information on science activities, see Chapter 5.)

Sand/Water Play Area

Water has an irresistible fascination for youngsters. Watch them wash their hands or get a drink. The splashing and squirting that often occur are part of the natural discovery process children use to learn about new things.

10. Arrange sand and water activities:
      _____ With enough accessories for several to play at once
      _____ To be used with minimum adult direction
      _____ Near source of water
      _____ For easy cleanup

Yet it is more than that. Water seems to have a mesmerizing quality. The smooth or bubbly feel of it . . . the gushing, gurgling sound of it . . . the way you can squirt it or spray it or pour it. Even children with short attention spans can play with it for hours. The hyperactive or unruly child often quiets down remarkably during water play. Its calming effect makes it an excellent quiet activity, a wonderful change of pace after a hectic morning.

The physical arrangement of the water play area, just as with the rest of your classroom, determines whether children can enjoy playing in water on their own, or whether there will always be squabbling, splashing, and the necessity for close adult supervision.

If you have a water table, put only an inch or two of water in it. Children can have fun with this much and still keep themselves and the room fairly dry. Have equipment for use in the water table on nearby shelves or hanging from a pegboard rack in the area. To avoid argument, be sure to have more than one of the favorite toys. Large plastic basters and eggbeaters are usually favorites. A supply of empty plastic squeeze bottles of various sizes, plastic pitchers, plastic bottles, plastic hoses, and nose droppers should be standard equipment. Plastic boats and figures of people are also popular.

Hanging on hooks or folded on shelves nearby should be the aprons the children can get by themselves to keep their clothes dry. Four children are about all a water table can accommodate at once. Place the number "4" or four stick figures of children in the area and let the children regulate themselves.

If you don't have a water table, use four plastic dishpans on a regular classroom table. The sink in the housekeeping corner makes a good, if small, water play area for doing the dolls' dishes or laundering doll clothes.

Put a squirt of detergent in the water at times and let children play with bubbles. They may want to blow through straws. Another day, let them use food coloring and droppers to mix colors.

One nursery classroom designed especially for children had clear plastic water pipes installed in the sinks so the children could watch the water in the pipes.

Water tables can easily be converted to sand tables for another activity children really enjoy. The same directions apply. Two or three inches of sand is plenty. Keep sand accessories and clean-up equipment in the area. Help children understand a few simple rules: keep the sand in the table; no throwing sand. Then enforce the rules with quiet, consistent firmness.

Woodworking Area

Wood is another medium especially attractive to children. You can see this in the way they handle wooden blocks. The fact that wood can be pounded and turned into something other than itself makes it as creative a medium as paint.

Both boys and girls love to pound. Thus, woodworking is an excellent channel for the acceptable venting of hostility. Children can pound wood and let off steam harmlessly.

11. Provide woodworking activities with:
_____ Usable pounding, sawing equipment
_____ Enough equipment for more than one child
_____ Wood scraps, nails, etc.
_____ Safety limits to protect children
_____ Necessary adult supervision
_____ Minimum adult direction

Not every early childhood program can afford a workbench, but I have found that tree-trunk sections are even more effective for pounding on or into. Just for the fun of pounding, let children nail things onto the tops of sawed-off tree sections. A box of nails of many sizes and another of pine scraps are enough to keep your woodworking area going for many days.

Some teachers substitute ceiling tiles for wood scraps because children have better control over hammer and nail and therefore more success using the soft tiles instead of the harder wood. Building-supply dealers will sometimes donate extra tiles. Children can also pound nails through leather scraps more easily than they can through wood. Tinkertoys can be used to pound nails through as well.

Woodworking tools can be stored in toolboxes, on shelves, or hung from pegboards with their outlines traced so that children can match shapes and return them easily.

Cooking Area

Many adults misunderstand the idea of cooking in the preschool classroom. This activity in no way purports to teach a child to cook. Cooking is, instead, an exceptional vehicle for promoting the many learning experiences thus far mentioned. Peeling shells from hard-boiled eggs offers unparalleled practice in fine motor skills. Scraping carrots, dicing potatoes, and turning the handle of an eggbeater provide additional fine motor practice.

Science observations and experiments can be carried on through almost any cooking activity: showing how heat changes things, demonstrating how liquids

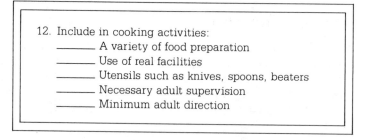

12. Include in cooking activities:
_____ A variety of food preparation
_____ Use of real facilities
_____ Utensils such as knives, spoons, beaters
_____ Necessary adult supervision
_____ Minimum adult direction

dissolve things, illustrating the changes produced by heating or freezing. Math learnings are promoted through weighing and measuring. Symbolization is strengthened through use of illustrated recipe charts.

Children's intense interest in food and food preparation provides motivation for immediate involvement. A teacher's or aide's ingenuity supplies the activities. There are no limits to the learnings implicit in a cooking area. Cooking is so important to children because it is a real activity, not a simulated one such as dramatic play. It is also satisfying because they can eat the results!

Cooking can take place in the regular classroom at a table set up for it, on a counter near an electrical outlet, or in the center kitchen. A teacher/aide who is comfortable with this activity will surely want it as a part of the classroom curriculum. (For more information on cooking activities, see Chapter 2.)

SEPARATES ACTIVITY AREAS AND PLACES THEM IN APPROPRIATE SPACES

Separating Activities

Most classrooms use shelves, cubbies, or large pieces of equipment as dividers to separate the activity areas from one another. Building a loft in the room gives you space under and on top. Use your ingenuity to section off your classroom areas. One teacher hung cargo netting from the ceiling to the floor with a mat at the bottom. Besides separating two areas of the room, it also provided for large motor development.

Finally, you need to arrange noisy areas away from the quiet activities. Dramatic play, block building, large motor activities, woodworking, and music are usually the noisiest. Be sure to place them at some distance from quiet areas such as the book corner.

Now step back and look at the way children use the classroom. Do they all crowd together in one area? Do they mill around in the center of the room without much direction? Do they have to walk through the block area to get to the bathroom? Are your clothing cubbies near the door where children enter? In order to arrange your activity areas so children can move to them freely and use them without difficulty, you need to determine how the room works in its present arrangement.

Floor Planning

Make a floor plan of the arrangement and record directly on it as you observe children during the free-choice period for ten minutes on three different days. Use some sort of symbol such as x's and o's for boys and girls. Record on the plan the individual children in each area for the ten minutes of your observation. Use arrows to show how children move from one area to another. Then sit down and discuss your findings with other members of your team. If movement, work, and play are not orderly, you may want to make some changes.

How much empty space do you have? How much do you need? Large areas of empty space encourage children to run around aimlessly. Would your program be better served if you sectioned off some of that space into activity areas? You may feel you need the space for circle time or whole group activities. Circle time could take place in the book area if you make it large enough. Whole group rhythm activities could take place in the block area, after the blocks are put away. These activities do not require permanent exclusive space when they can be combined with other areas. In other words, make the environment work to your advantage.

Some teachers locate all the tables in a large area in the center of the room. Is this necessary? Wouldn't the room be more interesting if the tables were scattered in different areas and the large space sectioned into activity areas?

Traffic Patterns

Now look at the traffic patterns. Can children move freely from one area to another? They should not have to squeeze between tables and room dividers or step over someone's block structure to get a library book. On the other hand, you want to avoid one long traffic lane that encourages running from one end of the room to the other. Simply move a room divider or a piece of equipment into the pathway to prevent this uncontrolled movement.

What happens when the children enter your classroom? If they remove their outer clothing inside the room, are their cubbies nearby, or must they cross the room to find a clothes hook? If there are activity areas near the entrance, be sure they are not quiet ones, for there will be much bustling in and out of any preschool classroom entrance.

Regulating Behavior

Does your observation indicate possible problems with regulating the number of children in any one area? Children can regulate themselves if you make a game of it. You can paste pictures of four fish on the wall by the water table, six construction workers in the block area, or four bookworms in the book area, with a hook under each. Then children who want to play in the particular areas can hang matching pictures on the hooks. Or, if this is too formal for you, use the number signs merely as suggestions.

The number of chairs at a table also regulates how many can play. Some teachers section off the floor of the block area with masking tape to delineate building lots, if children have been crowding into this area. Give your children some suggestions for this kind of regulation and ask them what they'd like to try. Some teachers prefer color coding, with a certain number of tags of one color to be used by that number of children in an area of the same color. The tags can be kept on a pegboard near the front of the room for the children to choose from.

Check your room after you have rearranged it, to see if movement, work, and play are more orderly than before. If not, you may want to try another arrangement. Make it on paper first, and discuss it with your team and your children—it is their room, as well.

ARRANGES EQUIPMENT AND MATERIALS SO CHILDREN CAN MAKE CHOICES EASILY AND INDEPENDENTLY

Careful arrangement of equipment and materials can also help promote the children's independence and self-direction. Materials for use in each activity area need to be placed within the area, on low shelves or pegboards, so children can get them by themselves. They should be arranged so the children understand what is available and can make choices. There is no need to display all the toys at the same time; this makes it too difficult for young children to choose. Keep a closed storage cabinet for extra supplies and materials.

Book Area

For example, your book area should display a moderate number of books arranged with the covers facing the children. Children can then see what is available and choose what to look at. If your shelves are not the type for displaying books with the covers showing, you may want to put out books flat on tables or hang them on a clothesline with clothespins. Books crammed on a shelf with only the bindings showing are not inviting for children. They cannot see what is available, and usually respond by avoiding the book area.

You may not want to keep all the books in one area. To encourage young children to go to books for information on their own, you may want to place certain books in other activity areas. How about a paperback fish book hanging from a cord next to the aquarium? All pet stores have booklets on goldfish and tropicals. Let your children have the fun of matching their own fish with the pictures. What about a gerbil or guinea pig book in your pet area? A book such as *What's Inside?* next to your incubator? *Mickey's Magnet* in your science corner? Books about farms or fire stations or post offices in your block area? Fasten a manila pocket folder to the wall in the particular area and place a book in it featuring the subject you are currently investigating.

Your purpose should be to get books and children together. It may mean locating the books where the children are, as well as attracting children to the book area.

Dramatic Play Area

In the dramatic play area, the dress-up clothes should be hung on hooks, pegs, clothes trees, or hangers at child-height so children can easily choose and later return their costumes. Clothes crammed into a box or drawer make it difficult for the children to see what is available and make choices. Prop boxes can be stored on low shelves, with pictures on the outside indicating their contents (for example, doctor's equipment, fire fighter's gear). Then children are free to select props for the roles of barber, beautician, supermarket clerk, doctor, fire fighter, or police officer on their own.

Keep this area neat if you want children to be attracted to it. When play is finished, have them help you get it back in order, with clothes on the dolls or on the hooks, a baby doll asleep in the crib, and the table set and ready for its next role players.

Manipulative Area

Puzzles and table games should also be on low shelves next to the table or floor area designated for manipulative play. Children can then choose the games they want to play with. When they are finished, they will have no difficulty returning them. Why should teachers make the choices for children? It strengthens children's independence and self-concept to allow them their own choices. If they find that a puzzle is too difficult, they can return it and take another. Let's set up our classroom to give children this opportunity.

Block Area

Blocks should be on low shelves, stacked lengthwise so children can decide easily what they need for their building. A cutout or outline of the block at the back of the shelf enables children to return the blocks to the proper shelves and stack them the right way during pickup. Every item of equipment in your classroom can be so designated. Cutouts or outlines of woodworking tools, rhythm instruments, water table playthings, house corner dishes, cooking implements, paint jars, etc., can be drawn or pasted on their storage shelves so children can choose them easily and return them to their proper places.

Pictures

Another way to help children work and play independently is to put pictures of items and activities in particular areas. In the block area, for instance, mount pictures of buildings, roads, and bridges at child height to motivate building. In the woodworking area, paste pictures of trucks, boats, and cars; in the dramatic play area, pictures of people in different roles; in the science area, pictures of pets, plants, light bulbs, magnets, rocks, and shells; at the water table, pictures of boats, waterfalls, and soapsuds; in the book area, dust jackets of favorite books or posters showing Brian Wildsmith's animals or Ezra Jack Keats's children. Cut out pictures from magazines or catalogs. Perhaps parents will help you save magazines or look for certain types of pictures if you let them know you need them.

Evaluating Room Arrangement

Your children's behavior in the classroom will tell you whether you have planned and arranged well for them. Large groups of children milling around aimlessly may mean there is too much open space or not enough activity areas. A great deal of running may mean that open areas need to be sectioned off with room dividers. Concentrated child involvement in the activity areas means your arrangement is working as it should.

Blocks should be on low shelves, stacked lengthwise for easy selection and return.

During the year, you may want to rearrange the room for variety or for new challenges. It is best to change only one or two areas at once. Young children are easily upset by abrupt changes. It helps to let them participate in the planning and rearranging, since it is their room as much as yours.

Before you begin moving heavy furniture, it might be helpful to plan your new arrangement on paper with the classroom team. A sketch such as that in Figure

3-1 allows you to try out different ideas without physical effort. Then, when everyone agrees on a new arrangement, you can make your move.

  With this careful planning and arranging, your program for children has taken its first giant step toward success.

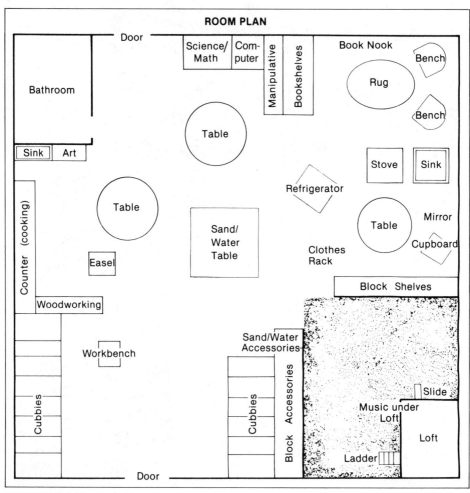

FIGURE 3-1 Room plan

SUMMARY

This chapter has provided ideas for setting up and arranging an early childhood classroom so that children will become self-directed in their learning. You will need to articulate your own program's goals in order to decide what activity areas to include in your classroom. Learning to use the Activity Area Checklist followed by your own Evidence List should help you understand how each activity area will promote your program's goals for young children. Since the physical arrangement of a pre-school classroom is the structure for an open and flexible curriculum, you will want to arrange your room carefully based on ideas from this chapter. Specific ideas for insuring that each area assists children in their learning include the use of a clothesline for displaying books in the library area and the use of a computer in the science/math area.

Ideas are presented on how to arrange the furniture in order to regulate disruptive child behavior or to help children use the activity areas more successfully. Children can make choices more easily and independently when material is placed with their needs and interests in mind. Teachers can determine the success of their arrangement through careful observation and recording of children's actions on a room plan.

LEARNING ACTIVITIES

1. Read Chapter 3, "Establishing a Learning Environment," and answer Question Sheet 3-A.
2. View Mediapak A, "Setting Up the Classroom," and answer Question Sheet 3-B.
3. Read one or more of the books listed under Suggested Readings, or view the sound filmstrip "Room Arrangement as a Teaching Strategy." Add ten cards to your file with specific ideas for setting up the classroom. Include the reference source on each card.
4. Make a floor plan of your classroom, and record on the plan the individual children in each area for ten minutes during free-choice period on three different days. Indicate boys and girls and the different days by color coding or symbols. Discuss the results with your trainer.
5. Visit another early childhood classroom and make a floor plan showing the areas children were using during your visit. Discuss the results with your trainer.
6. Use the Activity Area Checklist and Evidence List to assess your room arrangement. Set up a new area or rearrange an old one in your classroom based on the results. (The trainer can visit.)
7. Set up and implement a children's self-regulating method for choosing activity areas in your classroom as described in Chapter 3 or as decided by your classroom team. (The trainer can observe.)
8. Continue your Portfolio of evidence of your skills. Add one piece of evidence for each of the following Teacher Skills Checklist items:
   a. Determines what activity areas can and should be included in the classroom on the basis of program goals, space available, and the number of children.
   b. Separates activity areas and places them in appropriate spaces.
   c. Arranges equipment and materials so children can make choices easily and independently.
   Evidence should reflect what you, not another staff member, have done.
9. Complete the Chapter 3 Evaluation Sheet and return it and the answers to Question Sheets 3-A and 3-B to the appropriate college or program official.

QUESTION SHEET 3-A

(Based on Chapter 3, "Establishing a Learning Environment")

1. In what way does the physical arrangement of the classroom control the children's behavior?
2. What is one way your room arrangement can promote the children's positive self-image?
3. How can you determine what activity areas to establish in your room?
4. Why should you have a child's private area?
5. How can the arrangement of your block building area prevent squabbles?
6. How should you use the book area with your children?
7. What equipment might your dramatic play area contain after a field trip?
8. Why is it necessary to have large motor equipment inside the classroom?
9. Would you have rhythm instruments available for the children's free use? Why or why not?
10. When should you rearrange your classroom and how should you go about it?

QUESTION SHEET 3-B

(Based on Mediapak A, "Setting Up the Classroom")

1. What is one way you can arrange your classroom so children become more self-directed in their learning?
2. What can you do to help children make choices in the room?
3. How will you decide what block building accessories to provide?
4. How can you provide for the boys in your dramatic play area?
5. How should you arrange your dramatic play area to help children make choices?
6. How can children develop independence through art?
7. Why is it important to display children's art products attractively?
8. Where should children's manipulative materials be located?
9. How can your arrangement of the water play area promote children's independence?
10. How can you tell whether your room arrangement is successful?

SUGGESTED EVIDENCE FOR PORTFOLIO

1. Two floor plans of your classroom, one showing "before" and the other "after" you have rearranged your room to support your program's goals, with written explanation of the difference you hope your new arrangement will make.
2. Photographs of your classroom showing activity areas, with a written description of each photo and explanation of why the activity areas are set up this way.

3. A photograph or description of some innovative method you have used to divide the areas (such as the cargo net method), and a written explanation of why you chose the method.

4. Your observation floor plan with the marks showing children and traffic flow, along with your written interpretation of the observation, explaining how you corrected problem areas and the result.

5. A photo of an activity area showing how you arranged it for children to use independently, along with a written explanation of why this is important.

Each piece of evidence should be accompanied by a write-up explaining how this shows your competence in the area of **Learning Environment**, and how the activity is developmentally appropriate for your children.

SUGGESTED READINGS

Beaty, Janice J., and W. Hugh Tucker. *The Computer As a Paintbrush: Creative Uses for the Personal Computer in Preschool Classroom.* Columbus, Ohio: Merrill Publishing Co., 1987.

Cherry, Clare. *Creative Play for the Developing Child.* Belmont, Calif.: Fearon, 1976.

Cook, Ruth E., and Virginia Armbruster. *Adapting Early Childhood Curricula: Suggestions for Meeting Special Needs.* Columbus, Ohio: Merrill Publishing Co., 1983.

Forman, George E., and Fleet Hill. *Constructive Play: Applying Piaget in the Preschool.* Monterey, Calif.: Brooks/Cole Publishing Co., 1980.

Froschi, Merle, Linda Colon, Ellen Rubin, and Barbara Sprung. *Including All of Us: An Early Childhood Curriculum About Disability.* New York: Educational Equity Concepts, 1984.

Hill, Dorothy M. *Mud, Sand, and Water.* Washington, D.C.: National Association for the Education of Young Children, 1977.

Kritchevsky, Sybil, and Elizabeth Prescott. *Planning Environments for Young Children: Physical Space.* Washington, D.C.: National Association for the Education of Young Children, 1969.

Lindberg, Lucile, and Rita Swedlow. *Young Children Exploring and Learning.* Boston: Allyn & Bacon, 1985.

Magee, Patricia Boggia, and Marilyn Reichwald Ornstein. *Come With Us to Play-Group, A Handbook for Parents and Teachers of Young Children.* Englewood Cliffs, N.J.: Prentice-Hall, 1981.

Mainwaring, Sheila. *Room Arrangement and Materials.* Ypsilanti, Mich.: High/Scope Press, 1977.

Provenzo, Eugene F., Jr., and Arlene Brett. *The Complete Block Book.* Syracuse, N.Y.: Syracuse University Press, 1983.

CHILDREN'S BOOKS

Branley, Franklyn M., and Eleanor K. Vaughan. *Mickey's Magnet.* New York: Scholastic, 1971.

Cohen, Miriam. *Best Friends.* New York: Collier, 1971.

————. *Will I Have a Friend?* New York: Collier, 1967.

Garelick, May. *What's Inside? The Story of an Egg that Hatched.* New York: Scholastic, 1968.

Kessler, Leonard. *Mr. Pine's Mixed-Up Signs.* New York: Scholastic, 1961.

Oram, Hiawyn. *In the Attic.* New York: Holt, Rinehart & Winston, 1984.

Rockwell, Harlow. *My Nursery School.* New York: Puffin Books, 1984.

SOUND FILMSTRIPS

Beaty, Janice J. "Setting Up the Classroom," Medipak A, *Skills for Preschool Teachers.* Elmira, New York: McGraw Bookstore, Elmira College, 1979.

Dodge, Diane Trister. *Room Arrangement as a Teaching Strategy.* Washington, D.C.: Teaching Strategies, 1978.

CHAPTER 3 EVALUATION SHEET
ESTABLISHING A LEARNING ENVIRONMENT

1. Student _____

2. Trainer _____

3. Center where training occurred _____

4. Beginning date _____ Ending date _____

5. Describe what student did to accomplish General Objective

   _____

   _____

6. Describe what student did to accomplish Specific Objectives

       Objective 1 _____

       _____

       Objective 2 _____

       _____

       Objective 3 _____

       _____

7. Evaluation of student's Learning Activities
   (Trainer Check One)   (Student Check One)

       _____ Highly superior performance   _____

       _____ Superior performance   _____

       _____ Good performance   _____

       _____ Less than adequate performance   _____

Signature of Trainer: Signature of Student:

_____   _____

Comments:

4 Advancing Physical Skills

General Objective

To promote children's physical development by determining their needs and providing appropriate materials and activities.

Specific Objectives

☐ Assesses physical needs of individual children and makes appropriate plans to promote their development.

☐ Provides equipment and activities to promote large and small motor skills in and out of the classroom.

☐ Provides opportunities for children to move their bodies in a variety of ways.

T he physical growth and development of young children during their preschool years is such an obvious occurrence that we sometimes take it entirely for granted. Children will of course grow bigger, stronger, more agile, and more coordinated in their movements without outside help. It is part of their natural development. Then, we are suddenly caught up short by the four-year-old who cannot run without stumbling, or has trouble holding a paintbrush, or cannot walk up and down stairs easily.

We realize that individual differences in development account for many such lags. Some children are slower than others in developing coordination. Neurological problems or even lack of opportunity to practice skills may account for others. But no matter what the cause of developmental lags, classroom workers can help young children improve both large and small motor coordination by providing activities, materials, and equipment that will give them practice with basic movements.

ASSESSES PHYSICAL NEEDS OF INDIVIDUAL CHILDREN AND MAKES APPROPRIATE PLANS TO PROMOTE THEIR DEVELOPMENT

All children pass through the same sequence of stages in their physical growth, but some do it more quickly or evenly than others. Since individual children in a single classroom will be at many different levels of physical development, the teacher will want to determine at the outset each child's physical capacities to provide appropriate activities to promote his growth. To provide relevant help for your children, you should determine which large motor skills they already possess as well as the areas that need strengthening for each child. It is not necessary to have each child attempt the activities as you watch and record, since this tends to create a win-or-lose situation that makes children become self-conscious and less free with their movements.

Instead, make an informal assessment while the children play in the large motor area, on the playground, or in the block corner. Observe the children as they go up the steps and into the building. You will soon learn which children move with confidence and which have difficulty. Take a bean bag out on the playground and toss it back and forth to individuals. Put out tricycles for them to ride. You will soon have a comprehensive survey of each child's large muscle development.

The activities you plan as a result of this assessment, however, should not be singled out for a particular individual. There is no need to focus attention on an awkward child. All the children can benefit from practice with large body movements. But you will want to be sure children who need special help actually become involved with such activities.

Large Motor Assessment

The following checklist includes the large motor skills you will want your children to perform. Copy it onto a five-by-seven-inch card for each individual and check off items as they are accomplished. Add the date after each skill to keep a running record.

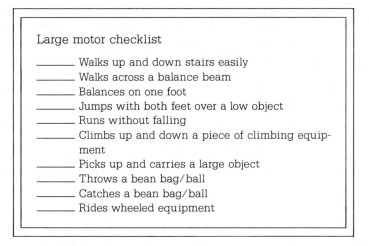

Large motor checklist

_____ Walks up and down stairs easily
_____ Walks across a balance beam
_____ Balances on one foot
_____ Jumps with both feet over a low object
_____ Runs without falling
_____ Climbs up and down a piece of climbing equipment
_____ Picks up and carries a large object
_____ Throws a bean bag/ball
_____ Catches a bean bag/ball
_____ Rides wheeled equipment

Walking

Uncoordinated children may still have trouble walking and need as much practice as you can give them. By playing walking games with small groups of children, you can make this practice fun for all. Play Follow the Leader with different kinds of walking, for example, tramping, striding, tiptoeing, strolling, shuffling, marching, waddling. You might say aloud the kind of steps you are making as you walk: "Tramp, tramp, tramp, shuffle, shuffle, shuffle," and so forth.

The children can also try to walk like certain animals (a duck, an elephant, a cat, or a mouse) and let others try to guess what they are. You can draw or paste a trail of stepping-stones on the floor and let the children step from one to another, or use squares of floor tile.

Walking up and down stairs calls for coordination and balance. A piece of commercial equipment that promotes this skill is the Rocking Boat, which, when turned upside down, becomes steps. Children can make their own steps with large hollow blocks pushed together and anchored firmly against a wall or with tape.

Balancing

To make any kind of movement with confidence and stability, a child must be able to balance himself. He must maintain body stability while stationary as well as during movement. To promote stationary balance, you can play Follow the Leader in the classroom. As leader, you can have the children stand still on one foot while holding the other, then shift to standing on the opposite foot. You can also put out large hollow blocks and have children try to stand on a horizontal block, then on top of a vertically placed block.

Another stationary balancing activity involves having the children pretend to be various animals or birds. Large pictures of animals placed around the room at children's eye level will help them choose which one to mimic. They might choose to be a bird dog pointing or a heron standing on one leg or a frog getting ready to hop. In a variation of this game, have one child from a small group pretend to be one of the animal pictures and let the rest try to guess which one he is portraying. The child who guesses correctly can be the next "animal."

Activities to promote balance while moving involve the traditional balance beam. This can be purchased from a school equipment company or made by fastening a long, smooth two-by-four-inch board to a block at each end that will raise it slightly off the ground. This equipment can have a permanent place in the large motor area, or can be brought out at special times for small groups to use. Children can practice walking across the wide side of the balance beam and then the narrow edge. They can first learn to balance while walking forward and later while walking sideways and backward. For a permanent balance beam on the outside playground, you can anchor a section of telephone pole lengthwise in the ground either in a shallow trench or bolted to end pieces.

As a substitute for a balance beam in the classroom, line up a row of unit blocks in a straight or curved line for the children to follow. Children must walk slowly and carefully because loose blocks are not stable. Another substitute is to have children walk a line rather than a board. The line can be drawn on your classroom floor or on a sidewalk or blacktopped area outside with chalk or masking tape. It can be straight or as intricate as you wish.

For another walking balance activity, the teacher cuts footprints and handprints out of contact paper and fastens them to the classroom floor in a series of "baby steps," "giant steps," "elephant steps," "frog hops" (i.e., both hand and footprints), and "tiptoes" for the children to follow during Follow the Leader.

Also include "crutch marks," "cane marks," and "wheelchair tracks" if you have physically impaired children in your class. Let the other children also have a turn to use crutches, cane, or wheelchair in your Follow the Leader activity. Commercial balance materials include the balance board, which is flat on top and curved underneath for a child to stand on and rock back and forth.

Can stilts can be purchased or homemade. These are tin cans for children to stand on, with long cords looped through the tops for the child to hang onto to keep the cans under his feet while walking.

For young children, you might start with tuna fish cans, which are flatter and easier to balance on. Be sure there are no jagged edges where the top has been removed. The children will be placing their feet on the covered end of the can, so puncture holes in each side near this end and string a cord through each can. Have a child stand on them to show you how long the cord loops need to be. Have parents save their tuna fish cans for your class and have a ''stilt-making bee'' when you have enough for everyone. The children can even have an extra pair to take home with them if they want. As their balance improves, you may want to make stilts out of taller soup cans.

Hopping, Jumping, Leaping

Once children have learned to balance on one foot, they can try hopping. The hopping movement is done on one leg. Children can practice hopping in place on one leg and then the other, or they can move forward with their hops. If you have made a footprint trail with cutout contact paper prints, place several single footprints in a row to the right and several in a row to the left. When the children come to these, they will have to hop first on the right foot and then the left foot. Games such as hopscotch encourage this movement as well. You can make up your own variation of a hopscotch pattern with or without numbers. Some teachers like to substitute symbols, such as geometric designs, or colors for the children to call out when they land on the space.

Jumping is the same as hopping with both feet together. It can be done in one spot, it can move the child forward, it can be used to go over something, or it can be done to get down from a height. Children can try to jump over ''the river'' you create in the classroom with two strips of masking tape or two chalk lines. Put them close together in the beginning. As the children develop jumping skill, you can make the ''river'' wider. Be sure the children are jumping with both feet together and not just leaping with one foot. Once they develop the skill of jumping over lines, let them try jumping over a block or some other raised object.

Children also enjoy jumping down from a height, but don't have it too high unless you have a mat for a landing pad. Jumping off a low chair is high enough. One teacher found that her children liked to measure and record their jumps—not to see who could jump the farthest, but to compete with themselves. She planned a ''jumping jack period'' once a week in which each child in a small group jumped off a low wooden box, another child marked the landing point with chalk, and then together they measured the length of the jump with a tape measure. The results were recorded with the teacher's help on each child's ''jumping jack chart.'' The children tried to better their previous record every time they jumped.

Children can also pretend to be various jumping creatures, such as rabbits, grasshoppers, frogs, or kangaroos. They can jump to music or to the beat of a tambourine. Your ''footprint trail'' can encourage jumping with pairs of contact paper prints placed together some distance from one another, so the children have to follow the trail. Jump ropes can also be used outside to promote this skill. You and a co-worker may need to turn the rope until children develop their own skills.

Leaping is easier than jumping for most children. It is done on one foot and can carry the child farther than a jump can. Again, children can pretend to be deer leaping through a forest or runners leaping over hurdles.

Running, Galloping, Skipping

Children who can run well spend a great deal of time doing so. It is the uncoordinated child who needs special practice running. When you plan running games for small groups, be sure all the children are included and encouraged to run. Games on the playground can include Follow the Leader, relay races, and circle games. To avoid stressing competition, the teacher should praise each child for his efforts, rather than make a fuss about the one who finishes first. If a child insists he won, you might comment, "You did very well. I like the way Beth and Andy ran, too." Be sure not to make races competitive, with winners and losers. The slower, uncoordinated children will not want to participate in activities in which they are certain losers. As with all games for young children, you need to stress fun, not perfection.

Inside the classroom, running skills can be promoted with body action chants that encourage running in place:

Trains

Huff, huff	(Run slowly in place)
Puff, puff	
Watch me go!	
I'm a locomotive	
Going slow;	
Chug, chug.	(Run slightly faster)
Tug, tug,	
Watch me pull!	
I'm a diesel engine,	
Pulling up the hill,	
Zip, zip,	(Run fast as you can in place)
Click, click	
Watch me come back!	
I'm a string of subway cars	
Zipping down the track,	
Whoa!	(Slow down)
Slow!	
Stop!	(Come to halt with a jump)

The galloping motion is a combination of a walk and a leap. The child takes a step with one foot, then brings the other one up behind it and leads off with the first foot again. In other words, one foot always leads. Children enjoy pretending to be horses and galloping around the room to music or tambourine beats.

Skipping is a much more complicated movement. Preschool programs should not be concerned with teaching children to skip. Most children do not master this skill before age five or six, nor should they be expected to.

Climbing

Climbing can be done either with legs or arms or both. To insure the safety of the children because of the height involved, you will want to purchase commercial materials from reliable firms. Any homemade climbing equipment needs to be tested carefully before children use it.

Indoor climbers include wooden jungle gyms, rung ladders (that can lead to a slide, a loft, or a horizontal ladder), and the climbing house or log cabin. Metal indoor climbers include nesting climbers of different heights that can stand alone or be used to support a walking board, a horizontal crossing ladder, a wooden sliding board, or even a teeter-totter. Indoor climbers are usually movable, rather than anchored to the ground like those on outdoor playgrounds. For safety's sake, classroom workers need to stand nearby when children are using them. Pads or mats should be placed underneath in case of falls.

Outdoor climbing equipment includes metal dome climbers, satellite climbers, jungle gyms, rung ladders, rope ladders, linked chain ladders, cargo nets, tires, and log cabins, to mention a few. The equipment your children use outside should be designed for preschoolers; you should not have large-sized playground pieces. Not only is large equipment dangerous for three- and four-year-olds because of its size, but the movements and skill required are beyond the capability of most young children.

Commercial climbing equipment is expensive. You can substitute your own outdoor equipment through donations such as an old rowboat, tree stumps, truck tires, and cable spools. Be sure the wooden equipment is splinter free and that any paint used is lead free.

Outside climbing equipment should be anchored firmly to the ground and cushioned underneath with either sawdust, wood chips, sand, or other soft material. (See Mediapak H, "Outdoor Play Equipment.")

Crawling, Creeping, Scooting

The crawling movement is made with the body flat out on the floor, with arms pulling and legs pushing. Children can pretend they are worms, snakes, lizards, beetles, caterpillars, or alligators. They can crawl to spooky music on the record player or to tambourine or drumbeats the teacher makes. They can also pretend to be swimmers who are swimming across a river or lake (the room). You can read the class a story about some creature and ask the children to move like the creature. You might play music while they are moving. Books such as Leo Lionni's *Inch by Inch,* about an inchworm, are excellent stimulators.

Creeping, on the other hand, is done on hands and knees with the body raised above the floor. Some children have difficulty creeping in a cross-pattern, that is, moving the opposite arm and leg in unison. If this is the case with any of your children, give them many opportunities to practice.

Children can pretend to be any one of a number of animals as they creep: dog, cat, horse, tiger, elephant, dinosaur. They can creep to music or drumbeats. They can creep through tunnels made from cardboard boxes, card tables, or two chairs tipped forward with their backs joined together. Commercial creeping equipment includes barrels and a fabric-covered Tunnel of Fun. You can create your own obstacle course around your room for creeping only, with the path marked out by masking tape or by handprints cut out of contact paper and stuck to the floor. Children can pretend to be an animal or a mountain climber as they creep through the course. A story such as *Just Suppose* by May Garelick that shows children pretending to be various animals can stimulate creeping.

Scooting is done by sitting, kneeling, or standing on something and pushing it along with the feet and legs. Children can sit on a piece of cardboard and push it backwards with their feet across a polished floor. A commercial Scooter Board is a caster-wheel board that children sit on and push around. Children also like to push themselves around on large wooden vehicles. This equipment can be kept in the large motor area of your room for daily use.

Picking Up/Carrying

Use a stack of hollow blocks or something similar for the children to pick up and carry one by one. When all the blocks have been moved in one direction, reverse the course.

Throwing/Catching

A great deal of practice is necessary for young children to become skilled at the arm movements of throwing and catching. Catching is the more difficult of the two. For children to experience success in your classroom, you should start with something easier to handle than a smooth round ball. Many teachers prefer bean bags. They can be purchased commercially or made. Bean bags can be thrown from one child to another, thrown high for children to catch, thrown at targets, such as a hoop, a barrel, a large cardboard carton with holes cut out of one end, or at a circle or square marked on the floor. Children can practice throwing both overhand and underhand.

Children can perfect their throwing skills with other objects, such as rings and a ring-toss board or bottles. Clothespins or almost any small object can be used to practice underhand throwing. Have children stand behind a line and try to toss the object into a can. The distance depends upon the children's skill. Have the can close at first, but move it back as children become more accurate.

After children develop the skill to throw and catch objects, you can introduce balls. Sponge balls, yarn balls, and beach balls are easier to catch than to throw because of their light weight. You might do the throwing, letting small groups of children practice catching. Keep the balls in the large motor area for individual practice.

Riding wheeled equipment helps children develop steering and balancing skills.

Finally, introduce rubber balls. Large balls promote the skills of throwing and catching with both hands. You might start with large ones, but introduce smaller balls as your children become skilled. Throwing and catching are skills often neglected in preschool classrooms. With careful planning and selection of activities to challenge your children without discouraging them, you can add immeasurably to their skills. Girls should develop the ability to throw and catch as well as boys. The fact that many do not often results from lack of encouragement and practice.

Although all of these movements can be practiced in isolation, they should eventually be used in combination. Give the children opportunities to move freely in their own creative ways by scheduling a "creative movement" activity at least once a week. Let them move to music, rhythmical beats, or even to stories or poetry. Put out props for them to use, such as animal hats, workers' hats, balloons, hula hoops, homemade wings, capes, streamers, and scarves, and let them express themselves in movement just as they do in art. You may have to be the model to get them started, but soon they should be showing you the way.

Riding Wheeled Equipment

Tricycles or Big Wheels help young children learn the skills of pedaling and steering. Some centers have halls that can be used for riding activities; others have sidewalks outside. If you do not have such a hard surface, consider asking a business or industry to donate an old conveyor belt to use as a trike path outside.

Making Plans for Individuals

Once your assessment of a child is complete, you should begin planning for his or her continued physical development. As previously mentioned, you should not single out a child who has a particular need, but instead plan a small group activity which will speak to that need and include that child. If the activity can focus on a skill that the child is good at, all the better. Whenever possible, you should begin with the strengths of a child in order to help him develop in an area of need. For example, five-year-old Andrew's large motor checklist, prepared by his teacher on a five-by-seven-inch card, showed the following:

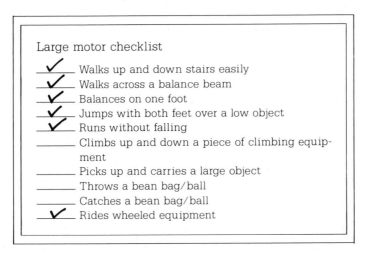

Large motor checklist

- ✓ Walks up and down stairs easily
- ✓ Walks across a balance beam
- ✓ Balances on one foot
- ✓ Jumps with both feet over a low object
- ✓ Runs without falling
- _____ Climbs up and down a piece of climbing equipment
- _____ Picks up and carries a large object
- _____ Throws a bean bag/ball
- _____ Catches a bean bag/ball
- ✓ Rides wheeled equipment

The teacher was surprised at the results, since Andrew's running and jumping skills were better than average, and he was such an active boy. He seemed to love balls and would try so hard to throw and catch, without much success. It seemed strange that his arms were not as strong or coordinated as the rest of his body. A conference with his parents revealed that Andrew's right arm had been injured in a car accident, and although it had healed, he did not use it as well as he should be able to. It embarrassed him not to be able to keep up with his friends in ball games.

The teacher decided to find a physical activity that would help to strengthen Andrew's arm. She discussed the problem with a physical education teacher who suggested playing tetherball. It worked very well because Andrew enjoyed any kind of ball game. This particular activity was so new to the whole class that no one was any better at it than anyone else. As the teacher noted on the back of Andrew's card, he spent a great deal of time playing tetherball, and his arm became much stronger.

Small Motor Assessment

Small motor abilities can be assessed in a similar manner. Copy the following checklist onto a card for each child.

Small motor checklist

_____ Inserts pegs
_____ Zips a zipper
_____ Laces a shoe
_____ Twists a nut onto a bolt
_____ Pours a liquid without spilling
_____ Cuts with scissors
_____ Cuts with a knife
_____ Pounds a nail with a hammer
_____ Paints with a brush
_____ Traces object with crayon, felt-tip pen
_____ Writes with an implement

Small motor coordination involves using the fingers with dexterity to manipulate objects. This is also known as eye-hand, visual-manual, fine motor, or perceptual-motor coordination. It is an important skill for young children to develop as a prerequisite for learning to read and write. Children who experience difficulty in these checklist areas often exhibit a lack of small motor coordination. Boys frequently show less dexterity with their fingers than do girls of the same age. As with girls and large motor skills, the lag may result from lack of encouragement and practice. Young children of both sexes can benefit from the small motor activities you provide for them.

Games for each of the small motor skills should be put out separately on different days. It is too confusing for young children to have to perform more than one skill at a time.

Inserting

Small motor activities help establish handedness in young children. Most of the children will already have exhibited a preference for either right- or left-handedness by the time they enter a preschool program. You should note which hand each child uses most frequently, and help them strengthen handedness through manipulative games. Children who seem a be ambidextrous and do not favor either hand can be helped to develop right-handedness (if this seems appropriate) by handing them things to be picked up and used with the right hand. A strongly developed preference for using one hand over the other helps children later in learning the left-to-right progression they must use when learning to read. Do not try to change a left-handed child. You can help him best by providing opportunities to become proficient with the left hand.

Picking up small objects with the preferred hand helps children develop and strengthen their handedness. It also promotes eye-hand coordination which allows them to grip the object they are viewing. It further helps strengthen finger muscles that will eventually be needed for grasping a writing implement.

Teacher-made sorting games are especially helpful in this area. In addition to promoting manual skills, sorting games help children develop cognitive concepts such as sorting and matching according to size, shape, or color.

Shoe boxes and plastic margarine containers are handy accessories for these games. Each shoe box can contain a separate game. Label each empty margarine container with the picture and name of the item it should contain. Then cut a hole in the top just large enough to permit the item to be dropped in. Have one extra container to hold the entire assortment of items. Label the outside of the shoe box so children can identify the separate games.

The idea of the game is to sort a collection of items by putting each one in the container where it belongs. Each shoe box game will contain a different collection. One can be a collection of beans of different kinds; another, a collection of seeds (large enough to pick up with the fingers); others, a collection of nuts, bolts, screws, and nails; buttons of various kinds; poker chips (to sort by color); marbles; magic marker pen tops; houses from an old Monopoly set; golf tees; tops to small plastic bottles; different kinds of macaroni; stones; seashells; nuts; and so forth. You can assemble any number of other collections from small items.

To begin, the children will want to pour out the collection into the top of the shoe box for easier sorting. Once they have finished, they will want to remove the plastic tops from the margarine containers to see how accurate they were in their sorting. If the game has truly captured their interest, they will want to pour the various items back into the top of the shoe box and start over again.

Plastic egg cartons can also be used for sorting. Either keep the top closed and puncture holes over every egg section, or let the children play with the carton open. Labels for the items can be pasted on the different sections or next to the holes. All of these games can be kept on the shelves of your manipulative area near the tables where they will be used.

Many commercial games also promote finger dexterity: Chinese Checkers, pick-up-sticks, wooden puzzles with knobs on each piece, Tinkertoys, Legos, pegboards, and so forth. Some Montessori equipment is also designed to promote this skill.

You can make your own pegboards by acquiring scraps of pegboard material from a lumber company and using golf tees as pegs. Another teacher-made board for promoting finger dexterity is the geoboard: pound headless nails equidistant (e.g., one inch apart) into a twelve-inch-square board. The children can stretch colored rubber bands over the nails to make various designs.

Puzzles require the same skill: picking up an item and inserting it into a space. The first puzzles for young children are the large wooden ones with only a few pieces to be inserted into a cutout wooden frame. Children who have never assembled a puzzle are more successful when each puzzle piece represents a whole rather than a part of the picture to be made, for instance, an arm, a leg, a hat, or a head rather than a part of an arm. Check your puzzles carefully. You will need a wide selection because of the children's range of abilities.

It is especially important at the beginning of the year to have puzzles that children who are new to the program can complete successfully. If they have had no previous experience with puzzles, you may need to sit with them for encouragement or actual help until the puzzle is completed.

A wide range of commercial puzzles is available, but you can also make your own. Enlarged photographs of each child can be glued to cardboard or wood, covered with clear contact paper, and cut with a modeler's knife or jigsaw. Make each piece large and different so children can put together the puzzle on their own. The puzzles can be stored separately in a manila envelope or shoe box in your manipulative area. You should put a small photograph of the puzzle picture on the outside of the box to give the puzzle maker an idea of what the completed picture should look like. If you use pictures of children, do not put out any of the puzzles until pictures of all are ready. It is distressing for a child to find that he has been left out.

Zipping

You can observe and record how the children zip their own clothing, or you can make a zipper board. Cut the zipper and the cloth around it from an old skirt or pair of pants, and staple or tack it to a board. Make more than one board with zippers of several sizes. Be sure to sand the wood so there are no sharp edges.

Twisting/Turning

Different small muscles must be developed to accomplish the skills of twisting or turning something with the hands. You can help by giving the children opportunities to use tools like eggbeaters, food mills, or can openers in their cooking activities. (Eggbeaters can also be used in water play with a small amount of detergent in the water. Be sure to have more than one beater to avoid squabbles.)

Start collecting small plastic bottles with screw-on tops. When you have several, wash them out and put them, along with their tops, in a shoe box for the children to try to put together. They must learn the additional skill of matching sizes before they can screw on the tops successfully.

You can also make a board with bolts and screws of different sizes protruding through the surface, with a container of nuts the children can screw onto the bolts. Squeezing oranges for orange juice is another activity that promotes the twisting and turning skill.

Pouring

If you use small pitchers, the children can practice pouring at the meal table. You may first want them to have experience pouring something other than a liquid. They can pour rice from a pitcher to a bowl and back again; salt, sugar, and sand are other possibilities.

Cutting with Scissors

You can help children who have not learned to cut in several ways. Show them how to hold the scissors with their favored hand. Then hold a narrow strip of paper stretched taut between two hands for the child to cut in two. Once he can do so without difficulty, have another child hold the paper and let them take turns holding and cutting. Another day, show the child how to hold the strip of paper in his own hand and cut with the other hand. Let him practice on different kinds and sizes of paper, including construction paper, typing paper, and pages from magazines. Finally, draw a straight (or curved) line on a sheet of paper and let the child practice cutting along a line.

Cutting with a Knife

Young children can learn to handle knives safely. Not only does cutting with a knife provide excellent small motor coordination practice, but it is a highly satisfying skill for children to accomplish. You can start with table knives and soft items. Children can learn to hold the knife in one hand with the sharp edge of the blade down while holding a hard-boiled egg, cooked potato, cooked carrot, peach, pear, or sandwich with the other hand. They may have to make a sawing motion to get started. After they have learned to control a table knife, they can begin learning to use a sharp paring knife for the same kind of cutting. Eventually, they should be able a cut such foods as raw carrots, apples, and celery.

Using a vegetable scraper is another satisfying skill to learn. Carrots are best to begin with, but children will soon be able to peel potatoes successfully. These are real experiences rather than games or simulations, and children understand the value of such skills because they have seen grownups practice them. It gives them great satisfaction to realize they can take part in and contribute to the adult world.

Their teachers can feel satisfaction, too, knowing what an excellent opportunity cooking experiences provide for developing children's small motor control. Other cooking tools such as shredders, graters, grinders, and melon ballers are also valuable in this respect.

Holding and Pounding

To pound a nail with a hammer takes well-developed eye-hand coordination even for an adult. Let children practice at the woodworking table with soft wood (such as plasterboard or ceiling tiles) and large-headed nails. They can pound pieces of wood together, or they can pound objects such as pieces of plastic foam onto a board.

Holding and Printing/Tracing/Painting

Many children have already learned to hold and use pencils, crayons, and paintbrushes before they enter preschool. Those who have should be able to continue their practice; those who have not should have the opportunity to learn.

Many teachers set up a writing table in the manipulative area with all kinds of writing or drawing tools and paper for children to experiment with. Threes and fours are most successful with primary-size pencils and crayons, and felt-tip coloring pens.

Let them practice scribbling and, eventually, tracing around their hands and other objects. They may want to color in their tracings, trying to stay within the lines. It is here in the manipulative area that coloring books belong, not in the creative art area. They are useful for helping children develop the small motor skills of holding and controlling writing implements. Moreover, children experience great satisfaction using the various writing implements.

Eventually, some children may want to try printing their names. Give each child a name card to copy with his first name printed as it will be in school (first letter capped, rest lowercased). Parents and preschool teachers often print in capital letters without realizing how confusing this may later prove to children when they enter school and have to relearn their names.

The paintbrushes in the art area should also be large enough for preschoolers to be able to grip them well. Easel brushes of this size are often too long for threes and fours to handle easily. Simply cut off and sand down the ends to a more manageable length.

Planning for Individuals

Once the small motor assessment has been completed, you and your classroom team will have a better idea of the activities you should provide. Although you will be planning for individuals, be sure not to single them out as being deficient in these skills. As with large motor activities, all the children can benefit from the small motor games you provide for certain children.

Handicapped Children

Retarded or physically handicapped youngsters should be encouraged to accomplish as many large and small motor activities as they can. Once you have assessed what they are able to do, you will be ready to make appropriate individual plans.

PROVIDES EQUIPMENT AND ACTIVITIES TO PROMOTE LARGE AND SMALL MOTOR SKILLS IN AND OUT OF THE CLASSROOM

We have described how to assess children's large and small motor skills. The same activities can promote large and small motor skills on a daily basis. Remember, the children will gain the most through individual and small group activities. Large group games with rules are not appropriate until later years.

Remember also when you purchase or construct equipment to try to make it serve several purposes at once. For example, one program invented what it called a Swiss Cheese Board for climbing and throwing both indoors and out. This was made from a sturdy pressboard with a frame around it and struts at the bottom to hold it upright. Holes of various sizes were cut through it to serve as hand- and footholds for climbing, windows for dramatic play, and targets for bean bags. The board was so popular with the children that three more were constructed, thus gaining walls for a playhouse as well as room dividers.

Although many of the activities in this chapter take place in the classroom, some should also be pursued out-of-doors. Young children need opportunities to run and play in the fresh air. Small motor as well as large motor skills can be pursued outdoors. Bring your paints and puzzles outside for a change, and see what renewed interest occurs on the part of the children.

The following motor activites and equipment discussed in this chapter can be used to promote motor skills both in and out of the classroom:

Walking	*Throwing/Catching*
Follow the leader	Bean bags
Walk like an animal	Ring toss
Rocking Boat	Sponge balls
Walking trail	Yarn balls
	Beach balls
Balancing	Rubber balls
Follow the leader	
Hollow blocks	*Riding Wheeled Equipment*
Be an animal	Tricycle
Balance beam	Big Wheel
Block beam	Large wooden vehicles
Contact footprints	Scooter
Balance board	Wagon
Can stilts	Conveyor-belt trike path

Hopping, Jumping, Leaping
Footprint trail
Hopscotch
Jump over the river
Jump off chair
Jumping jack period
Be a grasshopper
Jump rope

Running, Galloping, Skipping
Follow the leader
Relay race
Circle games
Body action chants
Be a horse

Climbing
Jungle gym
Rung ladder
Rope ladder
Cargo net
Climbing house
Nesting climber
Dome climber
Satellite climber
Linked chain ladder
Tires
Swiss Cheese Board
Rowboat
Tree stumps
Cable spools

Crawling, Creeping, Scooting
Spooky music
Tambourine
Drum
Tunnels of cardboard, card tables, chairs
Barrel
Tunnel of Fun
Masking tape obstacle course, contact paper handprints
Piece of cardboard
Scooter
Large wooden vehicles

Picking Up/Carrying
Large hollow blocks
Boxes
Unit blocks
Toys

Inserting
Shoe box collection
Egg carton
Chinese checkers
Pick-up-sticks
Wooden-knob puzzles
Tinkertoys
Legos
Pegboards
Golf tees
Geoboard
Frame puzzles
Photo puzzles

Zipping
Clothing with zippers
Zipper board

Twisting/Turning
Eggbeaters
Food mills
Can openers
Bottles and screw tops
Bolt boards
Orange squeezer

Pouring
Small pitchers and water, sand, salt, rice

Cutting
Table knife and cooked vegetables
Paring knife and raw vegetables
Shredder
Grater
Grinder
Melon baller

Holding and Pounding
Hammers
Nails, tacks
Soft wood
Ceiling tiles
Pieces of leather

Holding and Printing/Tracing/Painting
Pencil
Crayon
Paintbrush
Felt-tip pen
Tracing
Coloring book
Printing

PROVIDES OPPORTUNITIES FOR CHILDREN TO MOVE THEIR BODIES IN A VARIETY OF WAYS

Preschool classrooms in the United States seem to make less use of body movement than those in Europe, perhaps because we as adults are less inclined to express ourselves through our bodies. Or perhaps we are more inhibited and not as comfortable with our bodies.

Our children need not grow up feeling this way if we help them to be comfortable with creative movement activities. Until they can control their body motions, they will not feel free to move creatively. Some of the activities already described will help them to loosen up. Here are some other suggestions.

Imitating Animals

Begin by giving them something familiar to imitate. Let them move like familiar animals. Put up pictures of dogs, cats, birds, rabbits, mice, guinea pigs, snakes, beetles, and spiders around the room at the children's eye level. Let them try to move on all fours like one of the animals. Do it to appropriate music or a chant you make up such as:

> I am a bunny,
> Watch me hop,
> Here I go
> And never stop.

Encourage your children to watch how classroom pets move. Take the group to a pet store, a farm, or a zoo.

Perhaps one or two children will want to demonstrate their own movement while the rest clap a rhythm. You may want to tap on a tambourine or drum as children move like animals. They may want to try certain kinds of movements, such as crawling like snakes or worms, leaping like cats or tigers, or waddling like ducks. Picture books can also motivate children to move like animals. Read Leo Lionni's *Alexander and the Wind-up Mouse* to stimulate children to move like a live mouse and a wind-up toy mouse. The counting book *One Snail and Me* displays a lively assortment of animals who wriggle, squiggle, juggle, and spout in a little girl's bathtub. Your children may want to follow their lead after you read them the book.

Other Motions

The awkward or shy child can often be enticed to engage in movement activities if he has a piece of equipment to make a motion with—ribbons, scarves, paper streamers, hula hoops, balloons, or bubble hoops.

Soon the children will feel free enough to move like trees in the wind, like ocean waves, like lightning in a thunder storm. They can learn to move silently, heavily, slowly, rapidly. Eventually they can express emotions such as happiness, sadness, anger, and surprise in their movements. Accompanying mood music may help them.

Do not force children who are not ready to join the group. The activity should always be fun, not a chore. Leaving animal pictures and props in the music corner encourages individuals to try out body movements on their own.

Body Action Chants

Body action chants are like finger plays for the entire body. Teachers can lead children in all kinds of whole body motions while chanting. They can pretend to be carpenters standing on tiptoe to pound a nail in the ceiling, or elevator operators going up or down.

You Can Be a Carpenter

You can be a carpenter	(Stand, stretch arm above head)
Pounding in nails;	
Get them out of boxes,	(Bend over, reach down with right hand)
Get them out of pails;	(Reach down with left hand)
Pound them in the ceiling,	(Stand, stretch arm above head)
Pound them in the floor,	(Bend over, stretch arm to floor)
Put them in your pocket,	(Stand up, put hands in pocket)
And walk out the door.	(March in place)

Elevator Operator

Elevator operator	(Stand in place)
Going down, please;	(Squat down)
Down to the basement	
To look for the keys;	
Up to the first floor	(Straighten up halfway)
To let out the cat;	
Up to the second floor	(Straighten up all the way)
To take a nap;	
Up to the third floor	(Raise arms above head)
To find a friend;	
Up to the top floor,	(Jump up and sink down in squat)
And back down again.	

A teacher should lead the chanting. Do each one several times together if the children like them, and they will soon have them memorized. Body action verses like these are especially good to use as transitions between time blocks and while waiting for lunch or for the bus.

Let the children make up their own chants and follow them. They can choose an animal with distinctive motions or a worker such as a house painter, for instance. Then have them tell you the names or sounds of the motions that painters make—*splash, drip, step, stir, reach, bend*—then let them think of rhymes for these words: *splash—dash; drip-lip, tip; step—hep; stir—whir; reach—beach; bend—send.* Finally, try to put together some verses with body action in them:

Timothy is a painter,
Stir, stir, stir,
Likes to slap the paint on,
Whir, whir, whir,
Likes to climb the ladder,
Step, step, step,
Likes to carry buckets,
Hep, hep, hep,
Likes to mix the colors,
Splash, splash, splash,
Hopes he never spills them,
Then he'll have to dash!

Children can make up the motions they want to use for every other line. Not every word or motion will fit a single verse, but let them make up more than one verse. They will be more interested in acting out body chants they have invented themselves.

These movements are, of course, highly structured. You can begin with them, then move to more abstract motions. Play records of nursery rhymes with movements, such as "Jack Be Nimble" or "Jack and Jill," and let them act out the motions. Play records without words and let them create their own movements. Finally, children from other cultures or ethnic groups may also want to bring in records or tapes of their particular music. Perhaps a parent could be invited to demonstrate or teach the children a dance step from another culture.

SUMMARY

To promote children's physical development, determine their needs and then provide appropriate materials and activities. Informal observation of children using a checklist of large and small motor activities helps the classroom worker to assess more clearly where each child stands in the motor ability area. Then the teacher can make individual plans based on the child's needs, by using the child's strengths as a starting point. A child with particular developmental needs should not be singled out for special help, but should be included in small group activities designed for that child but worthwhile for others as well. Getting children involved in creative movement activities is also described, with special focus on imitating animals, using books to motivate movement, using props, moving to music or percussion beats, imitating movements in nature, expressing feelings, doing body action chants, and making up own movements.

LEARNING ACTIVITIES

1. Read Chapter 4, "Advancing Physical Skills," and answer Question Sheet 4-A.
2. View Mediapak H, "Outdoor Play Equipment," and answer Question Sheet 4-B.
3. Read one or more of the books listed under Suggested Readings, or view another of the sound filmstrips such as "Outdoor Play," "Manipulative Materials," or "Woodworking." Add ten cards to your file with specific ideas for helping children develop large and small motor skills. Include the reference source on each card.
4. Assess each child's large motor skills, using the checklist on page 86. Record the results.
5. On the basis of your results, construct a game, bring in materials, or conduct an activity to promote the large motor skills of children who need help. (The trainer can observe.)
6. Assess each child's small motor skills, using the checklist on page 94. Record the results.
7. On the basis of your results, construct a game, bring in materials, or conduct an activity to promote the small motor skills of children who need help. (The trainer can observe.)
8. Continue your Portfolio of evidence of your skills. Add one piece of evidence for each of the following Teacher Skills Checklist items:
   a. Assesses physical needs of individual children and makes appropriate plans to promote their development.
   b. Provides equipment and activities to promote large and small motor skills in and out of the classroom.
   c. Provides opportunities for children to move their bodies in a variety of ways.
   Evidence should reflect what you, not another staff member, have done.
9. Complete the Chapter 4 Evaluation Sheet and return it and the answers to Question Sheets 4-A and 4-B to the appropriate college or program official.

QUESTION SHEET 4-A

(Based on Chapter 4, "Advancing Physical Skills")

1. How can you provide for children who seem awkward when they walk and have difficulty balancing?
2. What should you do about children who have difficulty skipping?
3. How can you help your children develop the skills of throwing and catching?
4. If only one child in your classroom has difficulty throwing and catching, what should you do?
5. How can you best help a left-handed child?
6. How would you teach a child to cut with scissors?
7. How do cooking activities promote small motor development?
8. Describe a beginning activity to encourage creative movement with children.
9. How might you engage a shy child in movement activities?
10. What should you do if children refuse to join in a movement activity?

QUESTION SHEET 4-B

(Based on Mediapak H, "Outdoor Play Equipment")

1. What pieces of equipment would you choose for your outdoor play area? Why?
2. If you could choose only one piece of equipment, what would if be? Why?
3. If you had little money to spend, how could you provide climbing equipment?
4. How can you provide for digging in sand on your playground?
5. What different large motor skills can be promoted through use of slides?
6. In what different ways can the skill of swinging be promoted in an outdoor playground?
7. In what different ways can old tires be used on a preschool playground?
8. How can the skills of creeping and crawling be promoted in the outdoor play area?
9. In what ways can balancing be promoted?
10. What kinds of large motor skills can be promoted on a concrete or blacktop surface?

SUGGESTED EVIDENCE FOR PORTFOLIO

1. Include several of your child assessment cards, accompanied by an explanation of how you made each assessment, the plans you made for each child, and how successful they were.
2. Take a photo of one of the pieces of equipment you made or brought into the classroom. Explain how it helped improve your and your children's skill in this area.
3. Include one of your children's products or a photo of it (e.g., scribbling, writing, tracing) with an explanation of how you set up the activity to promote this skill and how it helped the child develop small motor skills.
4. Make a list of body action chants you and your children have made up or used, and explain how they stimulated body movement and large motor development.
5. Include an animal picture you have used to stimulate creative movement, along with a photo of a child moving like the animal. Explain in writing how this shows your competence.

Each piece of evidence should be accompanied by a write-up explaining how this shows your competence in the area of **Physical** and how the activity is developmentally appropriate for your children. Refer to Chapter 6, "Large Motor Development," and Chapter 7, "Small Motor Development," in *Observing Development of the Young Child* (Beaty, 1986) for developmental statements.

SUGGESTED READINGS

Atack, Sally M. *Art Activities for the Handicapped.* Englewood Cliffs, N.J.: Prentice-Hall, 1982.

Beaty, Janice J. *Observing Development of the Young Child.* Columbus, Ohio: Merrill Publishing Co., 1986.

Cherry, Clare. *Creative Movement for the Developing Child.* Belmont, Calif.: Fearon, 1971.

Frost, Joe L., and Barry L. Klein. *Children's Play and Playgrounds.* Austin, Tex.: Playgrounds International, 1979.

Gallahue, David L. *Developmental Movement Experiences for Children*. New York: John Wiley, 1982.

Sinclair, Caroline B. *Movement of the Young Child*. Columbus, Ohio: Merrill Publishing Co., 1973.

Sullivan, Molly. *Feeling Strong, Feeling Free: Movement Exploration for Young Children*. Washington, D.C.: National Association for the Education of Young Children, 1982.

Thompson, David. *Easy Woodstuff for Kids*. Mount Rainier, Md.: Gryphon House, 1981.

Torbert, Marianne. *Follow Me, A Handbook of Movement Activities for Children*. Englewood Cliffs, N.J.: Prentice-Hall, 1980.

Wilt, Joy, and Terre Watson. *Rhythm and Movement: 160 Experiences for Children Including Patterns to Use with Sticks, Cups, Balls, Rags, Hoops and Ropes*. Waco, Tex.: Creative Resources, 1977.

CHILDREN'S BOOKS

Aruego, Jose. *Look What I Can Do*. New York: Scribner's, 1971.

Briggs, Raymond. *The Snowman*. New York: Random House, 1978.

Bryan, Ashley. *The Dancing Granny*. New York: Atheneum, 1977.

Davis, Alice Vaught. *Timothy Turtle*. New York: Harcourt Brace Jovanovich, 1968.

Dragonwagon, Crescent. *Coconut*. New York: Harper & Row, 1984.

Freeman, Mae. *Gravity and the Astronauts*. New York: Scholastic, 1970.

Galdone, Paul. *The Three Billy Goats Gruff*. New York: Clarion, 1973.

Garelick, May. *Just Suppose*. New York: Scholastic, 1969.

George, Lindsay Barrett. *William and Boomer*. New York: Greenwillow Books, 1987.

Kepes, Juliet. *Frogs Merry*. New York: Knopf Pantheon, 1961.

Lee, Jeanne M. *Toad Is the Uncle of Heaven: A Vietnamese Folk Tale*. New York: Holt, Rinehart & Winston, 1985.

Lionni, Leo. *Alexander and the Wind-up Mouse*. New York: Knopf Pantheon, 1974.

———. *Let's Make Rabbits*. New York: Pantheon Books, 1982.

Roche, P.K. *Jump All the Morning*. New York: Viking Penguin, 1984.

Wildsmith, Brian. *The Circus*. New York: Oxford University Press, 1970.

SOUND FILMSTRIPS

Beaty, Janice J. "Outdoor Play Equipment," Mediapak H, *Skills for Preschool Teachers*. Elmira, N.Y.: McGraw Bookstore, Elmira College, 1979.

Manipulative Materials. Tuckahoe, N.Y. Campus Film Distributors.

Outdoor Play. Tuckahoe, N.Y.: Campus Film Distributors.

Woodworking. Tuckahoe, N.Y.: Campus Film Distributors.

CHAPTER 4 EVALUATION SHEET
ADVANCING PHYSICAL SKILLS

1. Student_____

2. Trainer_____

3. Center where training occurred_____

4. Beginning date_____ Ending date_____

5. Describe what student did to accomplish General Objective

   _____

   _____

6. Describe what student did to accomplish Specific Objectives

   Objective 1_____

   _____

   Objective 2_____

   _____

   Objective 3_____

   _____

7. Evaluation of student's Learning Activities
   (Trainer Check One)   (Student Check One)

   _____ Highly superior performance   _____

   _____ Superior performance   _____

   _____ Good performance   _____

   _____ Less than adequate performance   _____

Signature of Trainer: Signature of Student:

_____   _____

Comments:

5 Advancing Cognitive Skills

General Objective

To promote children's questioning, exploring, and problem-solving skills in order to develop their thinking ability.

Specific Objectives

☐ Helps children use all of their senses to explore their world.
☐ Helps children develop such concepts as shape, color, size, classification, seriation, number.
☐ Interacts with children in ways that encourage them to think and solve problems.

Advancing cognitive skills in young children involves helping them develop their intellectual or thinking abilities. Many preschool programs have overlooked or downplayed this area of development. Somehow we have the notion that we should not teach children to learn until they enter public school at age five or six. The preschool, we declare, should be concerned with play.

We seem to have overlooked the fact that young children are progressing in their intellectual development with or without our help. Cognitive development is just as important as physical or language development. In fact, they go hand in hand. It occurs at the same time and is integrated into every other aspect of the child's development.

We also seem to have forgotten that the principal direction of play for young children is not entertainment or recreation, as it is among adults, but learning. It is essential, therefore, that teachers of young children understand how cognitive abilities develop and how they can utilize play in their classrooms to promote cognitive development and give it direction.

HELPS CHILDREN USE ALL OF THEIR SENSES TO EXPLORE THEIR WORLD

A preschool child is a born explorer. Even as an infant and toddler, he comes with all the necessary equipment to be a great discoverer: eyes, nose, mouth, tongue, lips, ears, fingers, toes. In addition to this array of sensory apparatus, each child starts out with a strong natural drive or curiosity to put this equipment to good use. He is forever trying to poke, pry, bite, chew, lick, rub, pinch, sniff, stare at, listen to, or examine in great detail any object, person, or situation that gets in the way.

This is how children learn about themselves and their world. They have to try everything. They have to touch and test and pull things apart. (Putting them back together is not really a part of this initial investigation!) They may also drop or throw breakable objects, not to be naughty, but to find out what happens when they hit the floor. They are true scientific explorers of their environment. Thus, cognitive development for preschoolers involves use of their senses to examine things and to explore surroundings.

Yet some three- and four-year-olds seem to make no use of their sensory equipment in exploring the world around them. They don't seem to notice anything new or different in the classroom. In fact, they show little interest of any kind in their surroundings. Since we know they were born with a great natural curiosity, we can only surmise that somewhere along the way they lost it. Perhaps their curiosity was mistaken for mischief, and they were punished for it. Perhaps there were never adults around who took the time to answer their questions or support their exploratory activities. Whatever the reason, it is up to you—teachers, aides, and volunteers in preschool classrooms—to reawaken children's curiosity and sense of wonder if they have lost it, or to help direct it toward exploring their environment, if they have not.

Reawakening Curiosity

What about the children in your classroom? Do they still retain their natural sense of curiosity? Take a moment to observe their actions when they first enter your new environment. Listen also to the questions they ask. You should soon be able to identify those with a drive to explore and those who seem to have little interest in the new things around them.

Your job, of course, is to reawaken this curiosity and encourage them to find things out for themselves. To do so, you will need to serve as a behavior model, and help them learn how to explore with their senses through the interesting play activities you provide. You will need to put forth special effort to show your own interest in every new and different thing you see both in and out of the classroom.

Field Trips

The immediate environment of the center offers unlimited opportunities for children to explore and discover. Take the children on an outside walk around the building. Give them each a paper bag for collecting anything that strikes their fancy. Take a tape recorder with you to record the sounds of the environment. Take an instant print camera to record the scenes.

What will you find out? First of all, you will learn who are the curious children. Second, you will find out whether you yourself are tuned in to children and their interests. Was it a child who pointed out the dandelion growing from the crack in the sidewalk or was it you? Perhaps you will have to get down on your knees to look at the world from the perspective of a three-year-old before you can become a behavior model for exploring.

Field trips need not be elaborate, all-day, long-distance affairs. Brief ventures out around the building are best because this is the environment the children know best, and hence it is more meaningful to them. One class made exciting discoveries all year long on their weekly "field trip to a tree." They chose a maple tree on the playground and visited it once a week throughout the fall, winter, and spring. They took photographs, made bark rubbings, pressed leaves, collected and grew seeds, recorded the sound of wind in the leaves, and learned about the birds that nested in it and the insects that lived there.

A city program may not have trees, but you surely have other objects awaiting examination by young explorers. One city class visited a used car lot across the street. While such locations may not hold much interest for adults, they are new worlds to explore for young children. The teachers were surprised to find that the children were interested not so much in the cars as in their wheels. This should not have been surprising, since children tend to focus on things at their eye level.

Sensory Questions

What do you do on a field trip? If the children have not already begun to do so, you can start by asking questions involving the senses. "Close your eyes and what do you hear?" or "Does anyone smell anything different?" or "Put your hand on this. What does it feel like to you?"

When possible, take your lead from the children. Follow the direction of their interests. When they display little interest, then you may need to lead them. Look around you for things to explore with the senses. How do these objects look, sound, feel? Is there another one like the first? They may want to compare the two. How are they the same? How are they different? Take a photo of them. Make a rubbing. Make a tape recording of sounds. Take something back with you to the classroom to help children clarify and understand what they have seen and explored.

Materials in the Classroom

If children's curiosity is to be aroused, there has to be something to be curious about. Children will often bring in an interesting item from home or something they have picked up on the way to the center. This can be the beginning of their exploration, especially if it is displayed attractively so that attention focuses on it.

In the beginning, however, it is often up to the adult classroom worker to bring in new material to stimulate children's curiosity. A special table or counter top can feature a new or unusual item brought by you or the children. It could be labeled the "What's New?" table. To feature the new item of the week, you can place a piece of colored contact paper or construction paper underneath it.

Bring in an interesting piece of tree bark if you want to arouse the children's sense of touch, or if you plan to explore living trees by touch, or if you hope to do bark rubbings. Bring in a piece of driftwood or a seashell—but only if your community is near a river, lake, or ocean, where such items are common. It is essential to begin with something familiar to the children.

One teacher brought in a yellow fire hydrant top. She displayed it on a bright red piece of construction paper on her "What's New?" table. She had gone to the trouble of getting it from the fire hydrant foundry near the children's homes where many of their parents worked. The children were already used to the unusual items that appeared weekly on this table. Almost immediately some of the more aggressive children began talking about it and touching it. The teacher listened to their conversations to see how much they knew about it and whether they could discover more through their own senses. One boy tried to lift it and was surprised to find how heavy it was. Then all had to try.

But it was Christina, a shy girl who rarely played with the others, who finally identified the item. Her father worked in the foundry, and she was pleased to be able to share her knowledge about its products. This one item led to many weeks of sensory discovery in that particular classroom. The children explored colors, especially red and yellow as warning colors. Christina's father came to the class to tell about his job in the foundry. The children visited the shipping department (the only safe area for visitors) to see rows of new fire hydrants ready for shipment around the world. They explored more deeply the concept of metal and began looking for and identifying other metal objects.

You and your co-workers must decide in what directions you want the children to go during the year, what simple concepts you want them to explore. It is much more appropriate in preschool programs to start with the simplest and most basic kinds of things, then follow the children's interests as far as they will lead you.

For example, if your children are learning to identify colors in their art activities, you might ask the children to bring in something green for the "What's New?" table. If several children bring green items, display them all. If nobody brings anything, be prepared to bring something yourself, or have the children choose something green from the classroom to display there, for example, a plant (make sure it is nonpoisonous). Exploring plants can, of course, take you in many directions. Children might eventually discover that it takes sunlight to make a plant green. If you are still concerned with colors, you might feature a new one every few weeks until all the colors are thoroughly familiar to your children. It is up to you and your co-workers, however, to plan for something to happen. You will want your children to explore their surroundings. Again, start with something simple. For instance, we all need water to live. One teacher brought in some bottled water from the supermarket for her display table. This stimulated the children to wonder and talk about other kinds of water. They filled a glass full of water from the tap. They compared the bottle and the glass visually. They looked the same. The teacher posed this question to a small group who had gathered around the display table: "How else can we tell if there is any difference between bottled water and tap water?"

One child suggested smelling the two, and everyone wanted a turn. All decided there was a difference that was hard to put into words, but they agreed that the tap water smelled stronger. Of course, everyone had to taste the two. Most like the tap water better. The teacher recorded the results on newsprint after each child's name.

The simple display led to almost more activities than the teachers were prepared for. One child brought in muddy river water. Another brought a jar of greenish pond water. The word *pollution* became meaningful to preschoolers. The class traced the building water pipes to the meter in the basement and had the fun of watching the numbers change when somebody flushed the toilet! They eventually visited the city filter plant and later the reservoir. And all because of a bottle of water!

What this example points out is that you and your co-workers need to plan for something to happen, then you need to extend the activity according to your children's interests and needs. To determine their interests, listen closely to their comments and the questions they ask. Ask questions yourself about the activity to stimulate their thinking. Turn on your own imagination toward planning follow-up activities that will strengthen and extend their learning.

Other items about children and their surroundings you might bring in to display on your "What's New?" table from time to time include:

A sealed bottle of brown liquid (vanilla)
An open box of maple seeds
A brick
A hard-boiled egg
A sealed margarine cup full of navy beans
A baby's shoe
A cup of brown powder (chocolate drink mix)
A house painter's roller
An onion and a tulip bulb
A carpenter's level

To prepare for the children's possible questions and avenues of direction, you and your co-workers should make a list of free-association ideas for whatever object you display. For instance, whatever comes to your mind when you see an egg should be included in your list, no matter how improbable. This will help prepare you for possible areas your children may want to explore. Nevertheless, be prepared to be "out-associated" by the children! Unfettered children's minds are often more imaginative than those of many adults once they are turned on to wondering.

Here are some free-association ideas one classroom team came up with when they thought of an egg:

shell	yellow	nest	smell
chicken	smooth	sticks	Easter
hatch	round	fry	grass
warm	bird	omelette	hunt

These words will give you and your co-workers clues to possible directions for exploring activities involving eggs. Perhaps the children will want to hatch eggs in a homemade incubator. On the other hand, they may want to start exploring eggs by cooking them in different ways and eating them. Since Easter was one of the free-association words, this may tell you to save the egg experience until the Easter season. But whenever you do it, listen to what the children are asking about the egg on your "What's New?" table. This will tell you the direction your egg study should take. Your free-associating has merely prepared you for possible directions.

As you may have noticed, each of the ten items listed above can be explored with one or more of the senses. Let the children try out the items in their own way before you start with questions. Then go in whatever direction seems profitable for you and the class. If an item doesn't arouse interest, try a new one another day. Your own modeling behavior should, in fact, stimulate the children to (1) bring in their own items, (2) ask questions about them, and (3) test them out with their five senses.

Using the Senses to Examine Materials

Seeing, hearing, smelling, tasting, touching—these are the natural tools children use to explore and try things out. Even babies depend upon them. Taste seems to be one of the first senses developed. A baby almost always begins exploring new items by putting them in her mouth. Three- and four-year-olds do a great deal of touching, yet they are not beyond tasting when the occasion arises.

How do you as a classroom worker help children use their sensory abilities? You may want to start with the items on a science table. First, observe how the children themselves handle them. Are they doing sensory exploration (i.e., picking the items up, shaking them, smelling them)? If so, you need to support and encourage this by giving positive reinforcement: "Look what Joel's doing with the maple seeds. How did you discover they would fly, Joel?" or "You've discovered that the brown liquid has a smell, haven't you, Shelley? What can you tell us about it?"

If you find your children are not using their senses to explore new things, you will want to encourage them by serving as a model. You can start by touching the item yourself, picking it up, rubbing it, and so forth, all the while explaining your actions verbally. Or, you can start by covering your eyes with your hand (or a blindfold), then try to find out as much as possible about a new item without using the sense of sight. This can become a fascinating game for children in a small group around the science table. The children take turns being blindfolded and try to discover as much as possible about the secret items you have brought in a bag (for example, a hairbrush, a tennis ball, an hourglass egg timer). Be sure children feel comfortable about using a blindfold. It is a frightening experience for some preschoolers, and they would be better off covering their eyes with their hands.

Where else besides the science table can the children practice their newfound tools of discovery? Hopefully, they will apply them to exploring the environment of the classroom, the center, and the surrounding grounds or neighborhood. Once the children are familiar with their classroom, they may want to branch out by exploring the rest of the building. You should make arrangements or get permission ahead of time, if this is necessary.

We have mentioned following water pipes to a meter in the basement. Basements are always fascinating places for children. They may be interested in the furnace or water heater as well. If your program shares facilities with a school, church, or community center, the children will want to explore other parts of the building. It is best to go in small groups after discussing where you are going and using questions to predict what you might see.

It may be a bit overwhelming for threes and fours to try to explore a large building all at once; it is better to concentrate on one room or one area at a time. If you have a kitchen or food preparation space separate from the classroom, this may be a good place to begin.

Collecting, Comparing, Recording

In order to find out as much as possible about the object or idea under scrutiny, adult scientists collect similar things, compare and contrast them, and record their findings. Preschool children can do the same. In fact, once they are deeply involved in wondering, your children will want to follow up with collecting, comparing, and recording.

The possibility of collecting seeds of different kinds was already mentioned. Children can bring in seeds they pick up on their way to the center, or they can save the fruit seeds from their snacks or lunches. In this way, they will soon have a collection of maple seeds, linden seeds (tiny pealike balls), catalpa pods, acorns, orange seeds, grapefruit seeds, apple seeds, and even horse chestnuts (buckeyes) if they live where these are available. This can be an individual or group effort.

How will you display them? One easy way is to use the sectioned half of an egg carton and cover it with clear food wrap. The seeds can be labeled before the wrapping is put on. Each collector can fill his own carton. Another way is to place different seeds in plastic sandwich bags and hang them from a clothesline or tack them to a bulletin board in your science corner (with the name of the seeds and the child's name inside each bag).

What other kinds of collections can children assemble? Stones, seashells, fossils, nuts, buttons, berries, weed seeds, seed pods, leaves, soil, and bird feathers are a few possibilities. Whatever direction your science activities take will surely suggest other collecting ideas.

Then what? How can children's collections contribute to the method of sensory exploration they are developing? It can help them develop the thinking ability they need to view things logically. They will begin to understand not only how similar things are alike, but also how they are different. If Bernie brings in stones he has collected on his way to the center, you might ask, "What is it about all these stones that makes them alike?"

He may have to examine them closely, using his senses carefully to determine why they are alike. It is not their color. Some are gray, but different shades of gray. One is blackish, two are whitish, and one is sort of pink. Neither is it their size or shape. Some are large and round, some small and round, and some angular. So it must be their composition. Bernie calls it their hardness.

Next, you can ask Bernie how he will separate the stones for display. Posing this problem means he will have to determine how individual stones are different from one another. Ability to sort and classify according to a particular attribute is another facet of thinking. He may sort his collection on the basis of one of its most obvious attributes: color. Once the stones are arranged in groups according to color, you might ask, "How else could you sort out your stones if they were all the same color?" Will he be able to do it by size or shape? The more ways Bernie finds to classify objects, the more sophisticated his sensory exploration will become. He is developing not only his cognitive abilities, but a scientific mode of inquiry.

Scientists keep records of whatever they are investigating. They must record information such as where, when, how often, and how much. If we are serious about reawakening our children's sense of wonder and curiosity, we will want our preschool scientists to keep records as well. If they are making collections, they may want to record where or when they found the different items. It will be up to the adult classroom workers to do the actual writing. The record of a collection can be kept in an individual scrapbook with a page devoted to each item, or it can be kept on a wall chart.

For example, Bernie may want to keep a file card record for each of his stones. You might set up the following kind of record for him:

> Large White Stone
> Where found:
> When found:
> Description:

Let Bernie tell you the words to write down. Under "description" he may want to trace around the stone and color it in with white chalk.

Some children may be far enough along in scientific inquiry to actually identify rocks, but for most preschoolers, especially if they are picking up stones from the street or yard, it is not necessary or even appropriate to identify quartz or sandstone or limestone. The importance of recording lies in its ability to develop a more focused, in-depth kind of observation and questioning on the part of the child, as well as motivating her to continue the activity to find out all she can.

If your children are not collectors, start a simple collection yourself to get them started. Don't let it turn into a competition over who has the most or best; keep it strictly scientific. Later, you can help extend the activity by finding a simple science book with pictures that will help the collector identify some items. Again, the child must compare and contrast the pictures with the real items. You can help by asking questions such as, "What makes your stone like the one in the picture?"

Most preschool science books are not guidebooks for identification. You will have to select these from the nonfiction section of the library. Try to choose books with only one picture on a page, if possible, to make it less confusing for the children.

Other kinds of records might include simple graphs to show how much the children's plants have grown each week. Set aside a special time for every child to measure and record his plant's growth. A strip of construction paper can be used for measuring. Have the child cut it to the size of the plant and paste it on the chart. Graphs can be individual or group projects.

Children's height and weight can be measured and recorded if the class is involved with examining the growth of living things. Classroom pets can be weighed monthly and the results recorded. Seasonal changes in leaves, plants, and trees can be observed and recorded with words, line or bar graphs, or even photographs. Daily weather records can be kept with colorful symbols for sunny, rainy, cloudy, windy, or snowy. Once a few children start making records or scrapbooks, others will be motivated to begin their own scientific recording.

HELPS CHILDREN DEVELOP SUCH CONCEPTS AS SHAPE, COLOR, SIZE, CLASSIFICATION, SERIATION, NUMBER

As young children begin to perceive the world around them, they need some direction in organizing their perceptions to enable them to make sense of things and begin to think with clarity. Helping them develop certain concepts is an important way preschool programs can encourage this mental process. Concepts are the labels we give to mental constructs that describe groups of things that are alike in certain ways. Dean Spitzer, in *Concept Formation and Learning in Early Childhood,* calls concepts "the mental tools we develop to help us cope with our complex world."

Shape

Recent research shows that children develop concepts in a certain sequence. It is a good idea, then, for preschool programs to follow the same sequence in presenting concept activities. Shape is one of the early concepts to be formed. That is, young children can begin to discriminate objects on the basis of their shape quite early.

It is best to present activities about one concept at a time, and to give children plenty of time and opportunity to make that concept a part of their thinking process. In every instance, activities should involve familiar objects at first, and should be presented as games or play.

It is true that young children learn through exploring with their senses, but the way they do so is far different from adult scrutiny of a new object. Children learn through play. They try out a new object or new concept in a playful way to see what it will do or what they can do with it. Take, for example, a rattle. Adults know from past experience that a rattle should be picked up and rattled, that it will make a noise. Babies, toddlers, and young children who have never had experience with a rattle do not know how it is supposed to be used. They will playfully experiment with this new item, putting it in the mouth, hitting it on a surface, perhaps even throwing it, until they discover its most interesting aspect: the noise it makes when you shake it.

This is how young children learn concepts as well. Your classroom concept activities should provide children with all kinds of play opportunities for learning. For children to learn about circles, squares, and triangles, they will need to play circle games, sing square songs, make triangle hats, and have shape hunting games, lotto games, and puzzles. They can sort unit blocks on the basis of their shapes, cut out cookies or mold clay circles and squares, and saw wood into different shapes.

Color

Although they seem to talk about colors first, research shows that children develop the color concept shortly after that of shape, reflecting the fact that people around them make more reference to color than to shape. Children often name the colors before truly understanding what they mean. You can help them clarify color concepts by starting with one color at a time and providing them with all kinds of games and activities relating to that color. Start with the primary colors of red, yellow, and blue (plus black and white), since young children seem to recognize these most easily. Then introduce secondary colors—green, then orange, when Halloween comes.

Color songs, guessing games, pegboards, color lotto, food colors in water, paint mixing, and cutting colored construction paper are a few of the activities you can use.

Handicapped children can learn concepts along with the other children. Set up the activities as you do everything in your classroom so that children with physical and mental disabilities can participate. Keep many of the concept games on shelves in the manipulative area for the children to select on their own. Add to and exchange the various manipulative activities as the children learn more than one color.

Be sure to include picture books in your reading corner to motivate interest in colors. *Mr. Rabbit and the Lovely Present* is about a little girl who asks a child-sized rabbit to help her find a series of presents for her mother in the colors of red, yellow, green, and blue. *Anthony's Hat* is about a hat that is black and beautiful until a variety of items fall on top of it, turning it to white, red, green, and purple. This story can easily be converted to a flannel board activity by cutting out the items from an extra paperback book and pasting flannel or sandpaper to the back of each, for the children to use on a flannel board as you read the story aloud. Children can also play a game about Anthony's hat by acting out the story with real hats and clothing items.

A Rainbow of My Own is a book that will motivate children to create their own rainbow with a prism. Rainbow glasses can also be purchased in discount stores or toy stores. A book with stunning color photographs is Tana Hoban's *Is It Red? Is it Yellow? Is It Blue?* Color photographs of everyday objects at a child's eye level also include items that are orange, green, and purple.

Size

As the young child constructs his own knowledge by interacting with the objects and people in his environment, his brain seems to pay special attention to the relationships between things. Size is one of those relationships. The child must understand the property of size, like the properties of shape and color, in order to make sense of his world.

There are various orders of size, usually thought of in terms of opposites: big–little, large–small, tall–short, long–short, wide–narrow, thick–thin, and deep–shallow. Direct comparison of objects based on one of these aspects seems to be the best way for young children to learn size.

Yet most children can only relate to one aspect of an object at a time when they are comparing, contrasting, or categorizing. First they must learn the single concept, say, of "big," through many games and concrete activities (never worksheets!). Next they can contrast that concept with "little." But don't confuse them by bringing in thick or thin, or short or tall, all at the same time. Give them plenty of time to learn the concept "big" through all sorts of real materials before moving on to "little."

Classification

After learning simple concepts, children need to be able to apply them. Classifying has to do with sorting or separating objects into groups or sets on the basis of a common characteristic such as shape or size or color. This ability is necessary in cognitive development in order for the brain to sort out and process the wealth of incoming data obtained through the child's sensory activities. Sorting objects and materials in the classroom gives the children practice in this skill and involves identifying the similarities of objects as well as understanding relationships.

Piaget and other researchers have noted that children progress through a sequence of sorting skills, and each skill is more complex than the previous one as the youngsters' cognitive abilities develop.

The earliest sorting skill to appear is simple classification, which most threes can do. Children doing simple classification can sort or group objects that actually belong together in the real world. For example, they can group together all of the toy animals that live on the farm in one set and all of the toy animals that live in the zoo in another set if they have had previous experience with such animals.

In another type of simple classification, children place things that belong together into a group. For example, all of the toy trucks, cars, and motorcycles go together because "you can drive them." A more mature type of classification involves classifying objects into separate sets on the basis of a common characteristic like color, for example. The problem preschoolers have in doing this kind of sorting involves consistency. They may start out sorting on the basis of color but switch in the middle of the task to some other property like shape. Children need to practice with all kinds of sorting games as they develop this cognitive skill, and they enjoy this type of activity.

Bring in collections of items for children to sort out according to one attribute at a time. A box of buttons, for instance, can be sorted by size into margarine containers with slits on the lids. Use three margarine containers—one for large buttons, one for medium, and one for small buttons. At another time, let them sort the buttons by color, and still later, according to the number of holes in each button.

Other collections for sorting include shells, seeds, nuts, beans, rocks, leaves, toy cars, marbles, feathers, Tinkertoy sticks, and toy figures.

Seriation

Seriation involves arranging a set of objects in a certain order according to a certain rule; for example, from short to tall, light to heavy, loud to soft, light pink to dark red. Both commercial games and teacher-made activities help children learn such arrangements. Many Montessori materials involve seriation.

Young children usually are able to form a series if they are provided with cues. Montessori-size cylinders, for instance, are supposed to be arranged in a board with graded holes of the proper size. Children fit the cylinders from large to small in the increasingly smaller holes in this self-correcting activity. The youngsters match the size of the cylinders with the size of the holes and find out by trying which cylinders do or do not fit. Once they have learned the concept, many children are able to line up the cylinders in the proper order without cues from the board.

Stacking blocks, boxes, and rings work on the same principle of arranging items in a series from the largest to the smallest. Even toddlers soon learn that the largest item will not fit into a smaller one, and that if one item is left over, they need to start over again to find out their mistake. The point is that children should be allowed to play these learning games without your help, and then they will learn such concepts on their own, a necessary skill in their development of logical thought.

Numbers

Children encounter the spoken form of numbers long before they understand their meaning. Many can count accurately to ten or even twenty without having the slightest idea of what "six" or "thirteen" or even "one" means. Nursery rhymes such as "One, Two, Buckle My Shoe," and counting books such as *The Very Hungry Caterpillar* encourage this skill. Counting in other languages is fun for young children, too. If you have bilingual children, help them learn the number names in a second language. The picture book *Moja Means One* introduces the numbers one through ten in Swahili.

Next, children need to learn about number concepts; that "one" means one object, that "two" means two things. They can begin to count people, dolls, toys, or any other three-dimensional object that is meaningful to them. Don't start out with number symbols; they are still too abstract. Use stick figures or some other more concrete symbol. Once they have truly learned what oneness and twoness are all about, you can begin writing down number symbols.

The children may want to count their collections. You or they can record the amount in symbols of rocks or whatever. They may want to keep count of something: the number of cars or people that pass the center. Give them a file card and a paper punch, and let them punch a hole for every car or person they see. You may want to paste a picture of a car on one card, a truck on another. Another day, use pictures of people.

Once you have introduced true number symbols, be sure you give children many opportunities to play with them using concrete, three-dimensional materials, such as blocks, toy cars, or themselves. At this time you may want to change the signs in your activity areas that regulate the number of children allowed in each. Switch from stick figures or other symbols to real numbers. Let the children demonstrate what they mean.

INTERACTS WITH CHILDREN IN WAYS THAT ENCOURAGE THEM TO THINK AND SOLVE PROBLEMS

Your modeling behavior can be your most important contribution to this skill. If you demonstrate to children by your actions how interested and excited you are about the world around you, you will ignite their interest as well. It makes no difference whether you have any previous knowledge of plants, insects, or numbers. What makes the difference is that you show children you want to find out, too. Show your enthusiasm by your tone of voice, by the sparkle in your eye, by the questions you pose.

Children learn number concepts by counting things.

Questions: Open-ended and Closed

What kinds of questions are your children already asking? Get into the habit of writing them down so you'll have a concrete and specific take-off point in activities. Place some three-by-five-inch cards and pencils around your room, on top of shelves or room dividers, for you and your co-workers to reach when you hear a question, then write it down.

Joel asks, "Why do we always have to have orange juice for snack?" Later, he wants to know, "Where is Mrs. Appleton? Isn't she coming to our room anymore?" And still later, "Is that a piece of tree? It looks like the one in my backyard."

From this record of Joel's questions, you begin to realize that here is a curious boy who notices when the same thing is repeated as well as when things are not. He is even able to make comparisons. You will want to provide Joel with new opportunities to explore.

Shelley, on the other hand, asks only, "Can I play with the baby buggy now?"—a permission question, not a why or how question. She doesn't seem to notice the tree bark displayed on the science table, nor does she comment on the new arrangement of the dramatic play corner.

Questions children ask tell us many things about them. First of all, they tell us if the children are curious. Children who are not curious ask few *how, why,* or *where* questions. If we keep a record, we will soon know who they are; then it is up to us to help them start thinking in terms of questions.

We often have to be the ones who start the questioning process. Children closely imitate the adults around them. If we are successful in our questioning, many of the children should soon be copying us.

What kinds of questions should we ask? Open-ended questions seem the most valuable. These are questions that can be answered in many ways. They require the child to think and imagine and explore in order to come up with an answer. The answers to open-ended questions are never right or wrong, they are merely possibilities. Thus, such questions are not threatening to the child.

For example, Joel evidently discovered the piece of bark the teacher had displayed on the science table. If the teacher wanted to interest Joel more deeply in this item, she might ask an open-ended question, "What can you tell me about this?" This kind of question could result in many answers. On the other hand, a closed question such as, "What is this?" usually calls for only one answer, which will be either right or wrong. In this case, the teacher's closed question usually cuts off further discussion. Either the child is right, and that's the end of it, or he is wrong, and will seldom make a second attempt to answer.

If the teacher had noticed that Shelley was preoccupied with wheeling the doll buggy around and around in the dramatic play corner, she might have tried to stimulate Shelley's consideration of other possibilities with one of the following open-ended questions: "What else can you do with your baby buggy?" "How else could you give your baby a ride if you didn't have a buggy?" "What do you suppose your neighbors in the play corner are thinking when they see you go by with your buggy?"

Open-ended questions like these are provocative. They ask the child to look at an ordinary situation from a new perspective.

But, first of all, the teacher or aide needs to see things herself from a new perspective—the point of view of a scientist trying out and testing herself and the environment. It is not easy for most adults to pose open-ended questions. For example, what might you ask a child who has painted vertical red squiggles all over his paper? The questions we more frequently revert to are closed: "What is it?" or "Is your painting about the rain?" The classroom worker who is aware of the value of open-ended questions might ask, "What can you tell me about those red squiggles?"

Test yourself on your ability to pose open-ended questions. Suppose one of your children brought into class a woolly bear (caterpillar) he found on the way to the center. What could you ask him to stimulate his curiosity about the creature?

1. Do you know what it is?—a closed question that cuts off discussion and thinking, especially if the answer is no.
2. What do you call a caterpillar like that?—a closed question that ends with the answer.
3. What can you tell me about that fuzzy little creature?—an open question that allows for all sorts of possibilities.
4. Look how fast he crawls! Where do you suppose he is going?—open-ended and unlimited.

How did you score? Do you have the makings of an explorer? It takes thought and practice to ask open-ended questions.

Follow Up

Your children may not be able to answer these questions accurately any more than you can, but what fun it will be to find out the answers together. If you have involved them in the sensory exploration and concept development activities described, then you have the means for finding answers at your fingertips.

"Why is our aquarium getting all dirty on the glass inside?" What can you find out together about the growth of algae? That it is green algae and needs light to grow; that it also needs food to grow—waste matter (maybe you have too many fish; or maybe you feed them too much; or maybe your filter needs to be cleaned); that excessive algae needs to be removed in order to have a healthy fish tank; that certain creatures, such as snails and algae-eating fish, will remove it; that too much of it is a sign of pollution in rivers, ponds, and lakes—"Let's find out if our river is polluted!"

Be alert to questions and comments like this. When your children pose such problems, help them become involved in solving them by modeling your own interest and enthusiasm.

SUMMARY

This chapter has looked at ways to promote children's questioning, exploring, and problem-solving skills in order to develop their thinking skills. Early childhood classroom workers need to be aware of how children use their sensory apparatus to explore the world around them and need to set up classroom activities to promote such exploration. Using children's natural curiosity or reawakening it if they seem to have lost it should be the classroom worker's goal in the cognitive development of young children. Bring in new materials, pose questions about them, take children on nearby field trips, and be sure to record the questions the children are asking so that you will know what direction to take in planning cognitive activities.

Help children develop cognitive concepts such as shape, color, size, classification, seriation, and number through real activities in the classroom. Then they can apply these concepts to the exploration they are already doing as they collect, compare, and record interesting materials in their environment.

Interact with the children yourself to stimulate their curiosity and encourage them to think and solve problems. Ask open-ended questions and listen to the way the children answer them. This should give you clues as to what direction you should take with individuals and the group in providing them with new cognitive activities or extending the present ones.

LEARNING ACTIVITIES

1. Read Chapter 5, "Advancing Cognitive Skills," and answer Question Sheet 5-A.
2. View Mediapak G, "Preschool Science Experience," and answer Question Sheet 5-B.
3. Read one or more of the Suggested Readings or view another sound filmstrip, such as "Children Can Cook" or "The Community as a Classroom: Trips." Add ten cards to your file with specific ideas for helping children develop cognitive skills. Include the reference source on each card.
4. Take some or all of your children on a brief field trip to a nearby area. Follow up with a classroom activity to clarify concepts or support learning. (The trainer can go along.) Prepare lesson plan for presenting this activity.
5. Set up a "What's New?" table and record how you or the children use or explore the materials.
6. Help the children learn a new concept using ideas from this chapter. (The trainer can observe.) Prepare lesson plan and record results.
7. Bring in several children's books and use them to support the activities described in this chapter. Record the results.
8. Continue your Portfolio of evidence of your skills. Add one piece of evidence for each of the following Teacher Skills Checklist items:
   a. Helps children use all of their senses to explore their world.
   b. Helps children develop such concepts as shape, color, size, classification, seriation, number.
   c. Interacts with children in ways that encourage them to think and solve problems. Evidence should reflect what you, not another staff member, have done.
9. Complete the Chapter 5 Evaluation Sheet and return it and the answers to Question Sheets 5-A and 5-B to the appropriate college or program official.

QUESTION SHEET 5-A

(Based on Chapter 5, "Advancing Cognitive Skills")

1. Why is it important to help children develop cognitive skills during the preschool years?
2. How do children use their senses to explore the world around them?
3. What can we do to reawaken the curiosity of children who seem to have lost their sense of wonder?
4. How can field trips promote cognitive development?
5. How can you follow up on children's interests with materials in the classroom?
6. How can you use collections to promote cognitive development?
7. How would you help children learn a new concept such as "circles"?
8. How can children in your classroom learn the meaning of numbers?
9. Give two examples of open-ended questions about a guinea pig.
10. Why is it important for children to learn classification skills?

QUESTION SHEET 5-B

(Based on Mediapak G, "Preschool Science Experience")

1. What are three important goals for science in the preschool program?
2. Give an example of a broad science concept you might follow throughout the year.
3. How would you involve your children in your science planning?
4. How do children learn original information?
5. What form should your science activities take to insure that real learning takes place?
6. What is the most important aspect for children in their scientific exploration of a guinea pig?
7. How would you begin planning a study of the concept "we use water"? Why?
8. How can a cooking activity promote scientific exploration?
9. Would you have allowed your class to study plants when your plans called for a study of animal pets? Why or why not?
10. How can you remotivate your children once their interest in a science project begins to lag?

SUGGESTED EVIDENCE FOR PORTFOLIO

1. A photo or tape recording of a field trip you took with the children and a written explanation of how this shows your skill in helping develop children's cognitive abilities.
2. A photo or description of a collection the children have made and a written explanation of the sensory exploration they used and the concepts they learned.
3. A game you have constructed or a children's product that demonstrates how you helped children develop a particular concept and a written explanation of your role in promoting cognitive development.

4. A list of children's picture books in your classroom that promote cognitive development and an explanation of how this occurs.
5. A written explanation of one example of how you encouraged your children (or an individual child) to solve a problem on their own.

Each piece of evidence should be accompanied by a write-up explaining how this shows your competence in the area of **Cognitive** and how the activity is developmentally appropriate for your children. Refer to Chapter 8, "Cognitive Development: Classification and Seriation," and Chapter 9, "Cognitive Development: Number, Time, Space, Memory," in *Observing Development of the Young Child* (Beaty, 1986) for developmental statements.

SUGGESTED READINGS

Arnold, Lois B. *Preparing Young Children for Science.* New York: Schocken Books, 1980.

Beaty, Janice J. *Observing Development of the Young Child.* Columbus, Ohio: Merrill Publishing Co., 1986.

Brown, Sam, ed. *Bubbles, Rainbows & Worms.* Mount Rainier, Md.: Gryphon House, 1981.

Bybee, Rodger W., and Robert B. Sund. *Piaget for Educators.* Columbus, Ohio: Merrill Publishing Co., 1982.

Forman, George E., and David S. Kuschner. *The Child's Construction of Knowledge: Piaget for Teaching Children.* Washington, D.C.: National Association for the Education of Young Children, 1983.

Harlan, Jean. *Science Experiences for the Early Childhood Years,* 3rd ed. Columbus, Ohio: Merrill Publishing Co., 1984.

Kamii, Constance Kazuko. *Young Children Reinvent Arithmetic.* New York: Teachers College Press, 1985.

Osborn, Janie Dyson. *Cognition in Early Childhood.* Athens, Ga.: Education Associates, 1983.

Richardson, Lloyd I., et al. *A Mathematics Activity Curriculum for Early Childhood and Special Education.* New York: Macmillan, 1980.

Russel, Helen Ross. *A Teacher's Guide: Ten-Minute Field Trips, Using the School Grounds for Environmental Studies.* Chicago: J. G. Ferguson, 1973.

Siegler, Robert S. *Children's Thinking.* Englewood Cliffs, N.J.: Prentice-Hall, 1986.

Simon, Seymour. *Pets in a Jar: Collecting and Caring for Small Wild Animals.* New York: Puffin, 1975.

Stetten, Mary. *Let's Play Science.* New York: Harper and Row, 1979.

Wilt, Joy, and Terre Watson. *Listen! 76 Listening Experiences for Children, Including 60 Rhythm and Musical Instruments to Make and Use.* Waco, Tex.: Creative Resources, 1977.

_____. *Look! 70 Visual Experiences for Children, Including 35 Toys and Projects to Make and Use.* Waco, Tex.: Creative Resources, 1978.

_____. *Touch! 48 Tactile Experiences for Children, Plus 34 Art Media Recipes to Make and Use.* Waco, Tex.: Creative Resources, 1977.

CHILDREN'S BOOKS

Brown, Marcia. *Shadow.* New York: Charles Scribner's Sons, 1982.

Carle, Eric. *The Very Hungry Caterpillar.* New York: Crowell, 1971.

Ets, Marie Hall. *Gilberto and the Wind.* New York: Viking Press, 1963.

Feelings, Muriel. *Moja Means One.* New York: Dial Press, 1971.

Freeman, Don. *A Rainbow of My Own.* New York: Penguin, 1966.

Gretz, Susanna. *Roger Takes Charge!* New York: Dial Books for Young Readers, 1987.

Hoban, Tana. *A Children's Zoo.* New York: Greenwillow Books, 1985.

_____. *Is It Red? Is It Yellow? Is It Blue?* New York: Greenwillow, 1978.

Hutchins, Pat. *One Hunter.* New York: Mulberry Books, 1982.

Robison, Deborah. *Anthony's Hat.* New York: Scholastic, 1976.

Thole, Dorothy. *Tatum's Favorite Shape.* New York: Scholastic, 1977.

Zolotow, Charlotte. *Mr. Rabbit and the Lovely Present.* New York: Scholastic, 1962.

SOUND FILMSTRIPS

Beaty, Janice J. "Preschool Science Experience," Mediapak G, *Skills for Preschool Teachers.* Elmira, N.Y.: McGraw Bookstore, Elmira College, 1979.

Children Can Cook. New York: Bank Street College.

The Community as a Classroom: Trips. New York: Bank Street College.

CHAPTER 5 EVALUATION SHEET
ADVANCING COGNITIVE SKILLS

1. Student_____

2. Trainer_____

3. Center where training occurred_____

4. Beginning date_____ Ending date_____

5. Describe what student did to accomplish General Objective

   _____

   _____

6. Describe what student did to accomplish Specific Objectives

   Objective 1_____

   _____

   Objective 2_____

   _____

   Objective 3_____

   _____

7. Evaluation of student's Learning Activities
   (Trainer Check One)   (Student Check One)

   _____ Highly superior performance   _____

   _____ Superior performance   _____

   _____ Good performance   _____

   _____ Less than adequate performance _____

Signature of Trainer: Signature of Student:

_____   _____

Comments:

6 Advancing Communication Skills

General Objective

To promote children's verbal skills to help them to communicate their thoughts and feelings.

Specific Objectives

☐ Interacts with children in ways that encourage them to communicate their thoughts and feelings verbally.
☐ Provides materials and activities to promote language development.
☐ Uses books and stories with children to motivate listening and speaking.

M ost people now agree that the early childhood years, from birth to school entrance, are among the most important years of development. At no other time of life does development advance so rapidly in so short a time. Surely one of the most remarkable aspects of this period is the acquisition of a native language. From being totally nonverbal at birth, the young child develops the ability to think and speak in a native language by the time he or she enters school. If the family is bilingual, the child learns two languages.

How does this happen? Although psycholinguists advance several theories, the process is still something of a mystery. But we do know certain facts. We know that the drive to communicate is inherent in all human beings. We also know that children will strive endlessly to accomplish this goal of communication unless totally thwarted or frustrated by circumstances. And we know that if verbal ability is not developed during these crucial early years, it can affect a child's thinking and learning abilities the rest of his life.

Physical or mental disability may prevent language development from occurring at its normal time or rate. An abusive or uncaring home environment may discourage children from trying to express themselves verbally. The opposite is also true; if a child's every need is fulfilled without his having to utter a word, language is often delayed. Some twins satisfy the communication drive by developing their own verbal or nonverbal communication system, thus delaying native language development.

We also know that modeling behavior is as important here as in other aspects of development. Children from highly verbal homes seem to speak early and well, while children from homes where nonverbal communication is the norm are often delayed in learning to speak.

It is your role, then, as a teacher or aide in a preschool program, to promote language development in some of the following ways.

INTERACTS WITH CHILDREN IN WAYS THAT ENCOURAGE THEM TO COMMUNICATE THEIR THOUGHTS AND FEELINGS VERBALLY

For verbal communication to occur with preschool children, two factors seem to operate. First, there must be a stress-free environment that allows them to communicate, but does not force them. Children need to feel support from those around them in order to express themselves in their very personal but still imperfect mode of communication: language. Second, there must be a necessity. Children must have the need to communicate in the classroom.

Stress-Free Environment

For many children, verbalizing is a new and untried skill outside their home. Not only do they need opportunities to become proficient in it, but also encouragement. Children usually respond well to anything closely associated with themselves. Try playing name games to put them at ease and pique their interest:

> Bobby, Bobby dressed in blue,
> Tell us what you like to do
> On the playground.

> Jennifer, Jennifer dressed in red,
> Tell us what your good friend said
> In the house corner.

Play a follow-the-leader game in your classroom in which the leader touches and names items in the room and everyone who follows does the same. As children become proficient with one word, use two-word or three-word names (brown table, glass aquarium, little white telephone).

Praise them for their verbal accomplishments just as you would for a block building or a painting. "I like the way you said my name, Sharon. Sharon is such a nice sounding name, too."

A stress-free environment also means that you accept the children as they are—for themselves. This means you accept their language, no matter how poorly pronounced or how ungrammatical. Language is a very personal thing. It reflects not only the child's early stage of development, but also his or her family. Therefore, you must be especially careful not to correct a child's language. Telling them they are saying a word wrong is a put-down. Then how, you may ask, are they going to learn the "correct" pronunciation? They will learn it by hearing you and their peers use words, and by practicing new words in the many interesting language activities you provide.

A stress-free environment also means that your classroom is free from stressful situations for young children. They should not be put on the spot and forced to perform verbally, creatively, or in any other way. Offer them opportunities and encouragement, but do not force the shy or unsure children to speak.

Necessity

Do children have the need to communicate in your classroom? For what reason? You may want to list some of the reasons. If you are not sure, take time to observe and listen for communication opportunities. Your list may read something like this:

Giving a greeting
Asking a question
Giving a direction
Asking for permission
Telling what is happening
Inviting someone to participate
Reporting someone else's communication
Expressing an emotion
Relating an incident
Calling for attention
Expressing an inner thought, an idea
Pretending to be someone
Wondering about something

Next you need to provide opportunities for some of these types of communication to take place. Remember, you are the role model. You need to communicate verbally yourself whenever possible. Referring to your list, begin setting up opportunities for children to participate in talking.

Set aside a time of day when you greet the children and they greet one another. Have a small group or circle time in which the children have a chance to tell about something. A shy child might talk through a hand puppet at first. You can demonstrate how. Give your children a chance to pretend in the dramatic play area or with blocks or water. Ask one child to help another with a new tool or piece of equipment. Give children oral messages to carry to someone else in the room. Have them ask someone a question and return to you with the answer. Sit with the children at snack or lunchtime and start a conversation about something of interest to them.

Children need to hear words and how they are used in order to use them themselves. Make sure your classroom is full of talking. You can take the lead if no one else does. Describe in positive terms, for instance, what one of the children is doing. Then ask that child to describe what you are doing. Play games in which you give verbal directions to one child at a time to see if they can remember and carry them out. Start with one simple direction and add to it as the children become adept at playing: "Jeffery, can you go to the window, turn around in place two times, pick up a block, and give it to Kay?" Soon your children will be taking the lead themselves.

Verbalizing Feelings

Children also need to verbalize feelings. Whenever an emotional experience occurs in your classroom, take time out to talk about it with the individuals involved. Talk about feelings. If something nice has happened to a child or his family, get him to tell how he feels about it. If someone is angry or upset, help him express his emotion in words.

Books can promote discussions about feelings. *Let's Be Enemies* and *The Hating Book* can stimulate a discussion about how you feel when your best friend gets mad at you. *The Tenth Good Thing About Barney* explores feelings of grief when a pet dies. *Sometimes I Like to Cry* is a simple but effective display of times that call for tears. *Grownups Cry Too* shows that a person can express his emotions no matter how old he is. (This book is written in both English and Spanish.)

You might want to mount pictures of children laughing, crying, or feeling lonely in the area where you gather for group discussions. You might also photocopy and display some illustrations from the books mentioned to motivate children to talk about feelings on their own.

Child-Adult Communication

To promote good adult-child communication, you need to be an active communicator. This means you need to be a person the children are willing and able to approach. You must therefore be accessible to them. You may have to take the initiative with children whom you have assessed as needing language practice. They may lack the confidence to approach you on their own. Try stationing yourself in a particular classroom activity area near these children and create opportunities for conversation. If the children do not respond, you may need to talk for a while until the children accept your presence and realize that you accept them.

Observers of teacher behavior note that teachers usually respond to the children who talk the most. The quiet or inarticulate children, those who truly need conversational practice, are frequently ignored. You must therefore make a special effort to see that such children are not overlooked. Remember, patience, not pressure, should govern your approach.

What will you say in your conversations with individual children? Things of interest to them about themselves, the clothes they're wearing, the other children, their family, things they like to do, and classroom activities are always appropriate topics. Do not "talk down" to children in private conversations. They understand many more words than they use themselves. Instead, you should carry on a conversation just as you would with your own friends. Speak slowly and clearly, for in addition to stimulating children's speaking, you will be serving as a language model for them.

Bilingual Children

Bilingual children are fortunate to attend a preschool program that recognizes their native language as well as English because they will have the opportunity to become fluent in both languages during this period of language acquisition. At no other time in their lives will they be able to acquire another language so easily. In order to learn a second language, they must hear and practice it, and you must provide the opportunities for them to do so. If the majority of children in your class speak Spanish as a native language, they should be hearing and practicing English as well as the Spanish you or your co-workers and the other children speak. If only a few children speak a language other than English, it is that language you should give them extra help in, since children will learn to speak the language or languages they hear spoken around them.

We tend to think about learning a new language in adult terms: that it is extremely difficult for most people, and because it is so hard for adults, what must it be for a little child! The opposite is true, however; it is much easier for young children to learn a new language because they acquire it as they would a native language, not merely from books or formal teaching.

It is much more difficult for adults to acquire a second language because they have passed the natural acquisition stage in their development and have to learn it formally. In addition, adults must overcome the set language patterns of their native speech—something that is never entirely successful for most adult speakers, so they ultimately speak the second language with an accent.

You or a co-worker should be fluent in the second language. If one of you is not, ask for a volunteer from the community to visit regularly so the children will hear the language informally and practice using it. Perhaps one of the children's parents or relatives could do this. If you cannot find a native speaker to come in, locate a speaker and help him make tape cassettes using the second language. The speaker can tell a story or ask the children questions in the second language, and you can tape the children's answers and play them for the class.

You will also need to speak and write to the children's parents in their language. If you are not fluent, a language teacher from a local school might help.

Besides the many English language activities you provide for your children, you should plan specific activities using the second language, such as name chants and songs. The children can speak daily on the toy telephone with another second language speaker. A bilingual puppet can be part of your daily activities, talking to individuals and groups in both languages. Children can also learn to greet one another and say good-bye in the second language.

Dramatic play is one of the best vehicles for children's language development, no matter what the language, because natural conversation occurs. Be sure you allow enough time in your daily schedule for bilingual children to become involved in pretend play. If they seem shy, help them take on a role by playing alongside them until they feel comfortable with the other children.

Child-Child Communication

An important but frequently overlooked element in promoting and stimulating children's language in early childhood classrooms is the mix of children. Is your classroom composed of a single age group, such as all threes or all fours, or are these groups combined? Because children learn so much of their language through imitation of those around them, it is helpful for them to be around children more advanced than themselves. The language of three-year-olds will develop so much faster with fours in the same classroom. The same is true when deprived and affluent children are mixed together in a single classroom. The deprived child with limited language skills is soon expanding and improving his own speech.

There is one instance, however, where child-child communication is detrimental to the speakers' language development. This involves the previously mentioned phenomenon known as *twin talk*. It sometimes happens that young twins find a way to satisfy the drive to communicate by developing their own private language, a jargon that seems to be understood only by themselves and occasionally another close sibling. Once a youngster is communicating easily with another human being, his motivation to continue learning a new language is sharply reduced. Ordinarily, twin talk is a passing phase because other speakers in the home talk to and encourage the twins to respond normally.

Occasionally, however, when twins are left to themselves too much or the other family members accommodate them by learning enough twin talk to satisfy their needs, the twins will not develop their native language as rapidly or fluently as they should.

You can help twins who have delayed speech problems by placing each in a different classroom or by having them come to one class at different times. When this is not possible, make a special effort to involve each of them in different activities. Do not learn their twin talk yourself, but encourage them to learn normal language in the same manner you do with the others—by giving them a chance to listen to normal speech, providing them with incentives and opportunities for speaking, and involving them in experiences that give them something to talk about.

PROVIDES MATERIALS AND ACTIVITIES TO PROMOTE LANGUAGE DEVELOPMENT

To provide the materials and activities that will promote children's language development, you need to know at the outset each child's level of ability. As in every other aspect of development, the children in your preschool classroom will vary widely in speaking ability. This reflects their individual physical and intellectual development, the support they have received at home, the importance of verbal communication in their homes, the amount of practice they have had in speaking, and their own particular temperament.

The Language Assessment Checklist is a list of behaviors that most children with no physical or mental disability should be able to accomplish during their

---

Language assessment checklist

Child's Name_____

Time_____ Date_____

Observer_____

(Check items you see child performing. Use "N" to mean "no opportunity to observe.")

1. Confidence
   _____ Is confident enough to speak freely in surroundings other than home

_____ Speaks in normal tone of voice so others can easily hear

_____ Identifies himself/herself verbally by name

_____ Starts conversations sometimes

2. Articulation

_____ Speech is clear to other children

_____ Speech is clear to adults

3. Language production

_____ Speaks in simple sentences

_____ Asks questions; makes requests

_____ Converses informally at play or meals

_____ Responds to questions with more than one word

_____ Takes part in conversation

4. Vocabulary

_____ Uses names of people and things around him/her

_____ Uses simple verbs (come, go, see, etc.)

_____ Uses simple pronouns (me, him, her, etc.)

_____ Uses simple adjectives (big, little, red, etc.)

_____ Uses simple prepositions (in, out, up, etc.)

5. Communication

_____ Communicates wants and needs with words

_____ Talks with adults

_____ Talks with children

_____ Talks to animals, dolls, toys

6. Language understanding

_____ Follows teacher's simple directions

_____ Responds appropriately to another child's question or request

7. Word play

_____ Makes up nonsense words

_____ Enjoys doing finger plays; can repeat words

_____ Enjoys playing word and sound games

_____ Has favorite stories or songs he/she wants repeated

8. Listening skills

_____ Sits still and listens to someone talking or reading stories

_____ Can identify words and sounds which are alike or different

_____ Can find teacher when he/she calls from another room

_____ Can remember words and sounds when they are repeated

Permission is granted by the publisher to reproduce the Language Assessment Checklist for evaluation and record keeping.

preschool years. Although it is important to know the speaking and listening abilities of all the children in your classroom, you or your staff may want to begin this informal assessment with children who appear at the outset to need special help with language. They may be children who seldom speak or those you are unable to understand. By taking time to listen, observe, and talk with each child while he is involved in normal classroom activities, you should be able to complete the checklist for one child in one or two days.

Learning Prescription

After completing a child's Language Assessment Checklist, you will need to follow up with a Learning Prescription. First, list the areas of language strength and confidence; second, note the areas that need strengthening; and third, list the activities to help develop the areas of need.

A Learning Prescription for Sharon might read as follows:

Learning Prescription for _Sharon K._ Date _9/26_

Areas of Strength and Confidence

1. _Talks with adults_
2. _Follows teacher's simple directions_
3. _Talks to animals, dolls, toys_

Areas Needing Strengthening

1. _Confidence in speaking freely_
2. _Talking with other children_
3. _Taking part in conversations_

Activities to Help

1. _Involve her with toy telephone and another child_
2. _She could tell a newcomer how to use a toy_
3. _She could tell about guinea pig to another child_

Her prescription seems to be telling us that Sharon is comfortable and confident talking with adults and to animals, dolls, and toys. She is not yet all that confident talking to other children. The teacher will want to plan activities for Sharon that can help to involve her with perhaps one other child at first. Because she likes to play with toys, she might be willing to talk first to the teacher and then to another child on the toy telephone. The teacher might also ask her to tell a new child how to use a toy or piece of equipment such as the tape recorder or a computer program. Because she likes the guinea pig and talks to it every day, the teacher could ask her if she would tell a guinea pig story to one of the children she seems to get along with. In this way Sharon's language strengths can be used as the focus for improving the areas she needs to strengthen.

If, however, the activities seem to create pressure rather than pleasure, it may mean that Sharon is not yet confident enough to interact with another child. In that case the teacher should concentrate on helping the child feel good about herself by setting up activities she can succeed in and praising her for tasks accomplished. Language activities can come when the teacher feels they are appropriate. A discussion of each of the checklist items follows.

Confidence

The order as well as content of each numbered checklist item is worth noting. "Confidence" comes first, because a preschool child must feel at ease in the strangeness of the classroom environment and at ease among his peers in order to speak at all. The so-called nonverbal child is frequently one who lacks confidence to speak outside the confines of the home. You may want to talk with the parents to learn how much their child communicates verbally with them or siblings to assure yourself of the child's verbal ability.

Your principal task with the shy or uncommunicative child, then, will be to help him feel comfortable in the classroom. All the classroom workers need to be aware that overt efforts to help this child speak before he is at ease in the classroom may well produce the opposite result. Instead, all efforts should be concentrated on accepting the child as he is, using smiles, nods, and words of praise for positive accomplishments when appropriate, and leaving the child alone if necessary.

It takes a great deal of patience on the part of an early childhood classroom staff to allow the shy child to become at ease in his own good time, but this is often the only successful method. Weeks and even months are sometimes necessary for the extremely sensitive child to open up. If you have persisted in your "support without pressure" approach, you may be rewarded one day by a smile and even a whispered sentence.

Articulation

Articulation, the second area on the checklist, is difficult for the lay person to evaluate. Mispronouncing words is a common speech disorder. Nevertheless, articulation problems with young preschool children tend to be developmental lags rather than disorders. After all, at three and one-half years, many children have mastered only six consonants. What seems to you to be a disorder because you cannot understand the child may be merely a delay in the child's development. Certain speech sounds such as /l/ may still be impossible for them to pronounce, so they come as close as they can with /w/. They know how to form past tense by adding *ed,* so they apply the rule to every verb, regular or not, in an overgeneralized manner, saying, "I goed home" or "Baby taked her nap."

Preschoolers' speech develops in a distinct sequence at a definite pace. Modern linguists now realize that it is pointless for adults to try to correct a preschooler's speech by making him repeat sentences according to an adult pattern that he is not yet ready to use. Correcting is a negative response that tends to reinforce the unwanted behavior and, in addition, makes the child feel there is something wrong with him. Instead of improving a child's language, this technique often makes the child avoid speaking at all in the presence of the corrector.

Preschool classroom workers, instead, need to follow the positive reinforcement techniques used unconsciously by many parents and other adult caregivers in the home. They need to serve as good language models themselves, using clear words and simple sentences when they are around children. They need to support and encourage children's speaking efforts with smiles, praise, and repetition of words the child has used correctly. They need to provide opportunities for the young child to practice his speaking and listening skills.

If the other children in your classroom can understand the child speaker, you should be encouraged. It may take longer for you, an adult with set speech patterns, to become at ease with a child's speech idiosyncracies. Try hard to understand the inarticulate child without making him repeat everything. With practice and patience, you will find yourself able to understand the child as well as the other children do.

Again, your role is to be supportive, to be a good language model yourself, to provide opportunities for the child to practice speech sounds, and to give the child positive reinforcement in the form of smiles and praise when he is successful.

A warning is necessary whenever the preschool classroom worker deals with children's speech difficulties: Do not single out a child for special treatment. This may only accentuate the "problem." Instead, praise all the children for language accomplishments just as you do for their block building or painting. Give special help where necessary, but as unobtrusively as possible.

A classic example of the harm adults can cause by calling attention to so-called speech problems involves stuttering. Many children, especially boys, go through a phase at about three or four years of age when their speaking seems to be out of synchronization with their thinking. Hesitations at the beginning of a word cause them to repeat the first consonant in a stuttering manner. Parents sometimes feel they must force the child to slow down or he will become a permanent stutterer. This is exactly what they should *not* do. Their efforts in this direction only accentuate the "problem" and may actually cause the child to develop a real stutter. This nonfluent speech phase will usually correct itself *if left alone.* What the child really needs from the adults around him is a demonstration of love and acceptance.

Language Production

The third area of the checklist, language production, will help you recognize whether a child is producing sentences and taking part in conversations. It is necessary to check on this area with each child to make sure they have the opportunity to produce language daily. Do you or your co-workers initiate conversation on topics of interest to the children to which they can respond in answers of more than one word? Are you asking open-ended questions that require thoughtful answers, questions that begin with "how" or "why" or "what do you like about"?

An interesting classroom activity that always stimulates language production is puppetry. Young children use hand puppets differently from older children and adults. They seem to perceive puppets as extensions of themselves, rather than as separate doll-like toys. Notice how many times preschool children use a hand puppet as a "biter." We need to redirect this energy into using hand puppets as "talkers" too.

Rather than putting on a puppet show, preschool children should be encouraged to talk to one another through puppets. Again, you can serve as a model for this behavior. Put a puppet on your hand and talk to a child or small group through it. Use your own voice or, better, make a squeaky or deep voice, depending on the puppet character you are portraying.

You could have a boy character, Sammy, for instance, who comes to your classroom for the first time and wants to be introduced to the children. He could tell them how scared he feels coming there for the first time without knowing anybody. Maybe they will talk to him individually to help him feel better.

Or, you might have a bunny puppet who wants to meet your classroom animal pets and talk about how to care for rabbits or gerbils. He might ask each of the children what pets are their favorites and why.

When young children put a puppet on their hand, they tend to become that puppet. They will get deeply involved in the pretend situation—almost as if it were real. It offers the shy child an opportunity to talk through a "not shy" character, and it offers all children an unparalleled opportunity for language production.

Children with special needs can be involved in language through puppets with special needs. Have a puppet who speaks a language other than English visit your class. Motivation for this activity might come from the book *Maria Teresa,* in which Maria Teresa's Spanish-speaking puppet speaks to the American children in Maria Teresa's class and helps her make friends. You might even use a nonverbal puppet who can only point, and whom the children have to help learn to speak.

Vocabulary

Language delay in children may be caused by a deficient vocabulary, the fourth area in the checklist. Some children have not been around other children or adults who have used many words or encouraged them to. Their first words are usually nouns. If they are not also using simple verbs, pronouns, adjectives, and prepositions, you may want to get them involved in small-group games such as homemade lotto, which shows pictures of actions or qualities (e.g., a child running, a child sleeping, a small house, a big building). Children also learn many new words through imitation while interacting with their peers. You can promote interaction by arranging classroom areas to encourage small-group activities.

You might encourage vocabulary development by playing team language games with small groups. "Secret Whisper" is one example. Pair off four or six children into teams. In this game you secretly show one member of the team a picture of an object that you have concealed in a shoe box. This team member must then whisper through a cardboard tube (or softly through cupped hands) to his partner, telling what he has seen. The partner then says the name aloud, and gets to keep the picture if he is correct. Have plenty of pictures in the box, and keep going as long as you hold the children's interest. Let one of the children handle the "secret box" once everyone has caught on. Picture postcards or greeting cards can be used in the secret box as the children's ability to describe pictures increases.

Communication

Communication, the fifth checklist area, is closely connected with confidence. If children feel good about themselves, they will probably communicate with words. If they feel more comfortable with adults than with other children (as many youngsters do), the problem may be one of socialization rather than language. The child who talks only to "animals, dolls, toys" may be the shy, uncommunicative youngster already described under confidence. Besides giving support without pressure, your task will also involve easing the child into social situations with one or two other children, perhaps through role play or another activity that seems to attract him. You may need to be nearby in the beginning, but you can withdraw when you see the child playing comfortably with the others.

Toy telephones can help promote communication. Be sure to have at least two phones: one for the caller and one for the listener. For children who need special practice in speaking, you should put in a pretend call and talk with them every day. Other children will see you doing this and soon begin calling on their own. To make it more interesting, keep an old telephone directory in the area and pretend to look up the number.

Language Understanding

The next checklist area, language understanding, is related to listening skills and vocabulary. The child must be able to hear and know the words he is exposed to in order to respond with understanding. For children whom you have not been able to check off on either item, you may want to test for hearing problems.

Another teacher-made game that has proved a successful stimulus for language understanding uses a deck of playing cards to which the teacher has laminated pictures of children or objects cut out of magazines or catalogs. These can be covered with clear contact paper to keep them slick enough for shuffling and dealing. In this Talking Cards game, the teacher deals out a card to each child at the table. Each must name his picture aloud. If the child can name the picture, he can keep the card. The teacher deals again, and the naming continues until all the cards are gone. A more advanced form of this game requires the child to tell one thing (and later two things) about a card in order to keep it. A child can be the dealer after everyone understands the rules.

Word Play

We so often forget that learning through play applies to language. Children learn words through play just as they do roles. Early childhood classrooms need to encourage this kind of learning by providing opportunities for word and sound games, finger plays, songs, stories, and dramatic play. Encourage children to play with sounds and make up nonsense words on the tape recorder. If you don't have a tape recorder, you can jot down children's nonsense words and use a puppet to repeat them in a game at circle time.

Certain books stimulate children to have fun with words. They enjoy funny sounds, in words like "mush" from *Goodnight Moon,* and sound words like "plink, plank, plunk" from *Blueberries for Sal,* or the raindrop sound of "bon polo, bon polo" from *Umbrella.* Another favorite is sure to be *Mert the Blurt,* who blurts out funny family secrets to a colorful horde of animal characters.

Pat Hutchins focuses on this humorous word play in two of her books, *The Surprise Party,* in which each of the animals passes on to the next a whispered secret about Rabbit having a party, in a most distorted fashion as in the game Gossip, and *Don't Forget the Bacon!* in which a little girl with four things to buy at the store forgets not only the bacon, but garbles the rest of the directions as well, ending up with some surprising items.

In *Louie,* an Ezra Jack Keats book, a little nonverbal boy attends a neighborhood puppet show and speaks his first word. If your children respond well to Louie, they may want to make paper puppets of Gussie and Mouse as in the book.

Listening Skills

In order to speak, young children need to be able to listen and to hear. If you have reason to believe any of your children's hearing ability is impaired, their hearing should be tested. Parents may want to attend to it, but in many communities both auditory and visual screening are available for preschool programs. The earlier such problems are identified, the sooner the child can be helped to overcome them.

If it is a child's attention span that needs strengthening, you may want to devise activities of progressive lengths that will first focus attention, then help extend it. Games and stories that use the child's own name are always a good place to begin. Reading storybooks on a daily basis is an excellent method for developing attention. Some of the stories can be the children's own, which you write down as they dictate and later read back to them.

Good listening is a skill that adults seldom take time to develop themselves. To promote listening skills among your preschool children, you should make an effort to be a good listener yourself. Listen with interest to each child every day, especially those you have trouble understanding. To understand a child's speech, you need to learn to listen. At the snack table or book corner, seek out the child with articulation problems and encourage conversation. Good listening will promote listening on the child's part as well, just as a good language model promotes speaking.

In order to listen, you will need to stop speaking yourself. The child's utterances should be the focus of your attention. To encourage the child to continue, you should respond with smiles, nods, and short phrases. You need to look at the child and concentrate on what he is saying, and try to pick up a word or two you can understand, rather than ask him to repeat the communication. If you must ask questions, ask them as a friend would, not as a teacher who requires a correct answer.

The child will want to play listening games, too, if you present them in fun ways. At circle time, have the children listen quietly to the sounds around them. You may want to set a kitchen timer for one minute. How many different sounds will they hear before the buzzer sounds? The furnace rumbling, typing in a nearby office, the bubbling of an aquarium filter, and cars on the street outside may be some of the answers. If you have a tape recorder you can tape familiar sounds (a car door slamming, a refrigerator motor running, a kitten purring) and play them back for children to identify.

Once they are on the alert for them, children are likely to point out environmental noises and sounds you may not be aware of yourself. Adults take for granted so many things that children find new and intriguing. Give them the lead and see where it takes all of you!

Most of us are not used to verbalizing the simple, everyday actions we perform. Yet linguists have found this so-called self-talk to be an extremely helpful activity for preschool children during the long and complex process of learning a native language. Self-talk calls for you to put into words the actions you are performing, so the child hears and sees at the same time and thus learns what words mean.

For instance, as you prepare one of the classroom areas for a cooking experience with the children around you, you might say, "I'm getting out a big bowl to use for making gelatin. I'm putting it right here in the middle of the table. Let's see, we'll need a spoon to stir with. Here it is . . . a big spoon, a ladle. I'm putting the ladle on the table next to the bowl. We'll need hot water. Where is our teakettle? Oh, here it is. Joel, do you want to fill the teakettle with water? There, Joel is turning the water on to fill the kettle. Now I'm putting the teakettle on the hot plate to heat the water for our gelatin making. Tell me when you hear the teakettle whistle. Then it will be hot enough."

Parallel talk, in which adults verbalize the children's actions as they occur, also helps children learn to listen and understand the meaning of words by the way they are used. During the same cooking experience, you might make a running commentary of the children's actions by saying, "Joel is stirring the gelatin with a big spoon . . . a ladle. See how smoothly Joel stirs the gelatin, around and around. Joel, give the ladle to Sherry and let her have a turn. Now Sherry has the ladle and she is stirring."

Bilingual/Bicultural Children

You may have children in your classroom whose native language is not English but Spanish, Vietnamese, or a dialect such as black English. If a number of your children speak a different language or dialect, you should try to have a staff member or volunteer who speaks as they do. In addition, the children will be picking up English from the others. But if only one or two children speaks a different language which none of your staff speaks or understands, you should proceed as with nonverbal English-speaking children.

Just as English-speaking children can learn a second language easily and naturally at this language-learning stage, a foreign-speaking child can learn English without difficulty if he feels at ease in your classroom. You and the other children will serve as language models. You must not pressure the child to learn, but instead provide opportunities, support, and encouragement whenever possible. Word games like lotto are excellent aids if the cards show clear and simple pictures of objects or actions. But interaction with the other children during regular activities is perhaps the most valuable language activity the non-English-speaking child can have. Such a child is fortunate to be learning a second language during the language-learning stage of his life, instead of after the elementary years when language patterns are fixed and difficult to change.

As you can see, the development of language and listening skills on the part of a preschool child involves a great deal of speaking and listening by everyone. You must know each child's ability level in order to help him develop the necessary skills. Your efforts to assess each child and plan individual and group activities to support his growth are crucial during these preschool years, for lags in language development can cause learning problems a child may never fully overcome.

USES BOOKS AND STORIES WITH CHILDREN TO MOTIVATE LISTENING AND SPEAKING

One of the most important experiences a preschool child can have is a happy encounter with storybooks. If a preschooler is to meet with later success in learning and enjoying reading, he needs to become acquainted with books as early as possible. One hopes this pleasant acquaintance has begun in the home long before the child enters your classroom. The books and activities you provide will be a follow-up and expansion of the story reading that occurs at home. But for many children, the experience in your classroom will be their initiation into the exciting world of books and reading. You will want to make it a joyful one.

Children need to encounter books early in life for a number of reasons. Experiences with books help strengthen and reinforce their experiences with language. As they learn their native tongue orally, they will also be hearing and seeing words in books used in both familiar and new ways. They will eventually become aware of the concept of symbolization as they look at written letters that stand for sounds—the same sounds they are picking up in their oral vocabulary. They will also learn new

Children's books promote both listening and speaking.

words and new uses for familiar words as they listen to favorite stories read over and over.

When children see their parents and others reading, they begin to internalize the idea that reading is something that people around them like to do; it seems to be important and worthwhile. It is something they will want to learn to do when they go to school.

The adult who reads to a preschool child is saying something else very important: "I like you enough to take time out of a busy day to share something nice with you." It creates a good feeling for all concerned.

Characteristics of Preschool Children Useful for Book Selection

To bring children and books together successfully, you will need to know a great deal about both. Only a small number of children's books published annually are suitable for your three- and four-year-olds. How will you know which ones they are?

One of the simplest ways to choose suitable books is to focus on the principal characteristics of preschool children themselves, then select books that speak to the needs based on these traits.

An outstanding characteristic of young children is their egocentrism. They are very much concerned with themselves, their homes, their families, their friends. Thus, their favorite books will often be those in which they can readily identify with the main character, or in which the situation or the setting is familiar. Because children are involved with learning a language, they are fascinated with words and their sounds. At no other time of their lives will words and speech sounds be so new and so much fun for them. This means the books you choose to use with the children will be more enjoyable and meaningful for them if the words are interesting and distinctive. They like to hear rhyming words, sound words, nonsense words, and the repetition of words and phrases. Sometimes their attraction to a particular book is based entirely on one funny word in the story.

A third characteristic is their involvement with pretending and imaginative play. Young children spend a great deal of their time pretending to be someone else, trying out roles they see enacted around them in their homes, neighborhoods, or on television. They are therefore in tune with books that feature fantasy or imaginative situations or characters. Books with talking animals are more appealing to children of this age than any other age.

Children of preschool age are dependent upon parents or the adults around them. They also seek security at home. Books that feature warm family stories appeal to preschoolers. But no matter what the story, it should end happily and satisfactorily. Unhappy or unsettling endings are not suitable for children of this age. Unpleasant experiences with books can cause preschoolers to form negative attitudes that last a lifetime.

A fifth characteristic of young children is their short attention span. Books for preschoolers must be completed at a single sitting. Moreover, the story must have only a few words and a great deal of action. You will soon lose a preschooler's attention if the story is too long. Then, if he misbehaves and is reprimanded, the book experience is cast in a negative light for the child.

Because books for young children are picture books, their illustrations are another feature to examine in the light of children's characteristics and needs. Young children are attracted to bold, bright primary colors. The younger the child, the simpler and less cluttered the illustrations should be—with one prominent exception.

Preschoolers are also attracted to large pictures that show scenes in intricate detail. The *Madeline* books of Ludwig Bemelmans, with their detailed paintings of Paris parks and squares, Peter Spier's carefully done *London Bridge* or *The Erie Canal,* and Margaret Bloy Graham's line drawings of the city in Gene Zion's *Dear Garbage Man* or the inside of the house in *The Plant Sitter,* with all the tiny bugs, birds, and butterflies, for example, display the kind of detail that seems to intrigue many young children.

Young children also seem to prefer realistic illustrations to those of an abstract or stylized nature. Although adults usually select the books children read, often on the basis of adult sensibilities, we must remember that children will use the books. Their tastes should not be overlooked if we are to bring children and books together successfully. The illustrations and the text of a storybook should combine to help children identify with the characters, the situations, and the settings.

Choosing Books for Preschool Children

Every year between 2,000 and 3,000 new books are published for children. Bookstores display dozens of them. Library shelves are crowded with them. But it is up to tne staff of the preschool classroom to decide which ones are most appropriate for their children.

Once you know your children and understand their needs, you will want to learn a great deal about the available books to make the best selections. The following checklist, based on the characteristics of preschool children, has proved effective in helping teachers evaluate individual books. Although one book may not meet all the criteria listed, it should have most of them to be acceptable for use with

---

Book selection checklist

Title_____ Author_____

Illustrator_____ Publisher_____

Hardcover_____ Paperback_____   Date_____

_____ Main character children can identify with
_____ Situation familiar to children
_____ Setting familiar to children
_____ Illustrations bold, bright, attractive to children
_____ Words interesting, with distinctive sounds, repetition
_____ Action exciting, fantastic, fun
_____ Ending satisfying
_____ Story short enough to read at single sitting

preschoolers. For example, many of the *Curious George* books are a bit long for preschoolers, but their exciting action, along with the strong sense of identification children feel for the mischievous monkey George, more than make up for their length.

The thirty books that follow are listed alphabetically by author, and reviewed on the basis of this Book Selection Checklist. They have been chosen because they meet most or all of the criteria listed, and because they have been used widely and successfully with preschool children in the classroom.

You will want to start your own card file of books to use with children. The Checklist can be dittoed on the front of a five-by-seven-inch file card, and you can write comments about the book, the way you used it, and your children's reactions on the back.

The importance of becoming familiar with the books you intend to use cannot be stressed enough. Too many preschool teachers use books they are not really familiar with, books they have not actually opened until they sit down to read them to the children. The results are what you might expect—entirely up to chance. By accident, someone may have brought in a book suitable for preschool children, and you will have a successful experience using the book. On the other hand, the book may have been intended for older children, and your class will be bored and inattentive.

Because a book is a picture book does not make it suitable for preschool children. Picture books range in appeal and difficulty for children from infancy to third grade. That is why it is essential to know your children and your books before bringing the two together.

Because the book experience is so important for preschoolers, its success should be guaranteed at the outset. It is too important to be left to chance. Like every successful enterprise, it requires careful planning and extra time on the part of the adult to review the books to be used. Use the Book Selection Checklist to assess the books you presently have in your classroom. Do you find them all suitable? Remove those that are not, then become familiar with other good preschool books such as those listed here. You will need to handle them personally and read them yourself, though, to get to know them well enough to use with your children.

Review of Books for Preschool Children

Goodnight Moon by Margaret Wise Brown; pictures by Clement Hurd. New York: Harper & Row, Publishers, 1947 (hardcover), 1977 (paper).

A simple story about bedtime, with few words but detailed full-page pictures of a green bedroom on every other page, the bedroom grows progressively darker as the story continues. The main character, a small bunny in pajamas lying in bed, says goodnight to the many objects in his darkening room. Children can easily identify with the situation of going to bed before it's completely dark. But the outstanding element is the words, many of which rhyme and some of which delight young listeners because they sound so funny. This extremely short book can be read more than once at the same sitting to involve the listeners in finding the objects and repeating the giggly words.

Other Brown books: *Runaway Bunny.*

"I Can't" said the Ant by Polly Cameron. New York: Coward-McCann, 1961 (hardcover); New York: Scholastic Book Services, 1971 (paper).

This book, too, features word play rather than identification with a character. It involves the dilemma of a teapot that has fallen off the kitchen sink and is finally hoisted back up through the efforts of the ants, with clever comments by each of the objects in the kitchen. Each sentence of text contains two rhyming words and a line drawing of the object talking. The opposite page shows the entire kitchen with the objects in place as the action occurs. Children's attention is attracted by the humorous rhymes as well as a chance to participate once they know the story. This book should be read on a one-to-one basis or with small groups so the listeners can get a good look at the small red objects in the middle of each sentence.

The Very Hungry Caterpillar by Eric Carle. Cleveland, Ohio: Collins-World, 1967 (hardcover); New York: Putnam Publishing Group, 1986 (paper).

This story of a caterpillar who eats and eats until he turns into a cocoon and then a butterfly is in fact a clever counting book with bold illustrations of the fruit and food the caterpillar bores through as he progresses from one apple on Monday to a gigantic Saturday repast. Children are attracted to the pages of differing sizes with a hole actually punched through every piece of food. The bold, bright pictures of food against the white-page backgrounds are highly satisfying to the young child's visual sensibilities. The story is brief and fast-paced to accommodate the short attention span of its listeners. Children may not identify with a caterpillar, but they can appreciate his overeating and getting a stomachache. The book is not only a visual treat, but good fun.

Other Carle books: *The Grouchy Ladybug; Do You Want to Be My Friend?*

Will I Have a Friend? by Miriam Cohen; pictures by Lillian Hoban. New York: Macmillan, 1967 (hardcover, paper).

Children quickly identify with Jim and his situation as Pa takes him to nursery school for the first time, and he worries about finding a friend there. The familiar setting of a city preschool classroom with children of various racial backgrounds having fun with blocks and clay often compels children to adopt this book as their very own. Naturalistic illustrations cover the entire page, with the brief text tucked in blank spaces on the classroom walls. Even the words are childlike and fun. Best of all, this book can start children talking about their own uneasy feelings on the first day of school.

Best Friends by Miriam Cohen; pictures by Lillian Hoban. New York: Macmillan, 1971 (hardcover, paper).

The story of Jim and his best friend Paul in a city nursery school continues with a new adventure. Jim and Paul have a falling out until they are forced to work together to save the eggs in the classroom incubator when the light bulb burns out. Again, every item on the Book Selection Checklist can be checked. And once more, the story motivates a discussion about feelings and friendship.

Other Cohen/Hoban books: *The New Teacher; Jim Meets the Thing.*

Gilberto and the Wind by Marie Hall Ets. New York: Viking Press, 1963 (hardcover, paper).

Every classroom should have a copy of this book to be read on windy days. Most children, whether or not they are Hispanic, can identify with Gilberto in his adventures and misadventures with the wind. The pages are unusual in color—greenish-gray with simple black pencil drawings outlining Gilberto and his surroundings. The only other colors are the brown of his face and hands and the white of his kite, balloon, sailboat, pinwheel, and so forth. It is an effective use of simple colors. The story, with its series of windy encounters, is brief, action-filled, and interspersed with sound words whispered by the wind.

Play With Me by Marie Hall Ets. New York: Viking Press, 1955 (hardcover, paper).

Country children need stories and characters to identify with also. This book takes a little girl out into the meadow in an attempt to play with a grasshopper, a frog, a turtle, a chipmunk, a blue jay, a rabbit, and a snake. But all of them scurry away until the little girl learns to sit quietly and let them come to her. Again, simple line drawings with just a touch of color to the girl and animals make this a low-key story to look at and enjoy.

Other Ets books: *In the Forest; Talking Without Words.*

Corduroy by Don Freeman. New York: Viking Press, 1968 (hardcover, paper).

City children familiar with department stores and escalators quickly identify with the little girl who wants the teddy bear Corduroy for her very own. They can also appreciate Corduroy's attempt to replace the missing button on his overalls. The illustrations are realistic and colorful, the ending satisfying for all concerned. A multiethnic book.

Other Freeman books: *A Pocket for Corduroy.*

Millions of Cats by Wanda Gág. New York: Putnam Publishing Group, 1928 (hardcover); 1977 (paper).

This folktalelike story written in a storyteller's vernacular has been kept in print all these years because it is so well loved by its readers. Its rhythmical sentences and repetition of phrases are the outstanding features as the very old man sets out on his search to find a cat for the very old woman. The black and white prints that show him trudging over hill and dale are accompanied by simple text with the same rolling quality as the pictures. The "millions of cats" rhyme is repeated six times before the end of the book, with listeners eager to join in.

Other Gág books: *ABC Bunny.*

Nobody Listens to Andrew by Elizabeth Guilfoile; pictures by Mary Stevens. Cleveland: Modern Curriculum Press, 1957 (hardcover); New York: Scholastic Book Services, 1973 (paper).

This fast-moving modern story fulfills all the checklist criteria, as a frustrated Andrew tries unsuccessfully to get someone in his family to listen to him. Your classroom listeners will appreciate Andrew's dilemma, for they have surely heard the same excuses in their own families from people who have no time to listen. They are as delighted as Andrew's family is astonished to discover at last that there really is a bear upstairs in Andrew's bed! Then the fun begins as community helpers arrive with frantic sound words that children love to hear. Realistic illustrations in three colors place characters here and there on the pages adding to the excitement.

Bread and Jam for Frances by Russell Hoban; pictures by Lillian Hoban. New York: Harper & Row, Publishers, 1964 (hardcover); 1986 (paper).

Each of the "Frances books" is a warm family story addressing a familiar problem that many children experience. The characters are humanlike badgers illustrated in Lillian Hoban's sensitive two-color pencil drawings. The problem this time is Frances' refusal to try any new food. All she will eat is bread and jam—so her family lets her. Frances expresses her feelings in whispered songs and jump rope rhymes. The text of this story is longer than any reviewed so far, but a good story reader can usually hold preschool children's attention because of the novel references to a subject that commands children's attention: food.
> Other Hoban books: *A Baby Sister for Frances.*

Rosie's Walk by Pat Hutchins. New York: Macmillan, 1968 (hardcover); 1971 (paper).

In the shortest book mentioned so far, Rosie the hen walks through the barnyard in twenty-seven pages but only one sentence of text. What Rosie doesn't know, your listeners will quickly discover from Pat Hutchins' unique stylized drawings: that a sly fox is stalking her. Innocent Rosie leads the fox into one disaster after another, much to the delight of the listeners. This book demands one-to-one or smaller-group attention, since children at any distance from the pictures will miss the action.

The Surprise Party by Pat Hutchins. New York: Macmillan, 1969 (hardcover); 1972 (paper).

Again, animals in the same stylized drawings are the characters here in a delightfully mixed-up communication muddle reminiscent of the game Gossip. Rabbit whispers to owl that he is having a party tomorrow and it's a surprise. From then on, the message passed from one animal to another gets so garbled that it is truly a surprise for all at the end. Children love the nonsensical phrases the animals repeat, as well as the satisfying conclusion.
> Other Hutchins books: *Changes, Changes; Don't Forget the Bacon.*

The Snowy Day by Ezra Jack Keats. New York: Viking Press. 1962 (hardcover); New York: Penguin, 1976 (paper).

Children everywhere can identify with Peter, the little black boy who encounters snow for the first time. Readers and listeners alike see snow as a small boy might, in gigantic piles and weird shapes. They watch with delight as Peter makes footprints and tracks and a snowman and angels. They know how he feels when the snowball he has saved in his pocket melts into nothing. Keats's artwork fills every page with shimmering piles of snow against blue sky or pastel buildings, accenting Peter in his red collage snowsuit. It is the first of Keats's many "Peter books" and still one of the most popular with the preschool set because they can identify so closely with the situation and Peter's reactions.

Whistle for Willie by Ezra Jack Keats. New York: Viking Press, 1964 (hardcover); Puffin, 1977 (paper).

Peter wants to whistle for his dog Willie, but no matter how hard he tries, nothing comes out. Again, preschool children can identify closely with the characters and the situation. The sidewalks of the city are as colorful as before, with their collage buildings and graffiti-marked fences against a golden sky in Keats's full-page illustrations. And Peter behaves exactly as your listeners might when he tries to get away from his shadow by jumping or wears his father's hat to make himself more grownup.

Other Keats books: *Peter's Chair; Goggles; Pet Show; Louie.*

Leo the Late Bloomer by Robert Kraus; pictures by Jose Aruego. New York: E.P. Dutton, 1971 (hardcover); Windmill Books, 1971 (paper).

Preschoolers and adults alike are immediately attracted to this book for its feast of colors. A yellow owl, a blue elephant, an orange snake, a red plover, and a green crocodile prance across flower-filled pages performing all the feats poor little tiger Leo seems unable to do. "Are you sure Leo's a bloomer?" asks his anxious father. But his confident mother knows, "A watched bloomer doesn't bloom." Although preschoolers may not understand the term *late bloomer,* they have no trouble with the concept of parents worried because their child cannot read, write, draw, eat neatly, or speak—and when Leo does bloom, it's terrific!

Whose Mouse Are You? by Robert Kraus; pictures by Jose Aruego. New York: Macmillan Co., 1970 (hardcover); 1972 (paper).

Once again, children can identify with the little unloved boy mouse who fantasizes about his mother being inside the cat and his father in a trap just so he can rescue them and win their gratitude. Bright and extravagant pictures stand out against the white-page background. Most of the illustrations are double spreads, with only a brief sentence of text at the top of each page, making for rapid progress through the book. Mother mouse's reward—a fabulous banquet of cheeses—and father's—a race car of his own on a fantastic mountain track—will appeal to the youngsters' sense of justice. The exaggerations of the story may disturb some adults, but they need to ask themselves whether they are indeed in tune with young children's thinking. Children love the book.

Other Robert Kraus books: *Owliver; Mert the Blurt.*

The Carrot Seed by Ruth Krauss; pictures by Crockett Johnson. New York: Harper & Row, Publishers, 1945 (hardcover); New York: Scholastic Book Services, 1971 (paper).

Next to *Rosie's Walk,* this is the shortest and by far the simplest book reviewed here; also the smallest in size. A little boy plants a carrot seed, but his mother, father, and big brother inform him that it won't come up. He persists in weeding and watering it, and in fact it does grow into a huge carrot as big as the boy. Simple cartoonlike drawings on every other page opposite a sentence of text make the story faster moving than it would seem because of its simplicity. Young children are especially impressed by its satisfying ending and want to hear it again.

Frederick by Leo Lionni. New York: Pantheon Books, 1966 (hardcover, paper).

Because of their ability to pretend, preschool children truly love talking-animal tales like *Frederick,* the story of the mouse who stores up sunshine and colors instead of grain for the long winter months. Clever cutout pictures of the mice add a new dimension to Lionni's collage illustrations. The satisfying climax comes at the end of the winter, when the hungry mice press Frederick for his contribution. He paints them rainbow pictures of meadows and grain fields with words, holding them all enthralled. He is a poet—and he knows it.

Swimmy by Leo Lionni. New York: Pantheon Books, 1963 (hardcover); New York: Pinwheel Books, 1973 (paper).

Swimmy, the little black fish, is all alone in a blue, green, and purple watery world, portrayed by Lionni in full-page water colors with stamped designs. Paper doily stampings are "a forest of seaweeds growing from sugar-candy rocks. . . . " But Swimmy is too small to go on by himself. He finally persuades a school of little red fish to accompany him, by teaching them to swim in formation like the biggest fish in the sea. And then he informs them, "I'll be the eye." Black children especially identify with his leadership role, but all children love the story.

 Other Lionni books: *Inch by Inch; Fish Is Fish.*

Stone Soup by Ann McGovern; pictures by Nola Langer. New York: Scholastic Book Services, 1968 (paper).

There are at least two versions of this favorite folktale in print today. This one seems more suitable for preschoolers because it is shorter and simpler. *Stone Soup* is the story of a young man traveling through the countryside who stops at the house of a little old lady and asks for something to eat. When she refuses, he asks for a stone because you can make soup from a stone. The incredulous woman provides the stone in a kettle of bubbling water, and both sit back to wait for the soup to cook. As he tastes the soup from time to time, the young man suggests it would be better with some onions, then some carrots, then a chicken or two. Finally they sit down to a dinner fit for a king. Throughout the story, the little old lady makes comments, "Soup from a stone. Fancy that," which your listeners are soon repeating. Folktales do not necessarily fit the format of the Book Selection Checklist, but their read-aloud qualities, with much repetition and word play, make them favorites, nevertheless. This tale especially has additional possibilities for a cooking activity follow-up.

Curious George Goes to the Hospital by Margaret Rey and H.A. Rey. Boston: Houghton Mifflin Co., 1966 (hardcover); New York: Scholastic Book Services, 1971 (paper).

Here is another longer book with more text than is usually suitable for preschool children. This seems to make little difference with any of the *Curious George* books, the children love them so. They are very much attuned to the mischievous little monkey whose curiosity is always getting him into the same kind of trouble they have experienced. Yet he is loved and supported in the end by his caretaker, the man in the yellow hat. This particular version serves the additional purpose of helping to calm children's fears of doctors, nurses, and hospitals.

 Other Rey books: *Curious George; Curious George Rides a Bike.*

Where the Wild Things Are by Maurice Sendak. New York: Harper & Row Publishers, 1963. (hardcover); 1984 (paper).

For young children, Sendak's *Wild Things* remains one of the most popular picture books of all time, perhaps because of its unique blend of reality and fantasy in words and pictures that children can so strongly relate to. It is adults who have doubts about monsters. When Max is sent to bed without any supper for being such a wild thing, he fantasizes an entire world of gigantic wild things which he alone can tame with the magic trick of staring into all their yellow eyes without blinking once. Children are delighted; they share Max's feelings of adult rejection and the terrors of dream creatures. Yet they too want to return to the good graces of their loved ones and find supper waiting for them—while it is still hot.

Other Sendak books: *In the Night Kitchen; Chicken Soup with Rice.*

Sam by Ann Herbert Scott; pictures by Symeon Shimin. New York: McGraw-Hill Book Company, 1967 (hardcover).

Sam, the youngest in the family, faces the same dilemma as Andrew does in *Nobody Listens to Andrew.* Everyone in his family is too busy to play with him. Furthermore, each family member finds something to scold Sam about until he is reduced to tears. Not till then do they realize what they've done. Your children will empathize with Sam as his mother finally finds a highly satisfying job for him to do in the kitchen. Shimin's illustrations are the most impressive feature of the story—highly realistic and expressive drawings in charcoal against an orange background of this sad little black boy and his family.

Other Scott books: *On Mother's Lap.*

Green Eggs and Ham by Dr. Seuss. New York: Random House, 1960 (hardcover).

Preschoolers do not always understand the Dr. Seuss books, but they love them for their absurdly funny sounds, situations, and drawings. As with the other Dr. Seuss books, this is a rhyming story with the theme carried to exaggerated lengths. In it the little "boy" Sam-I-Am, tries to get his "father" to eat something he simply doesn't like—green eggs and ham—and, after a dozen hilarious attempts, finally succeeds. The role reversal with the little boy in charge is highly appealing to your listeners, as is the cumulative effect produced by the father each time he recounts where he will not eat green eggs and ham.

Caps for Sale by Esphyr Slobodkina. New York: William R. Scott, 1947 (hardcover); New York: Scholastic Book Services, 1971 (paper).

This classic tale of the peddler who carries his wares on top of his head is written in folktale style with much repetition, which children love. As with most folktales, the children do not necessarily identify with the main character; it is the action that holds them. They are intrigued by the tall stack of caps arranged in a certain order on the peddler's head, and are soon repeating this arrangement every time the peddler does. They love the tree full of monkeys who steal the peddler's caps and mimic the angry man when he shouts at them. They especially like to hear the sound the monkeys make—"tsz, tsz, tsz"—and want to try it themselves. Although the story is longer than many, it is specially good for dramatization.

Let's Be Enemies by Janice May Udry; pictures by Maurice Sendak. New York: Harper & Row, Publishers, 1961 (hardcover); New York: Scholastic Book Services, 1971 (paper).

Children respond with understanding to the brief story told by John about James, who used to be his friend but today is his enemy. The simple Sendak drawings with one line of text under each carry the story through to its satisfying conclusion and assist children in verbalizing their own feelings about friends and enemies. The book is tiny in format, another feature appreciated by preschoolers.

Umbrella by Taro Yashima. New York: Viking Press, 1958 (hardcover); 1970 (paper).

A little Oriental girl is the main character here, making this book a valuable addition to your multiethnic collection. Children everywhere can identify with Momo, who receives an umbrella for her birthday and can't wait to use it. Although the story is set in a large American city, the illustrations in crayon with slashes of rain scratched through give the book an interesting Oriental flavor. Children love to hear the sound of the rain as well: "bon polo, bon polo."

     Other Yashima books: *Momo's Kitten*.

Harry the Dirty Dog by Gene Zion; pictures by Margaret Bloy Graham. New York: Harper & Row, Publishers, 1956 (hardcover); 1976 (paper).

The little black and white dog Harry, featured in several Zion books, is a character preschool children can identify with. Here Harry refuses to take a bath, finally running away and becoming so dirty nobody recognizes him when he returns.

     Other Zion Books: *No Roses for Harry; Dear Garbage Man; The Plant Sitter; Harry By the Sea*.

Mr. Rabbit and the Lovely Present by Charlotte Zolotow; pictures by Maurice Sendak. New York: Harper & Row, Publishers, 1962 (hardcover); New York: Scholastic Book Services, 1971 (paper).

This book is written as a dialogue between a little girl who is looking for a birthday present to give her mother and a child-sized rabbit who agrees to help her. They walk off together through the countryside discussing colors as gift possibilities in a conversation so true to a child's way of thinking that it might have come from your own preschoolers. Sendak's watercolor illustrations on every other page pick up the colors as the two explore red, yellow, green, and blue objects.

     Other Zolotow books: *Flocks of Birds; The Hating Book*.

Books for Bilingual/Bicultural Children

A number of children's books are now available in Spanish for nursery school and kindergarten children. *Cultural Awareness: A Resource Bibliography* lists many, as well as posters, records, films, filmstrips, and other resources for Asian, Native American, Spanish-speaking, and black children. Early childhood book supply companies such as the Day Care Supply Company in Secane, Pennsylvania, and Gryphon House in Mt. Rainier, Maryland, list Spanish-language children's books in their catalogs.

Other children's picture books that focus on words in a second language are *Maria Teresa,* in which a Spanish-speaking puppet helps Maria Teresa make friends in her American class; *What Does the Rooster Say, Yoshio?,* in which a Japanese boy and an American girl tell each other the sounds the animals make in their two languages; *The Little Weaver of Thai-Yen Village,* in both English and Vietnamese, the story of a war-injured child who comes to the United States which, although for older children, still attracts preschoolers to the illustrations and the Vietnamese words; *Why Mosquitoes Buzz in People's Ears,* in which the listeners hear African sounds made by the animal characters as they move through the jungle; *Moja Means One: Swahili Counting Book,* which presents the numbers one to ten, and *Jambo Means Hello: Swahili Alphabet Book,* which gives Swahili words and their meanings for each letter of the English alphabet. Children need not be of Spanish, Japanese, Vietnamese or African heritage to enjoy learning words and sounds in these languages. They will reflect your own enthusiasm in trying out the interesting new names you introduce.

Wordless picture books are an excellent resource for use with bilingual children, because they can be "read" in either language. Both you and your children can make up stories in either language to go with the pictures in the books. You might want to record the children's stories on tape cassettes, to play when the children look at the books again. If you can write in the second language, you can record the children's stories on experience charts. Wordless picture books can motivate children to make up many stories in both languages.

Some excellent wordless books for preschoolers are: *What Whiskers Did,* featuring the adventures of a puppy who runs away in the woods; *The Adventures of Paddy Pork,* a humanlike pig who runs away with a circus; *The Circus,* showing all the animal and human performers; *The Bear and the Fly,* a three-bears story in which Papa Bear's flyswatter wreaks humorous havoc at the supper table; and *Do You Want to Be My Friend?* in which a mouse looks for a friend among a series of exotic animals.

Books for Children with Handicapping Conditions

Picture books that show acceptance of children with handicapping conditions by other children and adults can be instructive. You may want several in your reading corner for all the children to look at, if you think they will not cause the children to look at the handicapped child differently. *A Button in Her Ear* is a story about Angela, her hearing loss, and how she came to wear a hearing aid. *Darlene* shows that a little girl in a wheelchair can have the same kind of fun as the others in her family, and is an especially good book about not making the child seem different. *Tracy* is a photographic essay of a girl with cerebral palsy, in which she tells about her daily activities and life in a wheelchair.

Reading Books to Children

Plan your daily schedule to allow children to choose and read books on their own at sometime during the day. But you or one of your co-workers will be responsible for reading at least once a day to the children.

You may choose to read to a small group at a time while the rest of the children engage in another interesting activity. If so, be sure the others also have their turn to hear a story later on. Children need to sit as close as possible to the reader in order to see the pictures, to become personally involved in the story, and just because it feels good to sit close to someone who likes you. A small group makes it easier to accomplish this closeness. The reader also needs to sit at the children's level wherever possible, using a cushion, a small chair, or the floor.

You may want to invite guest story readers to your class as a special treat or on a regular basis. Parents, grandparents, older children (if you happen to be located in an elementary school), retired teachers, librarians, someone from a local bookstore—all are possible guest story readers the children would enjoy.

In addition to reading to small groups, it is important that you or your guest readers also read to children on a one-to-one basis. This is where language learning and the love for reading really have a chance to bloom and grow. When you read to a single child, you can reach him so much more effectively than you do when he is in a group. The experience takes on more meaning for the child because it is a personal one. It becomes meaningful to you as well, because you are able to get more closely in touch with the child. The book experience also becomes an active one for the child on your lap, for he is able to participate by saying words, finding pictures, and turning pages.

Although individual children will readily come to you on their own with books to be read, you may also want to approach a particular child with a book you have picked out especially for him to hear. A child whom you have previously identified as needing help in language can benefit by having stories read on an individual basis.

Know Your Book

To be a successful story reader, you will want to keep these hints in mind:

1. Know your book well.
2. Start with an attention-getting device.
3. Make your voice as interesting as possible.
4. Help children get involved through participation.

If you have chosen your book on the basis of the Book Selection Checklist, then you are already well acquainted with it. If not, skim through it, noting features such as:

1. Sound words for which you can make the sound rather than reading words.
2. Places where you might substitute the listener's name for the name used in the book.

3. Picture details you might ask a listener to look for if you are reading to one child.
4. Places in the story where you might want to pause and ask your listeners to guess what comes next.
5. Repetitious phrases where children can join in.
6. Items or objects the children will want to have concrete experiences with.

Attention-Getting Devices

Your story reading will not be successful unless you have your listeners' attention. It will be a poor experience for both you and the children if you have to stop to reprimand disruptive children. Better they should all be ready and eager for you to begin. You can be assured they will if you begin, not with the story itself, but with an attention-getting device that will help the children settle down and focus their attention on the book you are about to read.

One of the simplest and most effective devices is to use the cover of the book in some way. You might, for instance, ask the children something about the cover illustration. Here are some examples:

1. Today our story is *The Snowy Day*. Do you see the little boy in the snow? What do you suppose he is looking at?
2. This story is about a little fish named *Swimmy*. Do you see the little fishes on the cover? What different colors are they? Which do you think is Swimmy? You may be right. Shall we open the book and see?
3. The name of our story today is *Curious George Goes to the Hospital*. There's the little monkey George looking at some things. I wonder what they are? Does anyone know?
4. Today I'm going to read a story called *Rosie's Walk*. Rosie is a hen who is going for a walk through the barnyard. But someone is following her. Do you see who that is? What do you think might happen?
5. *Corduroy* is the name of the story I'm going to read today. Corduroy is a little teddy bear. He seems to be trying to reach something. Can you tell what it is?

Or you might use the title of the book to help the children focus on the story by asking them a question about the title. Here are some examples:

1. Our story today is *Nobody Listens to Andrew*. Here's Andrew trying to tell people something. And there are all the people walking away. What do you suppose Andrew is trying to tell them? Could you guess?
2. Today we're going to hear a story called *Will I Have a Friend?* It is about a boy named Jim. Where do you suppose Jim is looking for a friend? How can you tell?
3. This little book is called *Let's Be Enemies*. What is an enemy? Do you think the boys on the cover are enemies? How can you tell?

4. This story is called *Bread and Jam for Frances.* Do any of you like to eat bread and jam? What other things do you like to eat? Do you think Frances might like those things too?

5. Here is a story called *The Surprise Party.* What is a surprise party? Did you ever go to a surprise party?

An Interesting Voice

Do you enjoy reading aloud to your children? Your voice often reflects your feelings. If you are enthusiastic about story reading, the children will know it by the tone of your voice. They love to have the teacher dramatize the story by making her voice scary or whispery or way down deep! Can you do it? Most of us don't know until we try. Even then we're not sure how we come across. Turn on the tape recorder during story-reading time, and play the tape for yourself later, when you're alone, to hear how you sound. Do you like the way you read a story? Practice alone with the tape recorder on until you have improved as much as you want.

Child Involvement Through Participation

The egocentric nature of young children means they will enjoy stories better if they are somehow a part of them. You, the story reader, can get children directly involved in a number of ways. You might, for instance, ask a child to find a certain item in the illustrations. In *Goodnight Moon,* children can find a telephone, a red balloon, two little kittens, a pair of mittens, a little toy house, a young mouse, a comb, a brush, a bowl full of mush. In *Caps for Sale,* a child can point out the brown caps, the white caps, the gray caps, and the red caps. In *The Very Hungry Caterpillar,* a child can identify each of the food items the caterpillar eats a hole through.

It may be difficult to have direct child participation in a large group without disrupting the activity, because everyone will want a turn. That is the advantage of reading to small groups or individuals. But even with a small group, the story flows more smoothly if you ask a particular child to answer each time you ask a question, rather than have everyone respond.

Your entire group can participate by repeating rhyming words or repetitious phrases in unison. Children love to repeat the refrain in *Millions of Cats* about the hundreds and thousands and millions and billions of cats; in *Umbrella,* they can repeat the "bon polo" refrain; and in *Caps for Sale,* they can say the monkey sound, "tsz, tsz, tsz."

If you are reading to one child, you can substitute his name for the name of the character in the book. You can also have the child guess what will come next before you turn a page, or guess how the story will end.

For groups who are not used to sitting still and listening to a story, you may not want to interrupt the flow of the story with individual involvement for awhile. You need to decide whether your priority for the children is to complete a story without interruptions or to get the children involved by offering them opportunities to participate.

Extending the Book Experience

For books to be meaningful to children, you as teacher or aide need to be prepared to extend their book experiences into the total life of the classroom. Books should not be relegated to a reading corner alone. They can play a vital role in the entire curriculum if you are book-conscious enough to make them do so. When you notice children pretending to be fire fighters, after a visit to the local firehouse, place an appropriate book in the dramatic play area. A fish book should be stationed next to your aquarium and a gerbil book next to the gerbil cage. When you go outside looking for leaves in the fall, take a tree identification guide with you.

The storybooks reviewed earlier in this chapter can be extended into the life of the classroom as well. *Umbrella* can be read on a rainy day, but be sure to have a real umbrella with you for the children to handle. *The Snowy Day* can be read when it snows, *Gilberto and the Wind* when it blows. The latter book lends itself to a variety of fascinating activities: blowing up and sailing balloons, making and flying kites, picking apples, making and sailing sailboats, making pinwheels, blowing bubbles, raking leaves, and listening to or tape recording the sound of the wind.

Storybooks can also be a marvelous motivation for a number of food activities. *"I Can't" said the Ant* will help children learn about kitchen utensils and their use. *The Very Hungry Caterpillar* can introduce them to fruit, *Bread and Jam for Frances* may help them plan a lunch *Stone Soup* can be acted out in your classroom, with the children actually cooking stone soup, and *Green Eggs and Ham* can also be concocted in the cooking corner.

Many of the storybooks your children come to enjoy can be useful in teaching science or math concepts as well. *Caps for Sale* and *The Very Hungry Caterpillar* are counting books. If you read the *Hungry Caterpillar* to your children, be prepared to go out looking for caterpillars and collecting cocoons. This book also involves color concepts, as does *Mr. Rabbit and the Lovely Present* and *Goodnight Moon.* If you read *Best Friends,* be ready to hatch eggs in an incubator, as the children in Jim's classroom did.

Dramatizations of favorite stories are also fun for children when they are spontaneous and unforced. Certain stories lend themselves to dramatizing. If these are among your children's favorites, you might have them choose parts and make simple paper-bag costumes for their roles. The children then can act as you read. Books such as *Nobody Listens to Andrew, Stone Soup, Where the Wild Things Are,* and *Caps for Sale* make good plays. If your children are at ease with creative movement or free-dance activities, put on a record or tape of "mysterious" music and let them move like the monsters in *Wild Things.*

Story-dramatizing puppets are somewhat difficult for preschoolers, but can be used in kindergarten. Even puppet theaters operated by adults are not as effective for preschoolers as they are for somewhat older children. The young ones have difficulty sitting still to watch the action. They would much prefer participating by sticking their own heads through the stage opening or investigating what's going on behind the stage. One puppet alone used by an adult without a stage is much more effective in a preschool program, and that puppet can be used to read a story to your children with great success.

Many teachers like to use book records and filmstrips with their children. This is not nearly as appropriate or meaningful as the teacher's actual reading of a story. It is a passive experience for the children, with no chance for personal involvement. As with television, book records and filmstrips tend to provide an entertainment experience rather than a learning one, since as we know, young children do not learn much from sitting and listening, but from becoming actively involved.

Children will eventually want to compose their own stories. The teacher can take dictation from individuals or small groups who want to tell a story about a pet, a personal experience, a field trip, or a photograph. These stories can be made into books for inclusion in the book corner. Children gain an even greater appreciation for language and books when they create their own.

Books to Enhance Self-Image

Almost any book in which a child can closely identify with the main character can affect his feelings about himself. You can help strengthen positive feelings by discussing them with your listeners. Reading to one child only or to a small group makes it easier to carry on such a discussion. For instance, after you read the story, you might talk about the following:

1. Why do you think the ant said "I can't" in *"I Can't" said the Ant?* What would you have done?
2. How do you think Jim felt when Pa left him at the nursery school in *Will I Have a Friend?* Did you ever feel like that? What did Jim do about it?
3. How did Gilberto feel about the wind? Did you ever feel that way? What did Gilberto do about it?
4. How do you think Andrew felt when nobody would listen to him? Did that ever happen to you?
5. How do you think Sam felt when nobody would play with him? Did you ever have that happen to you? How did you feel? What did you do about it?
6. Did you ever get angry at your best friend like John did in *Let's Be Enemies?* Why did you feel that way?

Reading Multicultural Books

Invite family members and neighborhood volunteers to visit your classroom and tell stories from their culture. You will want to include appropriate picture books in your book area for children to look at and for you to read to them.

Inner-city black children enjoy reading about their culture in books like Eloise Greenfield's *She Come Bringing Me that Little Baby Girl,* or they may search for their African roots along with the girl who imagines what it was like in *Africa Dream.* Byrd Baylor has written a number of books featuring Native Americans of the Southwest. In *Everybody Needs a Rock,* an Indian boy tells how to find just the right kind of rock for a friend. Ann Herbert Scott's *On Mother's Lap* shows an Eskimo boy who learns that mother's lap has room for him, his toys, and even his baby sister.

My Aunt Otilia's Spirits, in English and Spanish, tells of a mysterious Puerto Rican aunt who comes to visit her nephew every summer. *Nini at Carnival* is about a little Jamaican girl who has no costume to wear for the Carnival celebration. In *The Wentletrap Trap,* a Bahamian boy tries to trap a rare seashell, and learns about taking care of himself.

Folktales from around the world are increasingly popular with young American children, and more and more tales are being written as picture books for preschoolers. *The Funny Little Woman* is a Japanese tale about a woman who liked to laugh and to make dumplings out of rice. Children can laugh along with the story of the woman's search for her runaway dumpling, and later make rice dumplings in the classroom. *The Banza* is a Haitian story about a little goat with a magic banjo that protects him from ten fat tigers. Your children will enjoy making up a tune for the Ten Fat Tigers song and helping the goat sing it every time he needs protection. They can make their own banjos out of foil pie plates, or you can invite a real banjo player to your class. *Bringing the Rain to Kapiti Plain* is an African cumulative tale told in the rhyming tradition of "This is the house that Jack built." The children may want to say the verse along with you, and point to the people and animals as the story progresses. Since this is a story about weather, the children may want to look for rain clouds.

A good source of information for other multicultural books is The Council on Interracial Books for Children, Inc., 1841 Broadway, New York, N.Y. 10023. For information on other cultures, see *Cultural Awareness: A Resource Bibliography* (Schmidt and McNeill, 1978).

Using Paperback Books

Most of the good storybooks for young children are available today in paperback. This has a number of advantages for preschool programs. First, paperback books cost less. If you are purchasing your own books on a limited budget, you can afford many more paperbacks than hardcover books. Names of paperback publishers are listed under most of the thirty books reviewed. Most bookstores now stock paperback picture books or can order them for you. Children can easily learn to handle them so they will not be torn or damaged.

A second advantage is their appeal to youngsters. There is something personal about a paperback book. They seem to belong to people rather than to libraries or schools. If you truly believe in bringing children and books together, then you should consider ordering paperback books just as you do art paper—to be used up by the end of the year. This means you will allow children to choose their favorite books to take home and keep.

The preschool book experience must extend into the home if it is to be truly meaningful. Parents should be invited into the classroom to participate by listening or reading to children themselves. Books should also circulate to the home.

Children should be encouraged to borrow books from the classroom to take home for someone to read to them. Many homes have no books of any kind; thus children are deprived of book-reading models during their impressionable years when they need them most. You may need two sets of books to allow this practice: one to read in the classroom and a duplicate set to circulate to the children's homes. This is possible if you purchase paperbacks, because of their low cost. When you consider what an important effect the happy acquaintance with books has on a child's later success in reading, you will surely find it worthwhile to purchase enough for home use.

Once the children's parents are aware of the importance of books for preschoolers and the joy of sharing them with their children, they may want to conduct a paperback book fair at a parent meeting, so they can choose and purchase their own, or they may want to stage a money-raising activity such as a rummage sale in order to buy books for everyone in the class.

The cost of hardcover books usually prohibits the purchase of more than one copy of a particular title. With paperbacks, you can purchase as many copies as you need of favorites. It is here that book records or cassettes can be used to best advantage. Set up a listening corner, and provide several copies of each book for each record or tape. Let the children listen on their own during the work/play period, with everyone looking at his own copy of the book as the record or cassette tape plays. It is a wonderful introduction to independent reading.

Multiple copies of favorite books have other good uses as well. You may want to make your own flannel-board characters from stories your children love. Cut them out of an extra paperback book and mount them on cardboard with flannel or magnetic backing. As someone reads *Caps for Sale,* for example, other children can participate by stacking the brown, white, gray, and red caps on the head of the peddler on your flannel board. Do your cutting when children are not around to avoid their ever trying to imitate you with other books!

If you are truly aware of your children's interests and needs and have developed a real acquaintance with good storybooks for preschoolers, then the meeting of children and books in your preschool classroom will be a happy experience for all involved. You will know you are successful when your children begin to say, ''Read it again, teacher.''

SUMMARY

Some of the activities discussed in this chapter to help children develop communication skills include:

Stress-free Environment	*Language Production*
Name games	Puppetry
Naming Follow-the-Leader	
	Vocabulary
Necessity for Speaking	Word Lotto
Greeting period	Secret Whisper
Hand puppet	Toy telephones

Oral messages
Verbal directions

Verbalizing Feelings
Feelings books
Pictures showing emotions
Photocopying books

Child-Adult Communication
Teacher station
Private conversation

Bilingual Children
Community volunteer
Family member
Tape cassette
Name chants/songs
Toy telephone
Bilingual puppet
Dramatic play

Child-Child Communication
Mixed age group
Guinea pig story

Language Understanding
Talking Cards

Word Play
Books

Listening
Listening games
Self-talk
Parallel talk

Reading Aloud

Extending Book Experiences
Food activities
Science/math concepts
Dramatization
Story-dramatizing puppets

Using Paperback Books
Books circulate home
Multiple copies
Use with tape cassette
Flannel-board stories

LEARNING ACTIVITIES

1. Read Chapter 6, "Advancing Communication Skills," and answer Question Sheet 6-A.
2. View Mediapak E, "Speaking and Listening Skills," and answer Question Sheet 6-B.
3. Read one or more of the books listed under Suggested Readings, or view another sound filmstrip, such as "Preschool Book Experience," "Puppets, Puzzles, Games and Fun With Children's Picture Books," or "Books and Stories." Add ten cards to your file with specific ideas for helping children develop communication skills. Include the reference source on each card.
4. Observe one of your children who is having problems with communicating, using the Language Assessment Checklist; make a Learning Prescription based on the results and implement it. Record the results.
5. Review twenty children's picture books and make file cards for each, recording the following information.
   a. Title, author, illustrator, publisher, date.
   b. Special features, such as sound words, rhyming words, repetitious phrases, picture details.
   c. Special time for using book (e.g. rainy day, Halloween, after field trip, when child is sad)
   d. Special activities to extend book experience (e.g., planting seeds after reading *The Carrot Seed*)

6. Read one of these books to a small group of children using attention-getting devices discussed in the chapter and child involvement activities. (The trainer can observe.)

7. Follow up the reading of a favorite book with a book extension activity. (The trainer can observe.)

8. Continue your Portfolio of evidence of your skills. Add one piece of evidence for each of the following Teacher Skills Checklist items:

   a. Interacts with children in ways that encourage them to communicate their thoughts and feelings verbally.

   b. Provides materials and activities to promote language development.

   c. Uses books and stories with children to motivate listening and speaking.

   Evidence should reflect what you, not another staff member, have done.

9. Complete the Chapter 6 Evaluation Sheet and return it and the answers to Question Sheets 6-A and 6-B to the appropriate college or program official.

QUESTION SHEET 6-A

(Based on Chapter 6, ''Advancing Communication Skills'')

1. How does the drive to communicate assist a child in his language development?

2. What factors other than physical ones can interfere with a child's normal development of language?

3. What factors seem to be important in order for communication to occur in the pre-school classroom? Why?

4. Why should you not correct a child's language? How, then, can you help him improve it?

5. Using one of the reasons for communication in your classroom, what kind of activity could you set up to promote that communication?

6. What kind of activity could you set up to help children learn to verbalize their feelings?

7. What does confidence have to do with children's speaking in a preschool classroom? How can you help strengthen it?

8. What can you expect in the way of articulation from the speech of a three- or four-year-old?

9. In what different ways can the use of puppets promote communication skills?

10. How can you help children who speak a language other than English?

QUESTION SHEET 6-B

(Based on Medipak E, ''Speaking and Listening Skills'')

1. Why is it necessary for a caring adult to be present during the early stages of a child's language development?

2. Why should you make an assessment of children's speaking and listening skills early in the program year?

3. What should you do with the assessment once it is completed?
4. How can you best help a nonverbal child improve language production?
5. How can dramatic play be used in promoting speaking and listening skills?
6. What kinds of activities during mealtime can promote language skills?
7. What should a teacher do to serve as a good language model?
8. How can room arrangement promote language development?
9. How does multi-age grouping promote speaking skills?
10. What kinds of language accomplishments should you comment favorably on? Give examples.

SUGGESTED EVIDENCE FOR PORTFOLIO

1. A list of activities you have provided in your classroom to promote children's communication, along with a written description of how your children responded.
2. A case study of an individual child who might have been nonverbal, bilingual, or shy, describing how you helped the child become verbal in English.
3. A photo or sample of a puppet you or the children made and a written explanation of how it promoted language development.
4. A list of your children's favorite books and an explanation of how you used them to promote language development.
5. A tape recording of a story your children have made up, along with a written explanation of how it originated and how it helped promote their language skills.

Each piece of evidence should be accompanied by a write-up explaining how this shows your competence in the area of **Communication** and how the activity is developmentally appropriate for your children. Refer to Chapter 10, "Spoken Language," and Chapter 11, "Written Language," in *Observing Development of the Young Child* (Beaty, 1986) for developmental statements.

SUGGESTED READINGS

Beaty, Janice J. *Observing Development of the Young Child.* Columbus, Ohio: Charles E. Merrill Publishing Co., 1986.

Cazden, Courtney B., ed. *Language In Early Childhood Education.* Washington, D.C.: National Association for the Education of Young Children, 1981.

Curran, Jean Stabenow, and Bryant J. Cratty. *Speech and Language Problems in Children.* Denver: Love Publishing Co., 1978.

Eisenson, Jon. *Is Your Child's Speech Normal?* Reading, Mass.: Addison-Wesley, 1976.

Glazer, Joan I. *Literature for Young Children,* 2nd ed. Columbus, Ohio: Charles E. Merrill Publishing Co., 1986.

Holzman, Mathilda. *The Language of Children: Development in Home and School.* Englewood Cliffs, N.J.: Prentice-Hall, 1983.

Jenkins, Peggy Davison. *The Magic of Puppetry: A Guide for Those Working with Young Children.* Englewood Cliffs, N.J.: Prentice-Hall, 1980.

Lamme, Linda Leonard. *Learning to Love Literature: Preschool through Grade 3.* Urbana, Ill.: National Council of Teachers of English, 1981.

Lindfors, Judith Wells. *Children's Language and Learning.* Englewood Cliffs, N.J.: Prentice-Hall, 1987.

Machado, Jeanne M. *Early Childhood Experiences in Language Arts,* 2nd ed. Albany, N.Y.: Delmar, 1985.

Peterson, Abigail. *The Communication Game.* Johnson & Johnson Baby Products Company, 1980.

Schmidt, Velma E., and Earldene McNeill. *Cultural Awareness: A Resource Bibliography.* Washington, D.C.: The National Association for the Education of Young Children, 1978.

Schon, Isabel. *A Bicultural Heritage: Themes for the Exploration of Mexican and Mexican-American Culture in Books for Children and Adolescents.* Metuchen, N.J.: The Scarecrow Press, 1978.

Sims, Rudine. *Shadow & Substance: Afro-American Experience in Contemporary Children's Fiction.* Urbana, Ill.: National Council of Teachers of English, 1982.

Thompson, James J. *Beyond Words: Nonverbal Communication In The Classroom.* New York: Citation Press, 1973.

White, Dorothy. *Books Before Five.* Portsmouth, N.H.: Heinemann, 1984.

Yawkey, Thomas Daniel, and Beatrice Villarreal. *Language Learning Through Pretend Play in Young Bilingual-Bicultural Children.* Arlington, Va.: 1979. (ERIC Document Reproduction Service No. ED 179 298)

CHILDREN'S BOOKS

Aardema, Verna. *Bringing the Rain to Kapiti Plain.* New York: Dial Press 1981.

───. *Why Mosquitoes Buzz in People's Ears.* New York: Dial Press, 1975.

Atkinson, Mary. *Maria Teresa.* Chapel Hill, N.C.: Lollipop Power, 1979.

Baylor, Byrd. *Everybody Needs a Rock.* New York: Scribner's, 1974.

Battles, Edith. *What Does the Rooster Say, Yoshio?* Chicago: Albert Whitman, 1978.

Carle, Eric. *Do You Want to be My Friend?* New York: Thomas Y. Crowell, 1971.

Carroll, Ruth. *What Whiskers Did.* New York: Scholastic, 1965.

Feelings, Muriel. *Jambo Means Hello: Swahili Alphabet Book.* New York: Dial Press, 1974.

───. *Moja Means One: Swahili Counting Book.* New York: Dial Press, 1971.

Fitzgerald, Judith. *My Orange Gorange.* Windsor, Ontario, Canada: Black Moss Press, 1985.

Garcia, Richard. *My Aunt Otilia's Spirits.* San Francisco: Children's Book Press, 1978.

Goodall, John S. *The Adventures of Paddy Pork.* New York: Harcourt Brace Jovanovich, 1968.

Greenfield, Eloise. *Africa Dream.* New York: John Day Company, 1977.

───. *Darlene.* New York: Methuen, 1980.

_____. *She Come Bringing Me That Little Baby Girl.* Philadelphia: J. B. Lippincott, 1974.

George, Jean Craighead. *The Wentletrap Trap.* New York: E. P. Dutton, 1978.

Hazen, Nancy. *Grownups Cry Too* (in Spanish and English). Chapel Hill, N.C.: Lollipop Power, 1973.

Hutchins, Pat. *Don't Forget the Bacon.* New York: Penguin, 1976.

Jeffers, Susan. *If Wishes Were Horses.* New York: E.P. Dutton, 1979.

Keats, Ezra Jack. *Louie.* New York: Scholastic, 1975.

Kraus, Robert. *Mert the Blurt.* New York: Simon and Schuster, 1980.

Litchfield, Ada B. *A Button in Her Ear.* Chicago: Albert Whitman, 1976.

Lloyd, Errol. *Nini at Carnival.* New York: Thomas Y. Crowell, 1978.

Mack, Nancy. *Tracy.* Milwaukee, Wisc.: Raintree Editions, 1976.

Maris, Ron. *I Wish I Could Fly.* New York: Greenwillow Books, 1986.

McCloskey, Robert. *Blueberries for Sal.* New York: Viking Press, 1948.

Morrison, Bill. *Squeeze a Sneeze.* Boston: Houghton Mifflin, 1977.

Mosel, Arlene. *The Funny Little Woman.* New York: E. P. Dutton, 1972.

Schubert, Dieter. *Where's My Monkey?* New York: Dial Books for Young Readers, 1987.

Scott, Ann Herbert. *On Mother's Lap.* New York: McGraw-Hill, 1972.

Stanton, Elizabeth, and Henry Stanton. *Sometimes I Like to Cry.* Chicago: Albert Whitman, 1978.

Tran-Khanh-Tuyet. *The Little Weaver of Thai-Yen Village.* San Francisco: Children's Book Press, 1977.

Viorst, Judith. *The Tenth Good Thing About Barney.* New York: Atheneum, 1971.

Wildsmith, Brian. *The Circus.* New York: Oxford University Press. 1970.

Winter, Paula. *The Bear and the Fly.* New York: Crown, 1976.

Wolkstein, Diane. *The Banza.* New York: Dial Press, 1981.

Zolotow, Charlotte. *The Hating Book.* New York: Scholastic, 1969.

SOUND FILMSTRIPS

Beaty, Janice J. "Preschool Book Experience," Mediapak F, *Skills for Preschool Teachers.* Elmira, N.Y.: McGraw Bookstore, Elmira College, 1979.

_____. *Puppets, Puzzles, Games and Fun With Children's Picture Books.* Elmira, N.Y: 3 to 5, P.O. Box 3213, 1980.

_____. "Speaking and Listening Skills," Mediapak E, *Skills for Preschool Teachers.* Elmira, N. Y.: McGraw Bookstore, Elmira, College, 1979.

Books and Stories. Tuckahoe, N.Y.: Campus Film Distributors.

CHAPTER 6 EVALUATION SHEET
ADVANCING COMMUNICATION SKILLS

1. Student⎯⎯⎯⎯⎯⎯⎯⎯⎯⎯⎯⎯⎯⎯⎯⎯⎯⎯⎯⎯

2. Trainer⎯⎯⎯⎯⎯⎯⎯⎯⎯⎯⎯⎯⎯⎯⎯⎯⎯⎯⎯⎯⎯

3. Center where training occurred⎯⎯⎯⎯⎯⎯⎯⎯⎯⎯⎯⎯⎯

4. Beginning date⎯⎯⎯⎯⎯⎯⎯ Ending date⎯⎯⎯⎯⎯⎯⎯⎯

5. Describe what student did to accomplish General Objective

⎯⎯⎯⎯⎯⎯⎯⎯⎯⎯⎯⎯⎯⎯⎯⎯⎯⎯⎯⎯⎯⎯⎯⎯⎯⎯⎯

⎯⎯⎯⎯⎯⎯⎯⎯⎯⎯⎯⎯⎯⎯⎯⎯⎯⎯⎯⎯⎯⎯⎯⎯⎯⎯⎯

6. Describe what student did to accomplish Specific Objectives

Objective 1⎯⎯⎯⎯⎯⎯⎯⎯⎯⎯⎯⎯⎯⎯⎯⎯⎯⎯⎯

⎯⎯⎯⎯⎯⎯⎯⎯⎯⎯⎯⎯⎯⎯⎯⎯⎯⎯⎯⎯⎯⎯⎯

Objective 2⎯⎯⎯⎯⎯⎯⎯⎯⎯⎯⎯⎯⎯⎯⎯⎯⎯⎯⎯

⎯⎯⎯⎯⎯⎯⎯⎯⎯⎯⎯⎯⎯⎯⎯⎯⎯⎯⎯⎯⎯⎯⎯

Objective 3⎯⎯⎯⎯⎯⎯⎯⎯⎯⎯⎯⎯⎯⎯⎯⎯⎯⎯⎯

⎯⎯⎯⎯⎯⎯⎯⎯⎯⎯⎯⎯⎯⎯⎯⎯⎯⎯⎯⎯⎯⎯⎯

7. Evaluation of student's Learning Activities
(Trainer Check One)   (Student Check One)

⎯⎯⎯ Highly superior performance   ⎯⎯⎯

⎯⎯⎯ Superior performance   ⎯⎯⎯

⎯⎯⎯ Good performance   ⎯⎯⎯

⎯⎯⎯ Less than adequate performance ⎯⎯⎯

Signature of Trainer: Signature of Student:

⎯⎯⎯⎯⎯⎯⎯⎯⎯⎯⎯⎯   ⎯⎯⎯⎯⎯⎯⎯⎯⎯⎯⎯⎯

Comments:

7 Advancing Creative Skills

General Objective

To promote children's creativity through playful expression and freedom of activity.

Specific Objectives

☐ Arranges a variety of art materials for children to explore on their own.
☐ Accepts children's creative products without placing a value judgment on them.
☐ Gives children the opportunity to have fun with music.

W hen we speak of a creative person, we generally mean someone who has original ideas, who does things in new and different ways, who uses imagination and inventiveness to bring about novel forms. Can young children be creative like this?

Not only can they be, they are. Creativity seems to be intuitive in young children, something they are born with. From the very beginning they have the capacity to look at things, to hear, smell, taste, and touch things from an entirely original perspective—their own.

After all, they are new and unique beings in a strange and complex world. The only way they have to make sense of things around them is to explore them with their senses: try them out, see what makes them the way they are, see if they can be any different.

Young children bring to any activity a spirit of wonder, great curiosity, and a spontaneous drive to explore, experiment, and manipulate in a playful and original fashion. This is creativity. It is the same impulse that artists, writers, musicians, and scientists have.

Yet, you may respond, not all children behave like this, as we noted in the chapter on cognitive skills. Some children show little interest in anything new. Some will not engage in activities unless directed by the teacher. These are the children who need our special assistance in recapturing the creativity they were born with.

Acceptance and Encouragement

Creativity flourishes only where it is accepted and encouraged. Infants, toddlers, and preschoolers who have been dominated by the adults around them and not allowed to do anything their own way will not show much creativity. They have already learned the sad lesson that experimenting with things only gets them into trouble. Children who have been the victims of neglect, lack of love, harsh discipline, or overprotection seem to lack the spark of creativity, as well.

It is extremely important that as a teacher or aide in a preschool program, you help to rekindle that spark. It is imperative that young children be able to use the creative skills of pretending, imaginative thinking, fantasizing, and inventiveness while they deal with the complex world around them. Strange as it may seem, these are the skills that will help them most in problem solving, getting along with others, understanding their world, and, eventually, in abstract thinking. Promoting creativity is an effective way to promote intellectual development in children.

Freedom

The key to setting up an environment that promotes creativity is freedom. Children need to be free to explore, experiment, manipulate, invent, and pretend spontaneously. Having an adult show them how or tell them what to do defeats this purpose. Adults do not see things or use things as children do. Young children need the opportunity to work out many ideas their own way, without adult direction or interference.

ARRANGES A VARIETY OF ART MATERIALS FOR CHILDREN TO EXPLORE ON THEIR OWN

When most adults think of creativity, the art area comes to mind. Yet, unfortunately for young children, this is often the least creative area in the entire program, because it is entirely adult-directed. Nothing happens spontaneously. Adults get out the art supplies, set up activities on tables, instruct the children how to use them, and stay at the tables to make sure they follow directions. This is not creative art. It is more a manipulative activity. Activities like these should not be banished from the classroom, since they are appropriate for promoting manipulative and direction-following skills; it is just that teachers and children should not confuse them with creative art.

As mentioned previously, the key to creativity is freedom. Children need to be free to explore, experiment, invent, and pretend with art materials just as they do with blocks or dress-up clothes. Adults rarely consider it necessary to remain in the housekeeping corner to make sure the children dress up ''properly'' or play their roles ''correctly,'' yet this all too frequently happens with art.

Process vs. Product

We need to step back and think: what is our primary purpose for having art in the classroom? Is it to have children paint a nice picture or make a lovely collage to take home to mother? If this is true in your classroom, then you have confused the product with the process. Most preschool children do not have the skills or the developmental level to turn out an accomplished art product without help. Our goal should instead be to assist children in becoming involved in the process of creating a product; it is the *process* of creation that is most important for young children.

We should not be faulted for making the mistake of focusing on the product. It is much easier to see a painting than a process. Moreover, no one ever told us this was not the proper way to ''teach'' art. After all, isn't everyone more concerned with the picture than the paints?

Not everyone. Take a look at the children in your classroom who are involved in painting. The only thing that seems to matter to them is the experience, the process. They focus on their product only after adults have made a fuss about it, after they have learned that this is the way to please adults. Before that, they seem more interested in things like smearing the paint around, slapping one color on another, moving the brush back and forth, covering everything they have painted with a new color. This is process—and this is how creativity is born.

Art Activities

Now that you know the true state of affairs, how can you set up your art activities to promote children's freedom to create? First of all, you need to keep some art materials permanently within children's reach. Most classrooms do this by having one or more easels available, with paper, paints, and brushes ready for use when the children arrive. Children can choose to easel paint during the free choice period. No teacher direction or assistance is needed. Children learn to handle the brush and control the paint by themselves.

Observe a beginner and you'll see how she manages. The new painter spends a great deal of time trying out which hand to use, the best way to hold the brush, how to get paint from jar to paper, how to move it around on the paper, how to control the drips. In other words, she is "manipulating the medium" rather than painting a picture.

To help your children manage this new medium, you might consider cutting a few inches off the long paint brush handle (most are the right thickness for pudgy fingers, but too long to manipulate easily). You might also want to put out only one or two jars of paint until children can handle more.

Art Supplies

If you have a permanent art area in your classroom, you should consider keeping certain supplies on low shelves next to the children's tables or work space. You will probably want several kinds of paper, paste, glue, scissors, crayons, felt-tip pens, finger paints, collage scraps, etc. Children should know they are free to select from the materials to use at the art table as they wish.

At other times you may want to set up the art activity before the children arrive and let them "play" with it creatively during free choice periods. Take, for example, dough. In the beginning, you may want to mix the dough and have it ready for the children to explore and experiment with. Perhaps you'll put out rolling pins and cookie cutters for the children to use by themselves. You can do this for a number of days with different implements. After they have exhausted the possibilities for manipulating the medium, you may want to involve them in the fun of measuring and mixing the dough themselves before they play with it. Another time, you might encourage them to add food coloring to the dough for an entirely different effect.

No matter what art materials you use, arrange them so the children can be creative with them on their own. Collage scraps, paste, and backing paper can be waiting for children on one of their tables. Food coloring, medicine droppers, and jars of water are another creative possibility.

Finger painting can be done on smooth paper, on tabletops, or on large sheets of butcher paper on the floor. The point is to set up the activity so that children can create with it on their own. Occasionally, you may have to get involved to get the children started, but then you can extract yourself and let them create on their own.

ACCEPTS CHILDREN'S CREATIVE PRODUCTS WITHOUT PLACING A VALUE JUDGMENT ON THEM

If freedom is the most important aspect of creativity, then acceptance is the second. You must accept whatever the child produces, unconditionally, just as you accept the child unconditionally. Not all children live up to the standards you expect, but that does not mean you don't accept them and value them as human beings.

As a professional in a preschool program, you are obligated to accept every child equally, whether they are clean or dirty, black or white, rich or poor, smiling or withdrawn—it matters not. They are all children. They have come to your center. They are yours to guide regardless of their qualities.

The same is true of their creative products. A smudge of brown covering an easel paper may mean a breakthrough to a child struggling to conquer the medium of drippy paint and awkward brushes. You must accept it for what it is: not a painting but a process, the results of a difficult struggle with the medium. But you must accept it honestly. What should you say? Not: "That's a beautiful painting, Charles," because it may not be to you. How about: "You surely used a lot of paint in your work today!" That is an honest appraisal of what happened, and the child should accept that.

On the other hand, a child may have done a representational drawing and want your reaction to it. Be positive but noncommittal when you are unsure of what to say. "What is it?" may be a real put-down, when the child knows it is obviously a fire engine. Instead you might say, "I like the way you used the red color. Do you want to tell me about your picture?"

Children don't always want to talk about the drawings and paintings they have done. They may not even want to show them to you. That should be their choice. You should, however, give them the opportunity to hang their work on the wall at their eye level, if this is where you display children's art. Let the child place it where she wants. You may give her the choice of mounting it first on backing paper to make it more attractive.

Stages of Art Development

You will become more accepting of children's art if you understand the various developmental stages children go through in drawing when they are allowed to express themselves spontaneously. From two to three years old, children mainly scribble. All children everywhere make these same markings, in the same way at approximately the same age (Kellogg, 1969). Sometime between two and four, the scribbles take on outline shapes, such as circles, ovals, squares, triangles, and crosses. Between three and five, children begin to make designs from the shapes they have been drawing. Although there are an unlimited number of possibilities, children usually draw only a

You must accept children's creative products without placing a value judgment on them.

few favorites. Some of their designs are suns (a circle), radials (a circle with rays), and mandalas (a circle with a cross inside).

Between the ages of four and five, their designs often take the form of people. People grow out of radials, with the rays of the sun becoming arms, legs, and hair, and the circle becoming the face and body. By five, many children are at a pictorial stage, creating representational drawings. Whether they continue developing talent in art during their elementary school years depends as much on the freedom and support they have received during the preschool years as it does on inborn skill.

It is important for you and the children's parents to know about this development, so the next time a three-year-old shows you a page of scribbles, you will not be tempted to dismiss it as "only scribbles." Instead, you will know it is the child's first exciting step in the developmental process of learning to draw.

Attitudes Toward Children's Art

Can you also accept artwork that is radically different from the norm? Some adults are uncomfortable with children's originality. They believe children should be taught to conform—that there is only one way to play with toys or paint pictures. They have great difficulty accepting red grass or purple sky.

This kind of attitude will quickly kill creativity in an early childhood classroom. Creativity demands a spontaneity that many adults do not exhibit because they have not allowed it to develop. Artists, on the other hand, have somehow escaped the inhibitions imposed on most of us. Preschoolers have the same great artistic potential because they have not yet experienced these inhibitions.

Give your children the opportunity to develop this most satisfying aspect of their nature while there is yet time. Do not insist that their paintings and drawings represent something. Many will not have reached this stage in their artistic development. Instead, give them your support regardless of the outcome of their efforts.

If they are in the process of creating a finger painting, for instance, let them complete the experience. Do not stop them when the painting looks "good" to you. The final result may eventually be a muddy smudge of colors, but it is their expression, not yours. Your support, in this case, has been your restraint from stopping them when the painting suited your taste.

If children have the freedom to experiment and create with color, you may be amazed at the results. Their abstract art compares well with that of professionals. Researchers who have studied this phenomenon believe it reflects the natural creative urge of all human beings. Most preschool children are able to express this drive in wholly original ways (as artists do) because they have not yet become inhibited by peers and adults and the conformity expected of them when they enter school. Sadly enough for many youngsters, this brief blossoming soon fades, and may not appear in their lives again until the retirement years, when the pressures of the workaday world have lifted and they are free once more to do things as they wish. Let us strive in our programs to keep creativity alive in young children as long as possible.

Some of your children may be ready to represent things in art. They, too, need the freedom to explore. Don't insist that they make blue sky and green grass. Let them play with painting a picture just as they do with building a block construction. One teacher tried without success to make a child paste cutout red "chimneys" on the roof of his house "where they belonged," instead of on the lawn beside the house. Finally the exasperated child looked up and declared, "They're firecrackers!"

GIVES CHILDREN THE OPPORTUNITY TO HAVE
FUN WITH MUSIC

Children need adult role models to dramatize to them how we want them to behave. This is as true in the creative arts as it is in eating food at the lunch table. The cliché is true: children will do as we do, not as we say. If you want your children to be creative, then it is up to you to lead the way.

Your creative actions should be as natural and spontaneous as you want the children's to be. In other words, don't direct the children to watch what you're doing and copy you. What you hope children will do is not an imitation but an original action spurred by your leadership.

Are you afraid to sing in front of others? Many of us are. Does it have something to do with our own improper introduction to music? We owe it to our children to avoid the same mistake with them.

Let's find a way to sing in the classroom. You don't need to be able to carry a tune; many of the children can't, either. All that really matters is that you have fun with sound. If you are having fun, the children are bound to. Start with a monotone chant. Make up your own if you don't know any.

Hap-py day,
Hap-py day,
Let's have a
Happy, happy day!

Clap while you are chanting. Some of the children may follow your lead and clap along with you. Repeat the chant a few times, and perhaps some of the children will join in. This isn't done during a formal "music period." Let's not make music formal. It can be done any time you feel like it. Maybe something makes you feel happy. Maybe everyone is busily working and it makes you feel good. You are doing your song or chant because it is the way you feel like expressing an emotion. Whether or not the children respond doesn't matter, but your acting in this spontaneous and creative way sets the stage for children to make up songs or chants when they feel good.

What other situations during the day can you convert to songs or chants? How about pickup time?

We're picking up the blocks,
We're picking up the blocks,
Clunk, clunk, clunk, clunk,
We're picking up the blocks.

We're picking up the trucks,
We're picking up the trucks,
Clack, clack, clack, clack,
We're picking up the trucks.

This can be chanted or sung to the tune of "The Farmer in the Dell." If the children join in, let them help you invent words for the other items to be picked up.

Singing or chanting directions can apply to any number of situations: putting on outside garments, setting the table, washing hands, or getting out cots for the afternoon nap (when you can whisper the chant).

You can sing or chant a welcome to the children in the morning, or when using their names throughout the day. Here are some beginning lines just to get you started:

> Where is Bobby? ("Where is Thumbkin?")
> Where, oh, where is nice little Lisa? ("Paw Paw Patch")
> Joel, Joel, come to lunch ("Skip to My Lou")
> Here comes Joyce, through the door ("This Old Man")

You can sing or chant about anything that happens in or out of the classroom. If the children look out the window and see it snowing, you can sing:

> Snow, snow, watch the snow,
> See it coming down,
> Silently, silently, silently, silently,
> Now it's on the ground. ("Row, Row, Row Your Boat")

You or the children may want to make up finger plays to go along with your songs. Sing a song at least once a day, and you'll soon be doing it more often. You'll know it was worth the effort when the children begin singing back to you.

Manipulating the Music Medium

What other kinds of musical experiences do the children have in your classroom? Do they consist mainly of records, with singers who tell the children how to move their bodies? This, of course, is not creative music. It compares closely to the manipulation of art materials we discussed earlier. There is nothing wrong with this per se; it just isn't creative music.

Children need to play with music as they do with blocks, trying out different combinations, breaking them up, and starting all over. And again, as with art, it is the process, not the product, that is important. Songs, the end result, may be highly satisfying, but if they are not arrived at freely and in fun, they may never be sung outside the classroom.

Initially, children will do with music just what they do with art: learn to manipulate the medium. This sounds strange when we talk about music, but it is the way young children learn any new skill if we give them the opportunity. In other words, they need the chance to play with sounds and rhythm. A book with excellent ideas and photos illustrating mouth sounds, clapping sounds, finger sounds, cup sounds, and stick sounds is *Rhythm and Movement*.

You can set up a sound-making table in a noisy area of the classroom. Sound makers can be a series of small containers, such as empty tuna cans, juice cans, margarine cups, and plastic covers, and a collection of seeds, beans, and pebbles the children can place inside the containers and shake. Have a record player or cassette recorder on the table that the children can handle by themselves, along with several records or tapes of rhythmic music. Let them try shaking the containers to music. They may want to record and play back the results.

Another time, use the containers as drums. Add a collection of Tinkertoy sticks and homemade drumsticks with cloth or tape wrapped around the ends (to cut down on noise), and let the children practice drumming to music.

You can also use all metal containers with large nails or spoons as drumsticks. Let the children fill a set of jars or glasses with varying amounts of water, and tap on them with a spoon. Put out a large collection of ''junk'' items and encourage the children to invent their own music makers. You may call this noise, not music, but don't tell the children that, if you want them to continue creatively. This stage compares to the scribble stage in art. After the children learn to manipulate the medium with ease, they may want to make their own rhythm instruments. *Your Children Need Music* tells how, and the book *Listen!* illustrates 60 different rhythm and musical instruments to make.

Instruments

Don't make the mistake of using rhythm instruments only as a group activity. Individuals need chances to make their own music alone as well as with the whole group. That is why it is important to maintain a music corner with a record player or tape recorder. Rhythm instruments can be hung on a pegboard for use during free choice periods. You can limit the record player's volume by taping down the knob, if this seems a problem.

Children do not need instruments to make music. They can sing, hum, clap, and tap their feet. You may want to introduce them to clapping during circle time. Let them clap out name chants: ''Here-comes-Bren-da,'' with a clap for each syllable. Or, children may want to play follow-the-leader with clapping patterns—one child claps out a rhythm, then the whole class imitates it. They can do the same by tapping their feet on the floor. How about letting them invent some ''foot music''? These games can be recorded and played back.

Adult-sized instruments need to be used cautiously with preschoolers. Always remember that it is the music maker who gets the most out of the experience, not the listener. Therefore, you should select adult instruments that children can also use, as well as those which are not overwhelming in sound.

This really rules out the traditional nursery school instrument, the piano. Think for a minute: who plays the piano? The teacher, not the children. How does it sound to preschoolers? Overwhelming! Even as accompaniment, it drowns them out. The skill it takes to play the piano seems so far beyond children's feeble abilities as to make learning music futile, indeed. The instrument itself is too big for them. Get down on your knees and look at a piano from a preschooler's perspective. In addition, the teacher has to sit with her back to the children, as if she is not even a part of the experience. Save pianos for older children, and use a more intimate instrument with preschoolers.

A guitar, for example, is better than a piano. The adult player is part of the group, and does not drown out the children's singing. A ukulele is even better than a guitar, because children can hold and strum it. Perhaps the best accompaniment of all is the autoharp. Anyone can play it by pressing down a cord button and strumming. Let the children learn to strum while you press down the button, and soon they will be doing both.

Harmonicas are also fun for children to use on their own. Buy enough small harmonicas for the entire class and give them a chance to play and march with them. You need to control this instrument, however, because of the possibility of transferring germs by mouth. When the children are finished, clean the instruments carefully with disinfectant wipes and put them away.

If you realize that many opportunities for individual play and experimentation with instruments are essential at the preschool level, your music program will take on an entirely different character.

Other Creative Activities

Every activity area in the classroom can promote creativity in children if you set it up so children can be self-directed and independent in its use. Sand and water tables are sources for imaginative play when interesting accessories are located within children's reach. Manipulative materials and table toys promote creativity when children are free to choose what they want and use them in different ways. Even the book area can be creative when teachers model the creative use of stories by making up their own and encouraging children to do the same.

Creative movement activities have been discussed earlier in Chapter 4, "Advancing Physical Skills." Dramatic play and block building, two other creative activities, will be discussed in Chapter 9, "Promoting Social Skills."

SUMMARY

This chapter has focused on the goal of promoting children's creativity through playful expression and freedom of activity in the areas of art and music. By allowing children to experiment with materials and colors, and then by accepting their artistic efforts and products as the beginning stages of a process,. we support their continued creative development. Teacher-directed art does have a place in the preschool curriculum to promote the skills of following directions and small motor manipulation. It should not, however, be confused with creative art in which the child is in control to manipulate the medium her own way in order to discover what she can do with it.

Music can also promote creativity in children when teachers use it themselves in a relaxed and enjoyable manner. In order to encourage music production in the preschool classroom, teachers must lead the way by chanting, singing, and providing musical toys and tools. Children need to become actively involved in creating their own music and not merely passive listeners to records. Clapping, tapping, and other rhythm activities can help lead children into song. Rhythm instruments can be made by the children and kept out for their use. Child-size instruments like ukuleles and harmonicas speak to this intuitive need within most children to express themselves in music.

LEARNING ACTIVITIES

1. Read Chapter 7, "Advancing Creative Skills," and answer Question Sheet 7-A.
2. View Mediapak A, "Setting Up the Classroom," and answer Question Sheet 7-B.
3. Read one or more of the Suggested Readings, or view another sound filmstrip, such as "Preschool Music for Non-Musicians," "Drawing," "Brush Painting," or "Paste and Collage." Add ten cards to your file with specific ideas for helping children develop creative skills. Include the reference source on each card.
4. Set up an art area the children can use independently. Observe and record what happens for three days. Discuss results with your trainer.
5. Allow children to paint (finger, easel, or table painting) on their own and observe the process. Discuss the results with the children in ways that show acceptance. Discuss this activity with your trainer.
6. Do a singing/chanting activity with children using ideas from this chapter. (The trainer can observe.)
7. Set up a sound or rhythm instrument activity for individuals or small groups to use. (The trainer can observe.)
8. Continue your Portfolio of evidence of your skills. Add one piece of evidence for each of the following Teacher Skills Checklist items:
   a. Arranges a variety of art materials for children to explore on their own.
   b. Accepts children's creative products without placing a value judgment on them.
   c. Gives children the opportunity to have fun with music.
   Evidence should reflect what you, not another staff member, have done.
9. Complete the Chapter 7 Evaluation Sheet and return it and the answers to Question Sheets 7-A and 7-B to the appropriate college or program official.

QUESTION SHEET 7-A

(Based on Chapter 7, "Advancing Creative Skills")

1. What is a creative person like?
2. What seems to kill creativity in children?
3. What can preschool teachers do to keep creativity alive in children? Why should they?
4. What is meant by the expression, "confusing the product with the process"? How can this affect children's art?
5. Why should children be allowed to "play" with art materials?
6. Why is it important to accept children's creative products even if they do not seem well done or attractive?
7. Why is it important to understand the developmental stages children go through in learning to draw?

8. How can you get the children in your classroom to sing?
9. What other ways can children become involved with making music?
10. How can or should adult instruments be used in preschool music?

QUESTION SHEET 7-B

(Based on Mediapak A, "Setting Up the Classroom")

1. How can a child feel good about his creativity in the preschool classroom?
2. How does the arrangement of the block area allow children to be creative in it?
3. How can children be creative in the dramatic play area?
4. What kinds of art equipment might you have available for children's use every day?
5. Why should art materials be kept on low shelves near the art tables?
6. Why should you hang children's art products on the wall at a child's eye level?
7. Can children be creative with manipulative materials? How does room arrangement encourage this?
8. What is one creative table game you could make for your children?
9. How can water play be arranged for children to use it creatively?
10. Why should children learn to use record players by themselves?

SUGGESTED EVIDENCE FOR PORTFOLIO

1. Take a photo of your art area and write an explanation of how you set it up so that children can get and use art materials on their own.
2. Include a sampling of one child's artwork over a period of time, explaining how you responded to each piece and how this promoted creativity.
3. Include a list of art activities you made up and an explanation of your children's responses, and how this shows your skill in this area.
4. Include a tape of a song, rhythm, or chant your children have invented and explain how you promoted their creativity.
5. Use a photo of your music corner and a written explanation of how you arranged it to promote the children's creativity.

Each piece of evidence should be accompanied by a write-up explaining how this shows your competence in the area of **Creative** and how the activity is developmentally appropriate for your children. Refer to Chapter 12, "Art Skills," in *Observing Development of the Young Child* (Beaty, 1986) for developmental statements.

SUGGESTED READINGS

Atuck, Sally M. *Art Activities for the Handicapped.* Englewood Cliffs, N.J.: Prentice-Hall, 1982.

Bayless, Kathleen M., and Marjorie E. Ramsey. *Music: A Way of Life for the Young Child,* 3rd ed. Columbus, Ohio: Merrill Publishing Co., 1987.

Beaty, Janice J. *Observing Development of the Young Child.* Columbus, Ohio: Merrill Publishing Co., 1986.

———, and W. Hugh Tucker. *The Computer as a Paintbrush: Creative Uses for the Personal Computer in the Preschool Classroom.* Columbus, Ohio: Merrill Publishing Co., 1987.

Bos, Bev. *Don't Move The Muffin Tins: A Hands-Off Guide to Art for the Young Child,* Roseville, Calif.: Turn the Page Press, 1978.

Burton, Leon, and Kathy Kuroda. *Artsplay: Creative Activities in Art, Music, Dance and Drama for Young Children.* Menlo Park, Calif.: Addison-Wesley Publishing Co., 1981.

Creative Associates. *Art, A Creative Curriculum for Early Childhood.* Mount Rainier, Md.: Gryphon, 1979.

Greenberg, Marvin. *Your Children Need Music.* Englewood Cliffs, N.J.: Prentice-Hall, 1979.

Haines, B. Joan E., and Linda L. Gerber. *Leading Young Children to Music,* 2nd ed. Columbus, Ohio: Merrill Publishing Company, 1984.

Haskell, Lendall L. *Art in the Early Childhood Years.* Columbus, Ohio: Merrill Publishing Co., 1979.

Jenkins, Peggy Davison. *Art for the Fun of It.* Englewood Cliffs, N.J.: Prentice-Hall, 1980.

Kellogg, Rhoda. *Analyzing Children's Art.* Palo Alto, Calif.: National Press, 1969.

Lehane, Stephen. *The Creative Child: How to Encourage the Natural Creativity of Your Preschooler.* Englewood Cliffs, N.J.: Prentice-Hall, 1979.

Moomaw, Sally. *Discovering Music in Early Childhood.* Boston: Allyn & Bacon, 1984.

Pugmire, M. C. Weller. *Experiences in Music for Young Children.* Albany, N.Y.: Delmar, 1977.

Uhlin, Donald M., and Edith De Chiara. *Art for Exceptional Children.* Dubuque, Iowa: William C. Brown, Publishers, 1984.

Wilt, Joy, and Terre Watson. *Listen!* Waco, Tex.: Creative Resources, 1977.

———. *Rhythm and Movement.* Waco, Tex.: Creative Resources, 1977.

CHILDREN'S BOOKS

Albert, Mary. *How the Birds Got Their Colours.* San Diego: Slawson Communications, 1983.

Berger, Barbara Helen. *When the Sun Rose.* New York: Philomel Books, 1986.

Bolliger, Max. *The Most Beautiful Song.* Boston: Little, Brown, 1977.

Duff, Maggie. *Rum Pum Pum.* New York: Macmillan, 1978.

Feeney, Stephanie. *Hawaii Is a Rainbow.* Honolulu: University of Hawaii Press, 1985.

Horwitz, Elinor Lander. *When the Sky Is Like Lace.* Philadelphia: J.B. Lippincott, 1975.

Keats, Ezra Jack. *The Little Drummer Boy.* New York: Collier, 1968.

Lionni, Leo. *Let's Make Rabbits.* New York: Pantheon, 1982.

Lloyd, Errol. *Nini at Carnival.* New York: Thomas Y. Crowell, 1978.

Martin, Bill. *Brown Bear Brown Bear, What Do You See?* New York: Holt, Rinehart & Winston, 1983.

Murphy, Jill. *What Next, Baby Bear!* New York: Dial Books for Young Readers, 1983.

Noble, Tinka Hakes. *Jimmy's Boa Bounces Back.* New York: Dial Books for Young Readers, 1984.

Spilka, Arnold. *Paint All Kinds of Pictures.* New York: Scholastic, 1963.

Shannon, George. *Lizard's Song.* New York: Greenwillow, 1981.

Stecher, Miriam B., and Alice S. Kandell. *Max, the Music-Maker.* New York: Lothrop, Lee and Shepard, 1980.

Stinson, Kathy. *Red Is Best.* Toronto, Canada: Annick Press, 1983.

Tomkins, Jasper. *The Sky Jumps into Your Shoes at Night.* La Jolla, Calif.: Green Tiger Press, 1986.

Wolkstein, Diane. *The Banza.* New York: Dial Press, 1981.

SOUND FILMSTRIPS

Beaty, Janice J. "Setting Up the Classroom," Mediapak A, *Skills For Preschool Teachers.* Elmira, N.Y.: McGraw Bookstore, Elmira College, 1979.

Benjamin, Jane. *Pre-School Music for Non-Musicians* (slides). Elmira, N.Y.: 3 to 5, P.O. Box 3213, 1979.

Brush Painting. Tuckahoe, N.Y.: Campus Film Distributors.

Drawing. Tuckahoe, N.Y.: Campus Film Distributors.

Paste and Collage. Tuckahoe, N.Y.: Campus Film Distributors.

CHAPTER 7 EVALUATION SHEET
ADVANCING CREATIVE SKILLS

1. Student_____

2. Trainer_____

3. Center where training occurred_____

4. Beginning date_____ Ending date_____

5. Describe what student did to accomplish General Objective

   _____

   _____

6. Describe what student did to accomplish Specific Objectives

       Objective 1_____

       _____

       Objective 2_____

       _____

       Objective 3_____

       _____

7. Evaluation of student's Learning Activities
   (Trainer Check One)   (Student Check One)

       _____ Highly superior performance   _____

       _____ Superior performance   _____

       _____ Good performance   _____

       _____ Less than adequate performance   _____

Signature of Trainer: Signature of Student:

_____   _____

Comments:

8 Building a Positive Self-Concept

General Objective

To help children improve their self-concept through your attitude and behavior toward them.

Specific Objectives

- ☐ Accepts every child as a worthy human being and lets him or her know with nonverbal cues.
- ☐ Helps children accept and appreciate themselves and each other.
- ☐ Provides many activities and opportunities for individual children to experience success.

T he formation of a self-concept begins at birth and is still very much in the developmental stage during a child's preschool years. How a child eventually comes to feel about himself is the result of an accumulation of contacts and experiences with other people and with the environment. If most of these contacts have been positive, the child should feel good about himself. If an infant has been loved and cared for, picked up and cuddled, fed and changed properly, provided with a stimulating environment, not neglected or left alone too much, not scolded too harshly or restricted too severely, not nagged at constantly, then he begins to develop, both consciously and subconsciously, a perception of himself as a likable human being. In turn, he will tend to like other human beings and behave as they want him to.

If, on the other hand, the child has accumulated an unending series of negative responses from other people and the environment, he will come to believe there is something wrong with him. Infants and young children are highly egocentric; they are concerned almost exclusively with themselves. If everything they do receives a negative response, they quite naturally assume it is their fault, that there must be something bad or wrong with them. This egocentricity sometimes carries children's guilt to extremes parents are totally unaware of. In cases of separation or divorce, the child frequently feels he is somehow to blame.

It is up to you and your classroom team to help your children experience as many positive interactions with people and things as possible. You need to be aware, however, that it is from an accumulation of responses and not just two or three that the self-image grows. You will therefore want to be consistent in your behavior toward a child so he receives a clear, ungarbled message of your positive feelings toward him.

ACCEPTS EVERY CHILD AS A WORTHY HUMAN BEING AND LETS HIM OR HER KNOW WITH NONVERBAL CUES

Your first step in helping a child accept and feel good about himself is to accept the child totally and unconditionally. This sounds so obvious you may wonder about its

189

inclusion. Of course you accept the unhappy child—you accept all the children in your classroom. But do you accept them totally and unconditionally? If you are human like the rest of us, you may have children you favor above others and children you do not like as well. You need to sort out and change your feelings before you can bring about change in the children's feelings.

A simple way to start is to make a list of all the children in your class. After each name, write down, as frankly and honestly as possible, what you like about each child and why; also write what bothers you about each and why. Then write down your reaction to the child in the classroom. For example:

Mary
Like: her quiet way of playing
Why: I like quiet children
Dislike: her uncleanliness
Why: I dislike dirtiness
My reaction in class: I leave her alone

Brian
Like: when he gives me a hug
Why: I like children to be affectionate
Dislike: His temper tantrums
Why: I don't like the way he disrupts the whole class when he doesn't get his way
My reaction in class: I often touch Brian, pat his head, hold him on my lap

When you finish, go back through the list and ask yourself for each child: Do I really accept this child totally and unconditionally? Do my day-to-day reactions convey to the child that I accept him as he is?

This does not mean you must accept disruptive and destructive behavior from the child. Instead, you should accept the child as an individual to be valued no matter what he looks like or how he behaves. It means you will help each child overcome negative behavior through your respect for them as individuals. If you find from your list that you do not, in fact, accept every child, then you need to begin by changing your attitude.

You might start by listing as many positive things as you can about each child whom you have not accepted totally. Keep a pencil and pad handy during the day and make a special effort to observe and record only positive things about the child. These notes, like your original list, are for you alone. They should be kept in a private place, to be disposed of when you finish with them.

Nonverbal Cues

You demonstrate your acceptance of children through nonverbal cues. Children understand how you feel about them by the way you act toward them rather than by what you say. Your tone of voice conveys as much or more meaning than your words. How do you sound to the child you seem to have trouble accepting totally? Switch on your cassette tape recorder when you are in an activity area with the child. After class, play back the tape and listen to yourself. Ignore everything on the tape but the tone of your voice. Play it low enough so you cannot even make out the words clearly. Are you satisfied with what you hear? If not, you may want to make a note to yourself about changing your tone of voice (perhaps making it softer, or keeping the scolding tone out of it). You realize, of course, that it is the accumulation of contacts with and behavior toward a child that help form his self-image, not one isolated instance.

What about your face? How does it look to a child? Do you scowl or frown very much? Do you smile a lot? Try smiling at the unhappy child. Children reflect and respond to the people around them. If nobody smiles at them, why should they feel like smiling themselves? Be persistent in your smiling. Eventually you will get a smile in return.

Touch and nearness are important cues of acceptance to preschool children. Affection is usually expressed through hugs, a hand on the shoulder, an arm around the waist, or sitting or standing close to someone. Most children crave this affection. Those who seem not to, who instead withdraw from touch or contact, may indeed have self-concept problems or may merely be shy, Your nonverbal cues of acceptance with these children may have to be smiles and a friendly voice until they feel better about themselves and/or become more at ease in the classroom.

It is important, therefore, for all the adults in the preschool classroom to behave consistently toward all the children. If you are the head teacher or team leader, it is your responsibility to make sure this happens. If you notice that a classroom worker seems to have a favorite child or seems to ignore another child, you may want to have a team meeting at which all of you do the exercise of listing the children's names, along with your likes, dislikes, and reactions. The harm created by an adult's showing favoritism toward a child in a preschool classroom lies in the nonverbal cues this action conveys to each of the other children. It says very clearly: this child is somehow more likable than I am; or, I am not as good as this other child.

Your acceptance of and positive reactions toward all the children in your class are thus extremely important aids to the growth of a child's healthy self-concept. Just as you make periodic assessments of children's feelings about themselves, you must also constantly check on your own feelings about the children.

HELPS CHILDREN ACCEPT AND APPRECIATE THEMSELVES AND EACH OTHER

How do children feel about themselves in your classroom? A child's self-concept is an elusive thing to pin down. One way to begin assessing self-concept is through observing the child and recording his behavior according to a checklist. The following Self-Concept Checklist can help you and your colleagues determine a child's perception of himself. (These behaviors should occur consistently, or they may not represent an accurate picture of the child.)

It is important at the outset that you attempt to determine how children feel about themselves. Since they have difficulty expressing this verbally, you must

> Self-concept checklist
>
> _____ Can identify himself/herself by first and last name
> _____ Looks at you without covering face when you speak to him/her
> _____ Seeks other children to play with or will join when asked
> _____ Seldom shows fear of new or different things
> _____ Is seldom destructive of materials or disruptive of activities
> _____ Smiles; seems happy much of the time
> _____ Shows pride in his/her accomplishments
> _____ Stands up for his/her rights
> _____ Moves confidently, with good motor control

determine it through observing and recording a child's particular responses or behaviors as he interacts with other children and activities. Add this information to each child's records and use it as you plan for individuals.

For children who have few checkmarks, you and your co-workers will need to provide special experiences for strengthening their self-concept. Perhaps the most critical indicator of a child's self-image is the entry "Smiles; seems happy much of the time." The child who does not smile or act happy demonstrates obvious evidence of troubled feelings within. What can you do to help?

Mirrors, Photos, Tapes

Besides accepting the child yourself, the most important role you can play is in helping children accept themselves and each other. Children need to know what they look like in order to accept themselves. A full-length mirror is a necessity in the classroom. Children will use it not only in the dressup corner, but at odd moments during the day. They are curious about themselves. Is this what they really look like? You will find they use mirrors quite differently from adults, who, after all, already know what they look like.

Young children are trying to sort themselves out and find out who they are. Hand mirrors serve the same purpose, giving a closeup view of the face for a child sitting at a table. Keep more than one in the classroom.

An instant-print camera is another good way to promote self-concept. Take many photos of each child during the program year. Instant prints are more meaningful to a child when he has just participated in the activity. Now he can see how he looks as the builder of a block house or dressed as a fire fighter.

Take photos of the child and his parents when you make home visits, to demonstrate your acceptance of both the child and his parents. Display the photos in the center or in personal scrapbooks the children may want to make.

Children need to know what they look like in order to accept themselves.

Photograph each child doing an art project, feeding a classroom pet, on a field trip, making a puzzle, going down a slide, or talking with a friend. Take individual pictures to be laminated and used by the child on an attendance chart. Enlarge each child's photo, glue it to wood, and cut it into puzzle pieces. Let children learn to use the camera and take their own pictures of each other.

A tape recorder may serve the same purpose. Spend time with individuals or small groups, recording each of their voices, playing it back, and discussing it. Children may want to tell something about themselves, tell a story, sing a song, pretend to be someone else. When they learn to use the recorder on their own, they can tape each other's voices.

Self-Concept Art Activities

Art projects can help children get in touch with their images through activities such as full-body drawings. Have the child lie flat on his back on a piece of newsprint on the floor, while another child traces around him. The child can then paint in features and clothes. These full-body drawings, cut out and mounted on the wall, make an attractive visual representation of the children in your classroom. Be sure you have drawings of everyone before you mount them. If you make them at the beginning and again at the end of the year, children can have the fun of comparing their changing looks and abilities over a span of time.

Other art projects include hand tracings or prints, finger printing with rubber stamp pads, foot tracings or prints or cutouts from contact paper, or a face collage made from eyes, noses, and mouths the children cut from magazines. Always be sure to label these body parts with the child's name. The child's name should also appear on labels on other things in the room: his or her cubby, name cards for places at the lunch table, science projects, art products.

Children's Books

Children can learn to accept themselves and others through stories about children who have these same concerns. *Will I Have A Friend?* shows Jim's familiar worry about finding a friend the first day of nursery school. *The Shy Little Girl* is older, but she has the same friendship problem. *The Very Little Boy* is not big enough to do anything interesting until he suddenly begins to grow. *Much Bigger Than Martin* is a humorous treatment of sibling rivalry on the part of the little brother, who finally finds a way to become much bigger than Martin. But Jason, the perfect little bear in *I'm Terrific*, has to become "the new me" in order to keep his friends.

Accepting Children with Special Needs

Children in your classroom who have special needs can develop a positive self-concept just as the others if you keep in mind these strategies: (1) acceptance; (2) stressing similarities to others, not differences; and (3) building on the child's strengths.

You must first accept the child as he is: his language, his culture, his clothing, or his handicap, if he has one. Show you accept him by your tone of voice, your smile, your words, your actions. Greet him cheerfully every day. Help him feel at home in your classroom.

You must then be careful not to stress his differences, but rather his similarities to the others. This child *is* just like the others. His skin color may be different, her language may not be the same, the child may have a physical handicap or learning disability. Nevertheless, all are children together, and all have the same need for your love, attention, and support.

You are the behavior model the children look to for a cue as to how they should behave toward a child they may perceive as "different." If the children see that you behave toward the child just as you do toward them, they will feel safe in doing the same. For instance, if the children discover that Alberto doesn't speak the same way they do, you can agree with them, pointing out matter-of-factly: "Many people in the world speak different languages. Would you like to learn some words from another language?"

In other words, you should deal with children with special needs just as you deal with every child in your classroom, for each of them has special needs, too. The child who is overly aggressive and the child who is shy also need your acceptance. They need to feel they are not different from the others, because "feeling different" usually means "feeling inferior," and often invites teasing and ridicule on the part of other children.

You should begin to help these individuals as you do all of your children, by identifying their strengths and building on them. A child who speaks Spanish can help the others learn to count in Spanish; the child who has a hearing loss can help lead the others in learning to listen quietly.

PROVIDES MANY ACTIVITIES AND OPPORTUNITIES FOR INDIVIDUAL CHILDREN TO EXPERIENCE SUCCESS

The activities and materials you provide can strengthen children's self-concepts if they find they can accomplish them successfully. Achieving success outside their home environment is very important for children. They need this kind of experience over and over again to build a good feeling about themselves.

You thus need to make sure that activities and materials are appropriate and at your children's levels of abilities. In other words, don't put out the most difficult puzzles, books, and activities at the beginning of the year.

You should not stress competition in your classroom. Your children will meet that soon enough in the outside world. Their experience in your classroom should give them breathing space, time to develop positive feelings about themselves as they accomplish the many interesting activities in your program Winning or losing can come later, when their concepts of themselves are stronger.

Although children should be able to choose from among any of the games and materials, you can steer those who have difficulties to the easier activities. All children need to experience success. For those who seldom sit still long enough to complete an activity, you might consider sitting with them and helping or encouraging them to complete it. Some children are so fearful of failure that they just won't try, so you may need to help them step by step to succeed.

Building on the Child's Strengths

Everyone can do something well. Help each child discover his particular skill, then build on it. Perhaps the child with poor motor coordination can grasp a spoon and stir well. It is up to you, then, to provide activities in which that child can experience similar success: mixing gelatin or powdered drinks or powdered paint or dough. Add other, similar, activities: let the children put together a fruit salad, with that child in charge of the melon baller. Think of other implements the child might use successfully: the paper punch to count the number of children in class each day; the pencil sharpener; the food mill to grind up cooked apples or pumpkins. Maybe that child can be a drummer in your rhythm band.

You may want to list such skills on individual file cards for each child, with space for the dates they accomplish something new. Parents need to know about your goals for their children, and you need to know about their goals for them. Discuss with them what their children are able to do in your classroom, so parents can encourage them to accomplish the same things at home.

Strengthening a Child's Independence

Children's concepts of themselves receive an exceptional amount of strengthening as they learn how to do things on their own. Some preschool teachers do not realize this, and think they are helping children by tying their shoes, zipping up their jackets, serving their food, and pouring their milk. Children do not protest. After all, they have been little and helpless all those years before coming to the center.

But now is the time for children and the adults around them to change. As children grow and change, the adults around them should, too. This is one reason for your child development center: to help young children grow and develop independence.

You might first list all the tasks a child in your center could accomplish successfully on his own; for example,

> Take off, put on outer garments
> Button, zip clothes
> Hang garments in cubby
> Choose activities to participate in
> Get out paints, puzzles, etc.
> Mix paints
> Help with cleanup, pickup
> Go to bathroom
> Wash hands
> Brush teeth
> Set table
> Fold napkins
> Serve food
> Pour drink
> Feed animal pet
> Help clean cage

Play musical instrument
Operate tape recorder, record player
Answer telephone
Hammer nails, saw wood
Cut with scissors
Cut with knife
Use vegetable scraper
Get out ingredients for cooking activity
Follow recipe chart
Print own name
Get out and put away cot
Fold blanket
Climb up and down climber
Operate computer

This is a partial list. Can your children do these things? More important, are they allowed to? Some teachers say, "I would never allow a three-year-old to use a sharp knife. He might cut himself." As many other teachers reply, "All my children learn to handle dangerous implements such as knives and saws so they won't get hurt. If they should ever slip and cut themselves, that too is a learning experience, and we have bandages and sympathy always at hand."

Some classroom staffs worry about children's using tape recorders and record players because they are expensive and easily broken. Others report that they try to purchase the most durable and least expensive recorders, those that will best survive children's handling. They believe it is of primary importance for children to use these recording tools by themselves. They are willing to spend as much time as necessary to instruct young children in their value and proper use, and to monitor the children until they are able to use these implements independently.

Parents' Expectations

Find out from both the parents and the children themselves what children can do on their own at home. You may be pleasantly surprised. If your and the parents' goals diverge sharply, you may want to find out why. Parents need to know what children of this age should be able to accomplish so they do not limit their children. You need to know what parents expect of their children at home to help guide your own expectations in the center. Both of you need to realize the importance of independent accomplishment in the development of a child's positive self-concept.

Society's Expectations

Children's accomplishments are as much a function of societal expectations as anything else. Certain societies, for instance, expect preschool boys to handle a two-foot machete (bush knife) safely and responsibly.

The point is that your children can accomplish whatever you and their parents decide is appropriate. It is hoped both of you will set your sights high.

Children's Books About Independence

Fictional characters who solve problems by themselves help strengthen preschoolers' feelings about their own abilities. *Sara and the Door* tells about a little girl who shuts the door on her coat and must handle the situation on her own. In *I Can Do It By Myself,* Donny overcomes his problems and fears to buy his mother a birthday present all by himself. *I'm in Charge Here* relates a little boy's humorous handling of household tasks while his mother is at work and his father can't be disturbed.

Children also appreciate *Leo the Late Bloomer* (or its Spanish equivalent, *Leo el Capulla Tardio*) about the little tiger who, according to his father, can't do anything right. With patience, Leo finally blooms, and is able to read, write, draw, eat neatly, and speak. Children love the book, but it is certainly intended for impatient adults as well!

Teacher's Role

You may agree with the theory of helping every child succeed at something, but wonder how you can implement such a concept when you have fifteen or twenty children in your classroom. No matter how many children you have, the concept is feasible if you have set up the physical environment along the lines discussed in Chapter 3 so that children can become independent and self-directed in their activities. The physical arrangement and materials should allow children to become involved with activities on their own, without your direction.

Your role in the classroom is to set up activities the group can enjoy, but which particular individuals will especially benefit from, then help involve those individuals in the appropriate activities.

Your role also involves stepping back and observing individuals and how they become involved, so you can decide what else you need to do and how else you should try to meet their needs. You are not in this alone. Whether you are a teacher, an aide, or a volunteer, you are a part of a team. When one of the team is leading a group project, someone else should be free to operate on a one-to-one basis with the child who needs special help improving his self-concept.

SUMMARY

This chapter has discussed methods for improving the self-concept of your children through your attitude and behavior toward them. First of all you must accept each of them and show them that you do, through verbal and nonverbal cues. Smile at them. Praise them. Let them know how you feel about them. Then you must find ways for them to accept themselves and each other. They begin to accept themselves in the classroom environment when they find that they can succeed in the games and tasks and interpersonal skills they must learn. Your modeling behavior of acceptance helps them to act in a similar manner toward one another. Then when they find that you give them opportunities to become independent in classroom activities, they develop pride in their accomplishments and receive a boost in their positive feelings about themselves.

LEARNING ACTIVITIES

1. Read Chapter 8, "Building a Positive Self-Concept," and answer Question Sheet 8-A.
2. View Mediapak C, "Self-Image and Self-Control," and answer Question Sheet 8-B.
3. Read one or more of the Suggested Readings. Add ten cards to your file with specific ideas for helping children develop a positive self-concept. Include the reference source on each card.
4. Assess the self-concept of every child in your classroom using the Self-Concept Checklist.
5. Make a list of all the children in your class, and after each name, write down frankly and honestly what you like about the child and why; what you dislike about the child and why; and your reaction to the child in class.
6. Choose a child you have perhaps not accepted unconditionally, and try to change your attitude by listing for three days all the positive things you see that child do. Show your approval with nonverbal cues and record the results.
7. Plan and carry out several activities with a child who seems to have low self-concept, based on ideas in this chapter.
8. Continue your Portfolio of evidence of your skills. Add one piece of evidence for each of the following Teacher Skills Checklist items:
   a. Accepts every child as a worthy human being and lets him or her know with nonverbal cues.
   b. Helps children accept and appreciate themselves and each other.
   c. Provides many activities and opportunities for individual children to experience success.
   Evidence should reflect what you, not another staff member, have done.
9. Complete the Chapter 8 Evaluation Sheet and return it and the answers to Question Sheets 8-A and 8-B to the appropriate college or program official.

QUESTION SHEET 8-A

(Based on Chapter 8, "Building a Positive Self-Concept")

1. How is a child's self-concept formed?
2. What is the first step you should make to help a child accept himself?
3. Why are nonverbal cues important to a young child?
4. What nonverbal cues can you give a child to show you like him?
5. What art activities can help improve a child's self-concept? How?
6. Why is it important for children to experience success? How can they do so in your classroom?
7. Why should you not stress competition in your classroom?
8. How does developing independence help improve a child's self-concept?
9. What do expectations–yours, a parent's, and society's–have to do with a child's self-concept?
10. What is your role in helping children with low self-esteem?

QUESTION SHEET 8-B

(Based on Mediapak C, "Self-Image and Self-Control")

1. What things make a child feel good about himself?
2. How does setting the table help strengthen a child's self-concept?
3. What kinds of things help a child develop a negative self-image?
4. How many positive incidents does it take to establish a good self-concept?
5. How does classroom arrangement affect self-image?
6. Why is it important for the child to have a private cubby?
7. What are some classroom activities that help a child develop positive self-image?
8. How can children's own ideas be used in the classroom to strengthen their self-concepts?
9. How can use of a camera help strengthen self-image?
10. How does the way the teacher handles children's negative behavior affect their self-concept?

SUGGESTED EVIDENCE FOR PORTFOLIO

1. Make a statement about the self-concept of each child in your classroom and how you have helped them toward developing positive self-concepts during the year.
2. Write about the results of keeping a list for three days of positive things a certain child did, how you supported him with nonverbal cues, and how your support made a difference.
3. Make a list of activities, or describe a particular activity in some detail, that you used to help children better appreciate themselves.
4. Write a case study (including a photo) of a child who seems not to have a positive self-image; describe the kinds of materials and activities you have provided to help that child experience success.
5. Describe books in the reading corner you have chosen to promote children's positive self-concept; discuss the children's response to them.

Each piece of evidence should be accompanied by a writeup explaining how this shows your competence in the area of **Self** and how the activity is developmentally appropriate for your children. Refer to Chapter 2, "Self-Identity," in *Observing Development of the Young Child* (Beaty, 1986) for developmental statements.

SUGGESTED READINGS

Bailey, Rebecca Anne, and Elsie Carter Burton. *The Dynamic Self: Activities To Enhance Infant Development.* St. Louis: C.V. Mosby Co., 1982.

Beaty, Janice, J. *Observing Development of the Young Child.* Columbus, Ohio: Merrill Publishing Co., 1986.

Borba, Michele, and Craig Borba. *Self-Esteem: A Classroom Affair.* Minneapolis, Minn.: Winston Press, 1978.

Bos, Bev. *Before the Basics.* Roseville, Calif.: Turn the Page Co., 1982.

Briggs, Dorothy Corkille. *Your Child's Self-Esteem.* Garden City, N.Y.: Doubleday, 1970.

Clemens, Sydney Gurewitz. *The Sun's Not Broken A Cloud's Just in the Way: On Child-Centered Teaching.* Mt. Rainer, Md.: Gryphon House, 1983.

Kranyik, Margery A. *Starting School.* New York: The Continuum Publishing Co., 1982.

Purkey, William Watson, and John M. Novak. *Inviting School Success: A Self-Concept Approach to Teaching and Learning.* Belmont, Calif.: Wadsworth Publishing Co., 1984.

Samuels, Shirley C. *Enhancing Self-Concept in Early Childhood.* New York: Human Sciences Press, 1977.

Texas Department of Human Services. *Culture and Children.* Austin, Tex., 1985.

Thompson, James J. *Beyond Words: Nonverbal Communication in the Classroom.* New York: Citation Press, 1973.

Yawkey, Thomas Daniels, ed. *The Self-Concept of the Young Child.* Provo, Utah:. Brigham Young University Press, 1980.

CHILDREN'S BOOKS

Castle, Sue. *Face Talk, Hand Talk, Body Talk.* Garden City, N.Y.: Doubleday, 1977.

Cohen, Miriam. *Will I Have a Friend?* New York: Collier, 1971.

Cooney, Nancy Evans. *The Blanket That Had to Go.* NY: G. P. Putnam's Sons, 1981.

Drescher, Joan. *I'm in Charge!* Boston: Little, Brown, 1981.

Frandsen, Karen G. *Michael's New Haircut.* Chicago: Children's Press, 1986.

Hutchins, Pat. *Happy Birthday, Sam.* New York: Penguin Books, 1978.

Jensen, Virginia Allen. *Sara and the Door.* Reading, Mass.: Addison-Wesley, 1977.

Kellogg, Steven. *Best Friends.* New York: Dial Books for Young Readers, 1986.

———. *Much Bigger than Martin.* New York: Dial Press, 1976.

Krasilovsky, Phyllis. *The Shy Little Girl.* Boston: Houghton Mifflin, 1970.

———. *The Very Little Boy.* Garden City, N.Y.: Doubleday, 1962.

Kraus, Robert. *Leo the Late Bloomer* (also in Spanish). New York: E.P. Dutton, 1971.

Little, Lessie Jones, and Eloise Greenfield. *I Can Do It By Myself.* New York: Thomas Y. Crowell, 1978.

Sharmat, Marjorie Weinman. *I'm Terrific.* New York: Scholastic, 1977.

SOUND FILMSTRIPS

Beaty, Janice J. "Self-Image and Self-Control," Mediapak C, *Skills for Preschool Teachers.* Elmira, N.Y.: McGraw Bookstore, Elmira College, 1979.

CHAPTER 8 EVALUATION SHEET
BUILDING A POSITIVE SELF-CONCEPT

1. Student_____

2. Trainer_____

3. Center where training occurred_____

4. Beginning date_____ Ending date_____

5. Describe what student did to accomplish General Objective

_____

_____

6. Describe what student did to accomplish Specific Objectives

Objective 1_____

_____

Objective 2_____

_____

Objective 3_____

_____

7. Evaluation of student's Learning Activities
   (Trainer Check One)   (Student Check One)

   _____ Highly superior performance   _____

   _____ Superior performance   _____

   _____ Good performance   _____

   _____ Less than adequate performance _____

Signature of Trainer: Signature of Student:

_____   _____

Comments:

9 Promoting Social Skills

General Objective

To promote children's social development by helping them learn to get along with others.

Specific Objectives

- ☐ Provides opportunities for children to work and play cooperatively.
- ☐ Helps, but does not pressure, the shy child to interact with others.
- ☐ Provides experiences that help children respect the rights and understand the feelings of others.

M any of us understand that young children are highly self-centered beings, and that this is a necessary step in the human growth pattern for the individual to survive infancy. We are also aware that as the child grows older, he or she needs to develop into a social being as well, in order to get along in society.

Children in your center must learn to work and play cooperatively, not only because we expect it of them, but because they are in a group situation that demands it. They need to be able to get along with the other children in their peer group. It may not be easy for some.

PROVIDES OPPORTUNITIES FOR CHILDREN TO WORK AND PLAY COOPERATIVELY

Three-year-olds, for instance, may be more attuned to adults than to other children. After all, they are not far removed from the toddler stage, when they were almost completely dependent upon an adult caregiver. Suddenly they are thrust into a group situation, where adults do not have time for them exclusively; nor do they expect children to act as dependent, self-centered beings. It is quite a shift for some children.

It is up to you and the other staff members to recognize this problem and help ease your children into becoming social beings who can work and play happily with other children. This is no chore for some children; they have learned these skills elsewhere. For others, you must work carefully to set up opportunities for them to become part of the group.

Dramatic Play

One effective opportunity is spontaneous role playing, often called "dramatic play" or "imaginative play" in preschool programs. Most classrooms have an activity area where children are encouraged to pretend and take on roles. Sometimes this area is called the "housekeeping" or "doll" or "family" corner, and contains equipment such as a play stove, refrigerator, sink, and dress-up clothes. These props encourage children to take on the family roles they see at home: mother, father, baby, sister, brother.

205

What is the point, you may ask? Why should we encourage children to fantasize? Isn't it bad for them? Not at all, respond child development specialists. Young children spend a great deal of time pretending, whether we encourage it or not. It seems to be their way of making sense of the people and the world around them.

In a preschool classroom, this kind of activity gives children an opportunity to be part of the group. If they are shy about interacting, they can become acquainted with others through the roles they take on, in the way of the shy child who hides behind a puppet. It is one of the most unique opportunities you can provide for learning social skills. To get along with the other players, they must learn to share, to take turns, and to wait their turn.

We know how important peer pressure is with older children. Child development research has only recently come to recognize how important peers are to younger children as well. They exchange information about the world around them; they offer suggestions on appropriate ways to behave; and some even try to impose their will on others in the group. Children are bound to learn what is expected, whether or not they decide to conform to this pressure.

Besides teaching them social skills, dramatic play also gives children the opportunity to try out the real-life roles they see enacted around them. It helps them understand what it is like to be a mother or a brother. They begin to see things from another perspective, often trying on for size the roles they will eventually play as adults. While they play these roles, they are becoming socialized in a much more effective way than any adult could provide. They learn to follow directions, to take leader or follower roles, to resolve conflict—all through spontaneous play.

Dramatic play also helps children master uncomfortable feelings. Adults are sometimes unaware of the frustrations children feel at being small and helpless in a grown-up world. Pretending to be an adult helps them gain some control over their world, and helps them work out fears and frustrations. They can pretend about going to the doctor and getting a shot, going to a strange school next year, or staying overnight with a babysitter, and thus lessen the trauma of the real event.

Furthermore, dramatic play helps children clarify new ideas and concepts about society and the world around them. As they gain information about unfamiliar people and situations, they are able to make it understandable by incorporating it into their imaginative play. The child who has a plumber come to her house plays out this situation in the housekeeping corner, and begins to understand it better. Dramatic play, in other words, gives concreteness to abstract ideas.

Finally, it helps young children develop creative skills by forcing them to use their imaginations. They make up the roles, the rules, the situations, and the solutions. The drama can be as elaborate or simple as the players make it. And, strangely enough, it is through imaginative play that children come to understand the difference between fantasy and reality. The real world becomes more real to children who have opportunities to pretend.

Dramatic Play Area

You will probably want to have a permanent area in your classroom for this kind of dress-up play. It can be a household area, such as a kitchen or bedroom, because those are the children's most familiar areas, thus encouraging them to play familiar family roles. Other dramatic play areas may also be appropriate from time to time. For example, you may want to set up a grocery store, shoe store, or post office, if the children visit one of these on a field trip. Children can bring empty cartons, cans, and boxes to fill the shelves.

Dramatic play can take place with smaller toys in many areas of the classroom, and serves the same socialization process. You can encourage it in the block corner by mounting at child's eye level pictures of buildings, roads, farms, or parks the children have visited, and providing appropriate toys to accompany the block play.

Do the same near the sand or water table and in the manipulative area. A supply of miniature people, animals, cars, trucks, and boats is essential if you are committed to promoting imaginative play. Many early childhood educators favor unpainted wooden miniatures because they put greater demands on the children's imaginations than do realistic figures.

It is not necessary to spend a great deal of money equipping your classroom. Large and small cardboard cartons can be cut down and covered with contact paper as buildings for dramatic play. Cutouts of figures and vehicles from magazines can be pasted to cardboard backings. Parents can donate old hats, shoes, purses, and wallets for dress-up accessories.

The book *Be What You Want to Be* is full of illustrated suggestions for using cartons, containers, tubes, cups, yarn, cord, bottle caps, and wallpaper paste to make props for play stores, offices, florists, or pizza parlors. The book gives directions for making everything from cardboard telephones and cash registers to typewriters and top hats.

Motivation

To stimulate children in their pretend play, you may want to take them on brief field trips around the corner or down the street. The most mundane places are exciting to young children, who see the world with fresh vision because it is new to them. A barbershop, laundromat, gas station, or even a parking lot can be the focus of fascinating imaginative play for these adventurers. It is up to you to provide the props for them to carry out their drama when they return to the classroom.

Another stimulus to pretending might be reading a book such as *Oliver,* about a little owl who loves to act out various roles with the enthusiastic support of his mother, or *Jim Meets the Thing,* in which a scary television program prompts the characters to pretend scary roles. All of Maurice Sendak's books feature pretending and imagination. *The Sign on Rosie's Door,* in which the children take roles and dramatize them, may be more appealing for somewhat older children, but *Where the Wild Things Are* and *In the Night Kitchen* are favorites of preschoolers.

Teacher's Role

Your initial role may be as an observer; you will want to determine which children take part in dramatic play and which never do. Who are the leaders? The followers? What roles do they play? How long do they sustain their roles? What do they know about the situations they are dramatizing?

Vicki, for instance, constantly refers to the "superman" in her apartment building whenever she plays house. Once you are aware of her confusion between the comic book hero, Superman, and the super (superintendent) of a building, you can help her understand the difference by discussing these terms later during a large-group activity.

Children's fear of doctors may also surface in dramatic play. If you observe that children have mistaken ideas about what doctors do, do not interrupt the play to "set them straight." Instead, take note of their misconceptions for future clarification. You may later want to read a story about a child who visits the doctor or a humorous animal adventure such as *Curious George Goes to the Hospital*. Or you may feel the children have been able to work out their fears satisfactorily in their dramatic play.

What happens in the dramatic play area is determined somewhat by how you set it up, what equipment and furniture are available, and what paraphernalia you put out. If the children have expressed fear of police officers, for example, you may want to put out appropriate props, especially after a visit from an officer.

If you observe that certain children are not participating in dramatic play, are not staying with a role, or are not really interacting with others in their roles, you may want to help them get involved by playing a role yourself.

"C'mon, Rob, let's visit Joyce's store. You carry the pretend money. What shall we buy?" When the child seems involved and comfortable, you can ease out of your role the same way you entered.

For new groups of children who seem to have no idea how to begin dramatic play, you may have to assign roles and start the play by taking a role. When things are going smoothly, you can withdraw.

To help a new child get involved, you might give him a prop to contribute to the play. "Sid, would you please deliver this box of shoes to Rachel's shoe store? They're the wrong size, and I need to exchange them for a size larger." Or simply give him a suggestion: "Knock on the door, Sid, and see if Rachel is there."

If the play begins to get wild or seems to disintegrate, you may need to step in and change its direction. "What do race car drivers do when the race is finished?" If you have the props on hand, you may be able to redirect the children into washing and polishing their race cars.

Prop Boxes

Some teachers like to keep paraphernalia for particular roles or situations in cardboard boxes, to have them handy when the need arises. They are especially good to follow up a field trip. You can assemble props for playing roles in a doctor's office, a supermarket, a car wash, a laundromat, a bus depot, a shoe repair store, a restaurant, a barbershop, and a beauty shop.

Block Building

The dramatic play area is one place where children's imaginative play can help them develop socially, emotionally, and intellectually. The block area is another. Children carry on their role playing in this area in a similar, but scaled-down, manner. Unit blocks are used realistically to construct roads, bridges, and buildings, or more abstractly as cars, planes, missiles, or anything else a child's imagination can conceive. Children play with the constructions they create both realistically and imaginatively, depending upon their experience with life, with blocks, and with pretending.

But before children role play in the block corner, they need to spend a great deal of time in exploratory play with the blocks. They need to handle and manipulate them, carry them around, push them and roll them, fill containers with them, and dump them out.

Very young children nearly always begin their initial experiences with blocks this way. They are exploring the medium. Even older children who have had no experience with unit blocks begin this way.

No matter how old they are, children seem to go through certain consecutive stages as they learn to use blocks by themselves. First attempts at building usually take the form of lining up blocks in rows on the floor, or stacking them vertically in towers. Children eventually learn through experimentation how to ''bridge,'' that is, connect the space between two blocks with another block. This breakthrough in construction techniques allows them to make more elaborate structures. Enclosing a space, a doll, a toy, or a car with blocks seems to be the next step. After they learn these basic techniques, children often go on to build complicated structures or line up blocks in intricate patterns. The key to their development here, as in other curriculum areas, is the freedom to explore the materials on their own, unhindered or undirected by adults.

Occasionally a child does not seem to know how to get started in block building. This would be an instance where you might want to intervene. How would you go about it? Sometimes simply your presence in the block corner will entice a shy or insecure child into the area. You might then ask the child to get you a long block from the shelf, if he doesn't seem to know what to do. Put the block down and ask him to get another block. Ask the child where to place it. Get him involved in selecting and placing other blocks one by one. Once he is involved, you can withdraw, as in dramatic play. Your role should be one of support for the shy or unsure child and that of observer for the rest.

You will soon become aware of which children build by themselves ''in solitary manner,'' who builds ''parallel to other children'' but not really with them, and who is able to build ''cooperatively with other children,'' the final step in the socialization process. Keep records of the children's progress on individual file cards.

It is important not to use pressure. It is not up to you to make Paul play with Mike. You need to provide the opportunity for both; they must make the contact on their own. This will often happen automatically after both feel secure in the block area. That means they need to experiment with blocks on their own. They need to do a great deal of solitary and parallel building before they gain the confidence to cooperate with another child.

Frequently, the first social contacts are ones of conflict. "He took my block!" or "She won't let me play!" Often, as teacher or aide, you will be drawn into the situation because the children want you to settle it. Situations of uncontrolled anger, destruction of materials, or harm to other children demand that you step in. Firmly but calmly, you must enforce previously established limits of not letting children hurt one another or harm equipment.

On the other hand, you can let the children handle many of their own problems with each other once they feel they have your support. Give them masking tape to mark off boundaries for building. Help them make a sign that asks others not to knock down the building. Help them set the kitchen timer to five minutes, so they can take turns with a favorite truck in the block area. Let a child give out tickets to other builders who would like to join in. You and your children can come up with dozens of similar ideas to help them solve problems on their own. You can anticipate such problems if you take a few minutes to observe the children in the block area.

You must remember, of course, that adult direction stifles children's imagination. You may need to encourage children at the outset to help them get started, but then you should tactfully withdraw. You may need to help redirect their play when it gets out of hand, but then step aside. For dramatic play to be truly effective, children need to manage these social roles by themselves.

HELPS, BUT DOES NOT PRESSURE, THE SHY CHILD TO INTERACT WITH OTHERS

For children who have difficulty interacting with others you may need to help them get started, but with great care and without pressure. If a child doesn't seem to participate in group enterprises, you will first want to assess the situation by observing.

Stages of Play

Does the child play happily by herself alongside the others? This solitary play is often the first step in socialization with peers. As the child gains confidence, she may become more involved with group activities even though still playing her own game—this is called parallel play. Eventually she will interact with the others in true cooperative play. You need not interfere to help the child work through the stages. It should occur automatically over a period of time if she is accepted and supported by you and her peers.

The Shy Child

The shy child or the newcomer, on the other hand, may need your help to get involved. One way to help the child get started, as mentioned previously, is to take a role yourself for a brief period, then extract yourself when the child seems comfortable playing with the others. You could say, "Come on, Jennie, let's visit Rob's grocery store and buy some food for lunch. You carry the purse, and I'll bring the baby. What shall we buy?" or "Shall we visit Rosa's house today, Jennie? You knock on the door and see if she is home."

Sometimes the seemingly shy child has other reasons for not interacting with others. One teacher learned that a boy who usually played by himself in a vacant corner and never wanted to go outside with the others was not shy at all. He came from a family of ten, and had no toys or space of his own; he needed to get off by himself. Someone from another program told about an extremely bright child who was reading at four, and was simply not challenged by the activities the others engaged in.

Children are individuals, as well we know. If the child seems happy in his self-contained play, invite but don't push him into a group activity. He may in fact do better on his own. We need to respect these differences in children as we do in adults. Don't give up entirely on the loner, however. Some children are simply overwhelmed by large groups. You might begin by inviting them to do something with a friend—look at a book together, help another pick up toys, set the table together, get out the cots for naps. The friends will eventually participate in group activities on their own.

Friendship

Friendship among young children is not necessarily the same as among older children or adults. Preschoolers value friends for their abilities (such as running fast) or their possessions (such as an interesting toy) rather than their personalities. Because young children are so self-centered, early friendships are often one-sided. A friend is valued if he satisfies certain needs of the other child.

For children who find it difficult to make friends, you might suggest they show another child how to do something they are familiar with (saw wood, make a puppet talk, make a puzzle, build with Tinkertoys), or ask another child to show them how to do something.

Classroom Materials

Classroom materials can help a shy child become involved with others. Materials through which he can project, yet not reveal himself totally, are best. A toy telephone, for instance, allows him to talk to another child indirectly until he feels confident enough for a more direct encounter. Puppets and dolls or toy animals also allow a shy child the same protection. Making friends with a pet guinea pig or rabbit can be the first step toward making friends with another child. Find out what the shy youngster is interested in, and use that prop to help him become involved with others.

Classroom materials can help a shy child become involved with others.

PROVIDES EXPERIENCES THAT HELP CHILDREN RESPECT THE RIGHTS AND UNDERSTAND THE FEELINGS OF OTHERS

A self-centered person, whether child or adult, has great difficulty seeing things from a point of view other than his own. Because of this, egocentric children often disregard the rights of those around them. If a child wants a toy another child is playing with, he may take it forcefully. He does not do this to be mean; rather, the social skills of sharing, taking turns, and waiting turns are simply not yet part of the young child's behavior, and must be learned.

Modeling

Children can learn from your example and that of other adults in the classroom. Make it obvious that you respect their rights and will stand up for them if necessary.

Make a point of thanking children who wait for a turn or share. Do this again and again, and some of the children will soon imitate this behavior.

Bring a special toy or activity to the classroom for sharing. Set a kitchen timer, or better still, have the children set the timer, so that each will get a turn. You can take a turn too, so the children are aware of the behavior you display while waiting.

Standing Up for Rights

You may need to help a shy or bilingual or handicapped child stand up for her rights. Children need to know you will respect each child's rights; then, you can help them stand up for their own rights.

When conflict arises, it is often impossible for the teacher to determine who was right and who was wrong. Try not to deal with children's conflicts on this basis; instead, redirect their interests. If one child claims another has taken her truck, put the truck away temporarily and give each child something interesting to replace it. Later, reintroduce the truck, and set up a situation for the two to take turns. Some teachers prefer not to remove the truck, but to offer the children the opportunity to resolve the conflict. "You both want the same truck. How can we solve this problem?"

Whatever you do, be consistent. The children will come to trust you, and to understand that you will treat each of them fairly in their dealings with one another.

Children's Books

Discussing problems of rights and feelings with individuals and small groups is another way to help children see things from a different point of view. You can sometimes motivate these discussions by reading an appropriate story. *Everybody Takes a Turn* explains this particular concept in simple, understandable terms. *Frederick,* about the little mouse who is different from others and gathers memories of sunshine and flowers instead of grain for the long winter months, might stimulate a discussion about a child who wants to be different. Other books dealing with this topic are *Oliver Button Is a Sissy,* about a little boy who liked to dance, and *Ferdinand* (also in Spanish), about a bull who was too gentle to fight.

Reading *Nobody Listens to Andrew* can lead to a discussion about how someone feels when no one will listen to him. *Sam* is about the same dilemma—no one in Sam's family allows him to get involved with them until he finally cries. *Ira Sleeps Over* can initiate a discussion about how it feels to be teased.

Marty McGee's Space Lab, No Girls Allowed is a wonderful story of a little girl and a baby sister who are quickly allowed in the space lab when it turns out that only they can make Marty's space helmet work. Children's treatment of one another is also the theme of *If He's My Brother,* a simple cartoonlike book in which a boy asks questions about how to treat his various material possessions and, finally, about how to treat his brother. Your children can have an interesting time trying to decide on some answers.

As these ideas become internalized through the children's experiences in the classroom, their social behavior should also change from self-centeredness to the cooperative, outgoing behavior of a socialized individual.

SUMMARY

This chapter has discussed ways to promote children's social development by helping them learn to get along with others. It is often difficult for children of this age, who are egocentric in nature, to work and play well in a group setting. Their experiences in the dramatic play area can provide opportunities for them to work out relationship problems with their peers. Through dramatic play children learn to see things from another's point of view. They exchange information with one another, often about appropriate ways to behave. They learn to share, take turns, and wait for a turn. To facilitate such play the teacher needs to observe and record information about who is playing cooperatively, who is not, and who needs help in getting involved. The teacher's role will be to motivate play in the first place by taking the children on field trips, putting up pictures, setting out props, and then supporting children in their efforts. When play disintegrates she may need to find ways to extend it further by posing a question or suggesting a new direction.

LEARNING ACTIVITIES

1. Read Chapter 9, "Promoting Social Skills," and answer Question Sheet 9-A.
2. View Mediapak D, "Dramatic Play," and answer Question Sheet 9-B.
3. Read one or more of the Suggested Readings. Add ten cards to your file with specific ideas for helping children develop social skills. Include the reference source on each card.
4. Observe the children as they engage in dramatic play, and note which children seldom or never play. Using ideas from this chapter, try to get one of the nonparticipants involved. Record the results.
5. Bring in props and set up a dramatic play situation around a new theme based on a new or different activity your children are involved with. Observe and record the results. (The trainer can visit.)
6. Bring in new pictures and accessories for the block building area to encourage nonparticipants to engage in block building. Observe and record the results. (The trainer can visit.)
7. Read to a small group of children a book about one of the following themes: being different, unfair treatment, standing up for rights, understanding people's feelings. Afterward, discuss with the children how they feel in similar situations. Record the results. (The trainer can observe.)
8. Continue your Portfolio of evidence of your skills. Add one piece of evidence for each of the following Teacher Skills Checklist items:
   a. Provides opportunities for children to work and play cooperatively.
   b. Helps, but does not pressure, the shy child to interact with others.
   c. Provides experiences which help children respect the rights and understand the feelings of other children.
   Evidence should reflect what you, not another staff member, have done.
9. Complete the Chapter 9 Evaluation Sheet and return it and the answers to Question Sheets 9-A and 9-B to the appropriate college or program official.

QUESTION SHEET 9-A

(Based on Chapter 9, "Promoting Social Skills")

1. Why should children have to change their egocentric natures when they come to your center?
2. How can you help bring about this change?
3. What social skills can children learn through dramatic play?
4. What stages do children seem to go through as they learn to play with unit blocks?
5. How can you help get a child involved who does not seem to know how to play with blocks?
6. How can you help a shy child get involved in playing with others?
7. How do friendships between preschoolers differ from those between older children?
8. How can the use of classroom materials help a shy child overcome his shyness?
9. How can preschool children learn to take turns?
10. In cases of conflict, how can you help a child stand up for his rights if you do not know who was right or wrong?

QUESTION SHEET 9-B

(Based on Mediapak D, "Dramatic Play")

1. What kinds of imagining or pretend play do young children do?
2. Why do children do this kind of pretending?
3. How does dramatic play help a child handle fears and frustrations?
4. How does dramatic play help a child clarify unfamiliar situations?
5. How does dramatic play help children to improve their communication skills?
6. How does dramatic play encourage socialization?
7. How should you set up the dramatic play area?
8. What should be the teacher's role in dramatic play?
9. How can the teacher extend children's learning in a play situation?
10. What can the teacher do when play disintegrates?

SUGGESTED EVIDENCE FOR PORTFOLIO

1. Describe how you set up a dramatic play area after a field trip, and the spontaneous social roles your children played.
2. Take photos of your children during their dramatic play and include them with a written explanation of how they resolved certain social problems, such as including an unwanted child in their play, or taking a role which no one wanted.
3. Write an explanation of how you helped a shy child become part of the group.
4. Describe the books you use with children to help them understand and overcome certain social problems.

5. Make a list of social problems that have occurred in your classroom and describe how you helped children cope with or overcome them.

Each piece of evidence should be accompanied by a write-up explaining how this shows your competence in the area of **Social** and how the activity is developmentally appropriate for your children. Refer to Chapter 5, "Prosocial Behavior," in *Observing Development of the Young Child* (Beaty, 1986) for developmental statements.

SUGGESTED READINGS

Beaty, Janice J. *Observing Development of the Young Child.* Columbus, Ohio: Merrill Publishing Co., 1986.

Creative Associates. *House Corner.* Mount Rainier, Md.: Gryphon, 1979.

Edwards, Carolyn Pope. *Promoting Social and Moral Development in Young Children.* New York: Teachers College Press, 1986.

Fiarotta, Phyllis, and Noel Fiarotta. *Be What You Want To Be!* New York: Workman, 1977.

Koste, Virginia Glasgow. *Dramatic Play in Childhood: Rehearsal for Life.* New Orleans, La.: Anchorage Press, 1978.

Perez, Carla, and Deborah Robison. *Your Turn, Doctor.* New York: Dial Books, 1982.

Provenzo, Eugene F.,Jr., and Arlene Brett. *The Complete Block Book.* Syracuse, N.Y.: Syracuse University Press, 1983.

Rubin, Zick. *Children's Friendships.* Cambridge, Mass.: Harvard University Press, 1980.

Smith, Charles A. *Promoting the Social Development of Young Children: Strategies and Activities.* Palo Alto, Calif.: Mayfield, 1982.

Webb, Roger A. *Social Development in Childhood.* Baltimore, Md.: Johns Hopkins University Press, 1977.

CHILDREN'S BOOKS

Alexander, Martha. *Marty McGee's Space Lab, No Girls Allowed.* New York: Dial Press, 1981.

Chislett, Gail. *Pardon Me, Mom.* Toronto, Canada: Annick Press, 1986.

Cohen, Miriam. *Jim Meets the Thing.* New York: Greenwillow, 1981.

Corey, Dorothy. *Everybody Takes Turns.* Chicago: Albert Whitman, 1980.

De Paola, Tomie. *If He's My Brother.* Englewood Cliffs, N.J.: Prentice-Hall, 1976.

————. *Oliver Button Is a Sissy.* New York: Harcourt Brace Jovanovich, 1979.

Guilfoile, Elizabeth. *Nobody Listens to Andrew.* New York: Scholastic, 1957.

Hughes, Shirley. *Alfie Gives a Hand.* New York: Mulberry Books, 1983.

Keats, Ezra Jack. *Regards to the Man in the Moon.* New York: Collier Books, 1981.

Kraus, Robert. *Owliver.* New York: Windmill and Dutton, 1974.

Leaf, Munro. *Story of Ferdinand*. New York: Penguin, 1977.

Lessac, Frane. *My Little Island*. New York: J. B. Lippicott, 1985.

Lionni, Leo. *Frederick*. New York: Pantheon, 1967.

Scott, Ann Herbert. *Sam*. New York: McGraw-Hill, 1967.

Sendak, Maurice. *In the Night Kitchen*. New York: Harper & Row, 1970.

_____. *The Sign on Rosie's Door*. New York: Penguin, 1972.

_____. *Where the Wild Things Are*. New York: Harper & Row, 1963.

Waber, Bernard. *Ira Sleeps Over*. Boston: Houghton Mifflin, 1972.

SOUND FILMSTRIPS

Beaty, Janice J. "Dramatic Play," Mediapak D, *Skills for Preschool Teachers*. Elmira, N.Y.: McGraw Bookstore, Elmira College, 1979.

CHAPTER 9 EVALUATION SHEET
PROMOTING SOCIAL SKILLS

1. Student_____

2. Trainer_____

3. Center where training occurred_____

4. Beginning date_____ Ending date_____

5. Describe what student did to accomplish General Objective

   _____

   _____

6. Describe what student did to accomplish Specific Objectives

   Objective 1_____

   _____

   Objective 2_____

   _____

   Objective 3_____

   _____

7. Evaluation of student's Learning Activities
   (Trainer Check One)   (Student Check One)

   _____ Highly superior performance   _____

   _____ Superior performance   _____

   _____ Good performance   _____

   _____ Less than adequate performance _____

Signature of Trainer: Signature of Student:

_____   _____

Comments:

10 Providing Guidance

General Objective

To promote the development of self-control in young children through positive guidelines and actions.

Specific Objectives

☐ Uses a variety of positive guidance methods to help children control their negative behavior.
☐ Helps children establish limits for their behavior.
☐ Helps children handle negative feelings through acceptable outlets.

C hildren who feel good about themselves are less prone to exhibit disruptive, negative behavior. Nevertheless, you and your classroom are not the only influences in the children's lives. Their interactions with others—parents, siblings, peers, neighbors, strangers—as well as their own personalities have a strong bearing on how they behave around you. Some children enter your classroom with as many as three or four years of accumulated negative experiences. How can you help those children control their behavior?

If you are aware that much of young children's negative behavior stems from insecurities and negative feelings of self-worth, you will eventually conclude that punishment, harsh treatment, and bitter words will not provide solutions. These responses are themselves negative behaviors, and only reinforce a child's poor image of himself. While punishment often stops negative behavior at least temporarily, it does not help the child build the inner, long-lasting control he really needs to get along in the world.

Preschool children have been sent to your classroom to develop manipulative skills, to improve large motor coordination, to learn social skills, to develop language, to develop creativity, to learn certain cognitive concepts, and to improve self-image. Learning to control their negative behavior should also be included as a learning goal. You should put this goal at the top of your list for certain children, and go about teaching it as you would any skill. Young children need objective—not emotional—direction in this area.

USES A VARIETY OF POSITIVE GUIDANCE METHODS TO HELP CHILDREN CONTROL THEIR NEGATIVE BEHAVIOR

Your role in teaching self-control is radically different from that as "preserver of order in the classroom" or "punisher of children with disruptive behavior." It is a time-consuming task: helping children develop self-control takes just as long as helping them develop motor control.

All behavior is learned, including negative behavior. Thus, undesirable behavior can also be "unlearned," that is, altered through learning. There are a number of ways to help children learn to behave positively rather than negatively. The teaching methods all focus on the *behavior* rather than on the *child*. The child is never considered bad, naughty, or inconsiderate; rather, it is the behavior that is negative. With patience and perseverance that can be changed.

Positive Reinforcement

Positive reinforcement helps the teacher focus attention on a child's desirable behavior and ignore his negative behavior. People usually focus on negative behavior because it is so attention-getting. The disruptive child is frequently crying out for adult attention, even if it means punishment. When we respond to misbehavior, even with punishment, we do not change it (even though it may stop temporarily), but only reinforce it. A response leads the child to believe: "If I do this, they will pay attention to me."

Therefore, we must shift our attention from the negative to the positive. This is no simple task—it will take a concerted effort on your part and that of the other staff members to shift attention to the positive and ignore the negative. This kind of shift requires changing a mind set. You must take a definite action to bring about the change in yourself first, before you can expect a child to change.

You can begin to accomplish this by making a list of all the positive behaviors a disruptive child displays during the day. Share the list with other staff members. Each time the child displays a positive behavior, reinforce him with a smile, a touch, or a word of praise. Each time he displays a disruptive behavior, try to ignore it. If you must stop it because it involves harm to another child or a piece of equipment, simply remove the other child or the equipment the disruptive child is bothering. Do not make eye or verbal contact with the disruptive child at this time. But as soon as the child exhibits desirable behavior, go to him and express your pleasure. Do this as soon as possible, so the child receives the message that you will respond to his positive behavior but not to his negative actions.

Be sure the other adults in the classroom will respond to the disruptive child the same way. There is no need to get angry, upset, speak loudly, or punish the child. Simply be calm, firm, and consistent in your actions. The child will soon get the message that negative behavior gets him nowhere in the classroom, but when he acts in a positive way, he receives attention and praise.

You must practice this new way of responding before you can expect results. Have another staff member watch you do it, then talk about it. Let that person try it, too. Work on this method until you make it work for you. It takes more time to get results than does forcing a child to stop his misbehavior, but in the end it is more worthwhile, because the behavior change comes from within the child rather than from outside. It is a step toward his developing self-control, and away from depending upon the adults around him to control his behavior.

When things get out of hand and one child hurts another, your first concern should be for the victim rather than the aggressor. You must, of course, stop the unacceptable behavior, but you do it by removing the victim. This is contrary to how adults usually act in cases of child conflict; ordinarily, the teacher rushes to the aggressor to stop him. But this tends to reinforce the child's misbehavior. If you go first to the victim, the surprised aggressor will get the message that he cannot gain your attention with such behavior. Do not forget, however, that as soon as the aggressor displays positive behavior, you must recognize that as well.

HELPS CHILDREN ESTABLISH LIMITS FOR THEIR BEHAVIOR

Young children need our help in learning to control their behavior. One of the things we can do is set simple limits and help children follow them. Children need to know they will not be allowed to hurt themselves or others, or to damage equipment. If you and your staff enforce these limits consistently and firmly, without harshness, the children will be more at ease and less likely to challenge you constantly.

Without limits, children will frequently test you to see how far you will let them go. They need to be satisfied that you will not allow destructive things to happen. They need to feel secure in this new environment in order to expend their energies on constructive activities.

The limits you set should be clear and simple. Having too many rules leads only to confusion, so begin with as few as possible. Do not announce the rules generally to the entire class. The only meaningful limits for young children are those that affect them directly and personally when something happens, but you and your co-workers need to have the limits clearly in mind. Other rules regarding number of children in activity areas, taking turns, and sharing materials, are regulated by the children themselves through the physical arrangement of the classroom and with the support of the adult staff.

If you have arranged your classroom as suggested in Chapter 3, you have taken a major step toward helping the children become self-regulating. The activity areas are arranged to accommodate a certain number of children, and the number or its symbol is clearly displayed. Another suggestion for helping children become self-regulating in activity areas is to use photographs of the children mounted on cardboard for them to hook in the area where they wish to play. The number of hooks in each area helps the children limit themselves. They can trade places on their own by mutual agreement, or wait for a prearranged signal to change. Masking tape is another simple but effective material to promote self-regulation. Tabletops in the activity areas can be divided into four or six sections with masking tape, if the children have been squabbling about how many can play with puzzles, dough, or paint. Sometimes chairs alone are not enough to help children regulate their numbers.

HELPS CHILDREN HANDLE NEGATIVE FEELINGS THROUGH ACCEPTABLE OUTLETS

What happens when a child becomes angry or upset? Don't wait for this to happen and then be forced to react negatively. You need to anticipate children's behavior, and be prepared for them to be out of sorts as you yourself are occasionally.

You can show your acceptance of children and their feelings by getting down to their level and listening to them.

Accepting Negative Feelings

Once you acknowledge that negative feelings are a natural part of a young child's growth and development, you will be able to take the next step more readily: that of *accepting* these feelings. Acceptance does not mean approval; it means only that you recognize this negative part of the child as well as his positive aspects, and understand that he has bad feelings at times just as you do. It means you are willing to help him change. Accepting a person's behavior is the first step in helping him control his negative aspects.

In addition, accepting negative feelings helps to defuse them. You need to display your acceptance by not becoming angry or upset yourself. You need to stay calm and respond to the child in a matter-of-fact tone of voice. Your even behavior is the first step in calming the child. Your actions say to him: "If she doesn't get upset, then it can't be so bad."

Verbalizing Negative Feelings

Next, you need to help the child express his negative feelings in an acceptable manner. Helping him find a harmless way to express these feelings defuses them. Otherwise, they may burst out again as soon as you turn your back.

Verbalizing feelings is one way to express them. Expressing anger, jealousy, or frustration in words helps relieve the emotion. Your calm voice saying, "How do you feel, Jennifer? Tell me how you feel," may be all it takes to resolve the problem.

Redirecting Negative Behavior

On the other hand, a hostile, crying child may not be able to respond verbally. Instead, a classroom activity may help him calm down and regain control of himself. Water play is an especially soothing activity. If you don't have a water table, you can fill the toy sink in the housekeeping corner or a plastic basin on a table for an upset child to play with.

Clay and dough are also excellent for children to use to work out frustrations. Encourage them to knead the material, or pound it with their fists or a wooden mallet if you feel this is appropriate. Bean bags serve the same purpose. Let children expend their negative energy harmlessly by throwing bean bags or a foam-rubber ball at a target.

Finger painting also helps children release negative energy. Consider keeping a quiet corner with a comfortable rocking chair and space for water play, dough, or finger painting. If children know you will help and support them in releasing negative feelings nondestructively, they will begin to assume more control themselves.

Books can sometimes be helpful in a stressful situation. For example, children often become upset when a new baby is born in the family, so it is a good idea to have several books that discuss this event. You will want to read and discuss the books with all the children, but they will give special comfort to the child who is directly affected. Popular books of this nature are *Peter's Chair*, *A Baby Sister for Frances*, *Nobody Asked Me If I Wanted a Baby Sister*, *When the New Baby Comes I'm Moving Out*, and *She Come Bringing Me That Little Baby Girl*.

Other books to help children get over feeling upset are *Alexander and the Terrible, Horrible, No Good, Very Bad Day*; *I Was So Mad!* (also in Spanish); *The Grouchy Ladybug*; *How Do I Feel?*; and *Sometimes I Like to Cry*.

Children's own behaviors will give you clues as to how to deal with them in strengthening their self-control. Here are some behaviors that actually occurred in preschool classrooms, as described by the teachers involved.

Destructiveness; Hitting

> Daryl is a real problem in the center. He is extremely destructive to the toys and equipment, and he endangers the other children when he hits or pushes them. When he hits them with the toys it can really hurt.

Compulsively hitting and damaging things may well be a tensional outlet for this boy. His teacher, Lynn, needs to be firm and consistent in not allowing Daryl to hurt other people or things. She needs to convey this idea to Daryl firmly but not harshly each time she stops him. Lynn needs to accentuate any positive behavior Daryl displays toward people or things by praising him. "Daryl, you and Bobby played so well together today," or "Daryl, I really appreciate how carefully you put the toys away." Finally, Lynn needs to redirect Daryl's negative behavior. Perhaps he can take out his negative energy on a homemade punching bag. On the other hand, Lynn may decide that Daryl needs most of all to calm down in order to control his inner frustrations. Playing at a water table may be a soothing activity for him. Lynn will undoubtedly have to try several approaches to see which works best for Daryl.

Whining; Tattling

> Nancy would be a likable child if only she'd stop her constant whining. She is always coming to the teacher with tales about other children doing things to her, and she always tells them in a whining voice. Nancy is four.

Already David, the teacher, has formed a judgment against Nancy by saying she "would be a likable child if only . . . . " David needs to start by changing his own attitude, then by showing Nancy that he accepts her as she is. The whining and tattling should be ignored as much as possible. Instead, David should concentrate on Nancy's positive behavior and praise her for ordinary things, for example, "Nancy, you and Sue played so well this morning." David may want to tape record Nancy's voice when she plays with others in the dramatic play area or converses at the lunch table. Later, Nancy and David can listen to the tape together, with the teacher making comments such as, "It really sounds nice when you talk so cheerfully, Nancy. Don't you like the way you sound?"

Biting

> Ronnie is a biter. Everytime someone does something he doesn't like, he'll give them a hard bite before they even know what's happening. Ronnie is four.

Here again, it sounds as though the teacher, Donna, needs to change her attitude. Already Ronnie has been labeled "a biter." He is undoubtedly a boy with great frustrations that need an acceptable outlet. As with Daryl, the teacher needs to stop Ronnie from hurting others and direct him into an acceptable channel for releasing his tensions. Since he seems to release energy through his mouth, perhaps he could chew on something when he gets upset. Calming activities such as water play might also be used. In addition, Donna needs to show Ronnie throughout the day that she cares about him and accepts him as a good person.

Thumb Sucking

Julie is a shy child who always has her thumb in her mouth no matter how many times you remind her about it. She is almost five.

An outside reminder is not going to help Julie stop sucking her thumb. For a teacher or parent to constantly call attention to this behavior only reinforces the behavior, and probably makes Julie feel bad that she is always doing something that offends others. Thumb sucking is a satisfying and tension-relaxing behavior for her. First, the teacher needs to accept Julie as she is; then, the teacher needs to help Julie find an acceptable substitute behavior. The adult in the classroom whom Julie most readily responds to should talk with her about thumb sucking and why people dislike it. Julie herself must want to stop before most efforts will be effective. Because she uses her fingers and mouth to release pent-up tension, the teacher should devise substitute activities for Julie's fingers or mouth. Perhaps she could chew gum. If this is not acceptable, perhaps she could hold some small object in her hand—a tiny doll or miniature car. Julie may also agree to have her thumb bandaged as a reminder not to suck it. Julie needs extra support and affection in the classroom to make her feel good about herself. In this instance, praise for not sucking may not be reinforcing. There may be too many relapses and therefore too much built-up guilt. The sensitive teacher may instead know when to ask Julie, "Is it working?" And if the answer is no, "Do you want to try something else?" Children are people too, and if treated with respect, can make such decisions to help themselves. (The same suggestions apply to nail biting and masturbation, both unacceptable tensional outlets in young children.)

Temper Tantrum

When Ricky can't have the toy he wants right away, he throws himself down on the floor and kicks and screams. He is three years old.

Some adults regard this kind of behavior as that of a "spoiled child." It is, instead, a release of great tension. Not much can be done for a child during the duration of the tantrum. It is best to move other children away and go about the business of the classroom. Afterwards, the teacher needs to comfort the child and suggest other outlets. Perhaps Ricky could pound on a pillow or kick a ball. Lynn, his teacher, might do well to purchase a tether ball for just such occasions. She can fasten it on a short rope to a low place in a corner for children to kick when they are out-of-sorts like this. Lynn will need Ricky's cooperation, though, to achieve any kind of success. Perhaps he will be willing to cooperate when he realizes he is warmly accepted and loved in the classroom despite his moments of rage. Patience will be necessary on everyone's part. There will undoubtedly be many lapses before Ricky learns to substitute ball kicking for tantrum throwing.

Rocking

> Sherry is a quiet, almost nonverbal child of three and one-half. She often sits in a little rocking chair and makes it go. Even when she sits in a straight chair, she rocks her body back and forth. On her cot at nap time, she always rocks back and forth until she falls asleep. It is also difficult to get Sherry to participate in any activity, and she never seems to smile.

The teachers in this case were perfectly willing to let Sherry continue her rocking—they were just worried about it. Did it mean there was something wrong with her? Not necessarily. This too is a tensional outlet, although a rather extreme one. It is a so-called stereotyped movement that many creatures (including animals) resort to if they have been isolated or neglected for long periods of time when they were young. They then sometimes withdraw into themselves and rock, or even bang their heads against something, as a tensional outlet. Children with autistic tendencies also exhibit this behavior, but not because of neglect or isolation. Autistic children seem unable to make or keep contact with other human beings and often resort to mechanical behavior.

In Sherry's case, the day care staff would do well to bring in an outside specialist to observe, perhaps a child psychologist familiar with such behavior. The staff should help Sherry feel accepted and loved, but at the same time should not put pressure of any kind on her to conform or participate. They should make a home visit, if possible, to talk with Sherry's parents to find out if the same behavior occurs at home. This should be done as tactfully as possible. A case conference may then decide how best to deal with the situation.

Overaggressiveness

> Lyle seems to take pleasure in hurting others. He looks around the room to see which boys are doing something interesting, then goes over to them and breaks up their building, throws something at them, takes away their toys, or pushes them down. He is a new boy at the center and hasn't made any friends.

In fact, Lyle has been trying hard to make friends. Some children use this aggressive technique to do so. They are making contact as best they know how, even though it produces negative results. The teacher, David, has passed judgment on the behavior ("Lyle seems to take pleasure in hurting others") without understanding the reason for it. David will need to change his attitude to succeed in helping Lyle control his behavior. David will first need to accept Lyle as a worthy person.

Since Lyle seems desperate to make a contact with another boy, perhaps David can ask Lyle and one other boy to do some chores for him, or put Lyle in charge of a group activity such as woodworking. With time and patience, this problem should work itself out as Lyle becomes accepted by the group. David should set an example, though, by demonstrating his own acceptance.

Jealousy

Jill is excessively jealous over her younger sister, Sue, who is three and one-half. Jill is almost five. Both are in the same day care center classroom. Jill is cross, cries a lot, and throws temper tantrums if anyone makes a fuss over Sue, who is the cuter of the two sisters, but so helpless.

Jealousy toward a younger sibling is a natural occurrence. The teacher may want to ask the parents how they deal with it, but she will also want to change her attitude toward the two girls to a more objective one. "Cuteness" is often in the eye of the beholder. The teacher may need to give Jill extra love and attention until she adjusts to her younger sister's presence in the class, and perhaps put Jill in charge of some activities or give her the added responsibility an older child can handle.

Taking Turns

All the children in the classroom have trouble taking turns, and are always squabbling about it. But John and Mickey have real fights on the playground over who gets to ride the tricycle first.

Here is a behavior problem that preschool classroom workers can anticipate and be prepared for. Most children of this age have trouble taking turns and sharing. It is a natural expression of their growing individualism. Teachers should first look over the classroom and playground for materials that might cause this kind of squabble. A tricycle is often a favorite piece of equipment, and if you have only one, you can expect many hours of turmoil. It is better to acquire a second tricycle or get rid of the one. Even with two, you will need to work out a system for taking turns. You can draw names out of a hat, have children sign up for turns, or flip a coin. Some teachers like to use a kitchen timer or three-minute hourglass to regulate each child's turn. The "waiters" can have fun keeping track this way.

Modeling Behavior

To help children control their negative feelings, you must first control your own. Just as with the children, "controlling" does not mean "not expressing." There is no sense in hiding strong feelings. Children need to know how others feel about the things they do. You would not be honest with them if you did not let them know. It is their behavior that angers you, not them personally. You should express your anger verbally, being firm, specific, and matter-of-fact—not hostile, harsh, sarcastic, shaming, or loud. You need to state clearly how you feel and what specifically made you feel that way: "Sheila, I feel very angry about your breaking that record! I can't let you damage our classroom materials that way!"

You should avoid certain behaviors, however, and if parents or other classroom workers rely on any of these negative ploys to make a child behave, talk to them about it. Try to interest them in reading this chapter.

Some of the following actions do "make a child behave"; they do not, however, strengthen self-concept or help a child develop control of behavior.

Things to Avoid

1. Do not talk to a parent or other adult about a child where the child can hear you.
2. Do not use judgment words such as *good, bad, stupid* or *slow* when referring to a child.
3. Do not constantly nag or scold.
4. Do not correct a child's speech.
5. Do not embarrass or humiliate a child.
6. Do not compare a child with siblings.
7. Do not accentuate negative things about a child.
8. Do not stress competition between children where someone wins and someone loses.
9. Do not withhold food (such as dessert) as punishment.
10. Do not use physical punishment against a child.

Your efforts to improve the children's self-control will be rewarded as they learn to control their behavior in the center. Parents, too, may note their children's growth in this regard and help support your efforts at home. The child with special behavior problems may require concerted and cooperative effort on the part of both home and center to effect a change. It is surely worth the effort.

SUMMARY

The goal of guidance should be to promote the development of self-control in young children. This is accomplished through helping children to feel good about themselves by focusing on positive rather than negative behavior. Each time a disruptive child displays a positive behavior you can reinforce him or her with a smile, a touch, or a word of praise. His or her negative behavior needs to be ignored as much as possible or responded to matter-of-factly without making eye contact. It takes practice to respond to disruptive behavior in this way, but in the long run, it helps a child to develop inner control.

Setting limits on behavior and helping children stay within these limits are other important methods for helping children to control their own misbehavior. Children also need to have acceptable outlets for their negative behavior. Expressing anger, jealousy, or frustration in words helps to relieve their emotions. Using water play, dough, finger painting, and bean bags can help children defuse intense feelings in a nondestructive manner. Your own modeling of calm yet firm behavior should help children feel less upset in times of stress.

LEARNING ACTIVITIES

1. Read Chapter 10, "Providing Guidance" and answer Question Sheet 10-A.
2. View Mediapak C, "Self-Image and Self-Control," and answer Question Sheet 10-B.
3. Read one or more of the Suggested Readings or view one or more of the Sound Filmstrips. Add ten cards to your file with specific ideas for helping children develop self-control. Include a reference source on each card.
4. Observe a disruptive child for a day, and write down all the positive behaviors he or she displays. Show that you approve by smiling or giving a word of praise. Record the results.
5. Set up a new area of the classroom so children can limit and regulate themselves. Record the results. (The trainer can observe.)
6. Bring in a material or set up an activity through which children can express or work out negative feelings. Record the results. (The trainer can observe.)
7. Read an appropriate book to a child who displays negative feelings. Record the results.
8. Continue your Portfolio of evidence of your skills. Add one piece of evidence for each of the following Teacher Skills Checklist items:
   a. Uses a variety of positive guidance methods to help children control their negative behavior.
   b. Helps children establish limits for their behavior.
   c. Helps children handle negative feelings through acceptable outlets.
   Evidence should reflect what you, not another staff member, have done.
9. Complete the Chapter 10 Evaluation Sheet and return it and the answers to Question Sheets 10-A and 10-B to the appropriate college or program official.

QUESTION SHEET 10-A

(Based on Chapter 10, "Providing Guidance")

1. How can a child "unlearn" negative behavior?
2. Why should the teacher focus efforts on a child's behavior rather than on the child?
3. How does it help to ignore a child's negative behavior?
4. Why should you not punish a child for negative behavior?
5. Why should your first concern be for the victim rather than the aggressor when two children are in conflict?
6. How does "redirection" work?
7. What limits should you establish in your classroom and how can you enforce them?

8. Why should you allow children to express negative feelings?
9. What are acceptable outlets for children's negative feelings?
10. Although scolding a child makes him behave, why should you not scold?

QUESTION SHEET 10-B

(Based on Mediapak C, "Self-Image and Self-Control")

1. What does self-image have to do with the way a child behaves in the classroom?
2. Why is it important in the development of self-control for a child's peers to show they accept him?
3. How does coping with the environment affect a child's self-control?
4. How does classroom arrangement affect a child's self-control?
5. What does a child's participation in classroom chores have to do with self-control?
6. What has to happen in order for children to assume control over their behavior?
7. What is the best way for a teacher to enforce limits in a classroom area when children get out of hand?
8. How should the teacher deal with negative behavior on the playground?
9. What rule should you follow in order for children to gain the teacher's attention?
10. Do you agree with the statement "self-control and self-image go hand in hand"? Explain.

SUGGESTED EVIDENCE FOR PORTFOLIO

1. Include a photo of an area of your classroom arranged for children to be self-regulating and explain how it works and how the self-regulating process leads to self-control on the part of the children.
2. Discuss the behavior limits you have set in your classroom and describe how children respond to the limits.
3. Describe the activities you use to help children channel negative behavior in nondestructive ways.
4. Make a list of books you have chosen to help children handle negative feelings.
5. Write about a child in your class who has been able to develop self-control as the result of your efforts.

        Each piece of evidence should be accompanied by a write-up explaining how this shows your competence in the area of **Guidance** and how the activity is developmentally appropriate for your children. Refer to Chapter 3, "Emotional Development," in *Observing Development of the Young Child* (Beaty, 1986) for developmental statements.

SUGGESTED READINGS

Beaty, Janice J. *Observing Development of the Young Child.* Columbus, Ohio: Merrill Publishing Co., 1986.

Briggs, Dorothy Corkille. *Your Child's Self-Esteem.* Garden City, N.Y.: Doubleday, 1970.

Cherry, Clare. *Please Don't Sit on the Kids: Alternatives to Punitive Discipline.* Belmont, Calif.: Pitman Learning, 1983.

_____. *Think of Something Quiet: A Guide for Achieving Serenity in Early Childhood Classrooms.* Belmont, Calif.: Pitman Learning, 1981.

Crary, Elizabeth. *Without Spanking or Spoiling: A Practical Approach to Toddler and Preschool Guidance.* Seattle, Wash.: Parenting Press, 1979.

Essa, Eva. *Practical Guide to Solving Preschool Behavior Problems.* Albany, N.Y.: Delmar, 1983.

Kersey, Katharine. *Helping Your Child Handle Stress: The Parent's Guide to Recognizing and Solving Childhood Problems.* Washington, D.C.: Acropolis Books Ltd., 1986.

Marion, Marian. *Guidance of Young Children,* 2nd ed. Columbus, Ohio: Merrill Publishing Co., 1987.

Mitchell, Grace. *A Very Practical Guide to Discipline with Young Children.* Marshfield, Mass.: Telshare Publishing Co., 1982.

Rice, Mary F., and Charles H. Flatter. *Help Me Learn: A Handbook for Teaching Children from Birth to Third Grade.* Englewood Cliffs, N.J.: Prentice-Hall, 1979.

Twiford, Rainer. *A Child with a Problem: A Guide to the Psychological Disorders of Children.* Englewood Cliffs, N.J.: Prentice-Hall, 1979.

CHILDREN'S BOOKS

Alexander, Martha. *Nobody Asked Me If I Wanted a Baby Sister.* New York: Dial Press, 1971.

_____. *When the New Baby Comes I'm Moving Out.* New York: Dial Press, 1979.

Bodsworth, Nan. *Monkey Business.* New York: Dial Books for Young Readers, 1986.

Carle, Eric. *The Grouchy Ladybug.* New York: Thomas Y. Crowell, 1977.

Greenfield, Eloise. *She Come Bringing Me That Little Baby Girl.* Philadelphia: J. B. Lippincott, 1974.

Hoban, Russell. *A Baby Sister for Frances.* New York: Harper and Row, 1964.

Keats, Ezra Jack. *Peter's Chair.* New York: Harper and Row, 1967.

Marzolla, Jean. *Uproar on Hollercat Hill.* New York: The Dial Press, 1980.

Simon, Norma. *How Do I Feel?* Chicago: Albert Whitman, 1970.

_____. *I Was So Mad!* (also in Spanish). Chicago: Albert Whitman, 1974.

Stanton, Elizabeth, and Henry Stanton. *Sometimes I Like to Cry.* Chicago: Albert Whitman, 1978.

Viorst, Judith. *Alexander and the Terrible, Horrible, No Good, Very Bad Day.* New York: Atheneum, 1972.

Wilhelm, Hans. *Let's Be Friends Again!* New York: Crown Publishers, 1986.

SOUND FILMSTRIPS

Beaty, Janice J. "Self-Image and Self-Control," Mediapak C, *Skills for Preschool Teachers.* Elmira, N.Y.: McGraw Bookstore, Elmira College, 1979.

Converting Conflict to Calm. Ypsilanti, Mich.: High/Scope Foundation.

When "I've Told You A Thousand Times" Isn't Enough. Ypsilanti, Mich.: High/Scope Foundation.

CHAPTER 10 EVALUATION SHEET
PROVIDING GUIDANCE

1. Student _____

2. Trainer _____

3. Center where training occurred _____

4. Beginning date _____ Ending date _____

5. Describe what student did to accomplish General Objective

   _____

   _____

6. Describe what student did to accomplish Specific Objectives

   Objective 1 _____

   _____

   Objective 2 _____

   _____

   Objective 3 _____

   _____

7. Evaluation of student's Learning Activities
   (Trainer Check One)   (Student Check One)

   _____ Highly superior performance   _____

   _____ Superior performance   _____

   _____ Good performance   _____

   _____ Less than adequate performance   _____

Signature of Trainer: Signature of Student:

_____   _____

Comments:

11 Promoting Family Involvement

General Objective

To encourage family involvement in center activities to promote their children's positive development.

Specific Objectives

☐ Involves parents in planning and participating in children's program.
☐ Communicates frequently with parents.
☐ Respects parents' views when program goals differ from parents' goals.

P arent involvement has long been a part of most preschool programs, but only in recent years have we come to realize how important this involvement can be. Research shows us that programs with a strong parent component have the longest lasting positive effects on children. Not only do children change and improve their skills as a result of their preschool experience, but their parents change as well.

Parents who are directly involved in the preschool programs their children attend are much more likely to encourage their children's development at home, and to support their learning during the later school years.

INVOLVES PARENTS IN PLANNING AND PARTICIPATING IN CHILDREN'S PROGRAM

Parents can be involved in many ways and at many different levels in early childhood programs. These are only several of the possibilities:

1. Visiting the program
2. Learning to practice child observation
3. Being invited to the classroom team meeting to help plan for child
4. Volunteering as a teacher's assistant to work with individual children
5. Receiving training and working as a paid classroom aide
6. Helping the classroom staff on field trips
7. Making equipment for the center
8. Putting on a money-raising project for the center
9. Bringing their culture into the classroom by teaching a song, a dance, making a food, or teaching words in another language
10. Visiting the classroom as a community helper or to demonstrate an occupation
11. Becoming a member of the Policy Action Council or other decision-making body
12. Serving as the Parent-Community Representative on the Local Assessment Team for a staff member's CDA assessment
13. Carrying out at home with their child an activity they have learned from the center
14. Joining a parent club and attending meetings
15. Taking instruction in nutrition, cooking, parenting, or another topic in a workshop or class sponsored by the center

Most parents will not become involved automatically. You must take the initiative, letting them know they are welcome and helping them find a comfortable way to contribute to their child's welfare while in your program.

If parents' only experience has been with public school programs, they may not realize how important their role is for their child's success in your classroom. Parents of preschoolers are their child's most important role model. If they ignore or downplay their child's preschool experience, the child may not take it seriously himself. If they do not know what learning is going on in the preschool, they can hardly support or extend that learning at home.

Thus, it is vital to find a way to involve the parents of each child in some aspect of your program. It may not be easy, especially with parents who work or whose own school experience has left them with negative feelings about classrooms and teachers.

Focus on the Child

The most effective approach is to focus on the child, not the program. Parents are concerned about their children's welfare, and if you focus on this from the beginning, you will quickly capture their attention.

The intake interview or enrollment process is often conducted by someone other than a member of the teaching staff. Your first contact with the children's parents may well be at the program's beginning in the fall. You will want to structure the opening days so as to have time and opportunity to get acquainted with the children and their parents, at the same time giving them a chance to get acquainted with you.

Beginning School

Many programs begin with a staggered entrance process so all parents and children do not come on the same day at the same time. Half the children may come on one day and half the next, or half in the morning and the other half in the afternoon. On those first days, each half of the class stays only part time. Parents or other family caregivers can be invited to bring their children and stay for the brief class session. You and your staff will divide your time between the parents and their children. The children and parents should be invited to explore the room. You can set up puzzles or a water table for them, as well as the permanent activity areas.

In the meantime, one of you can talk with the parents, asking them about some of the things their child likes to do at home and what the parents hope to see the child accomplish in preschool. Jot down this information on a file card for each child.

It is helpful to have a handbook to give to each parent at this time. Go over it with them, clarifying what will happen if their child becomes ill, other emergency procedures, and what kinds of things the child will do in the program. They may already have talked to the parent worker about this, but it is still a good idea for the classroom staff to reinforce the notion that the program cares about them and their child, and will go out of its way to express this care.

Invite them to stay until the child feels comfortable without them. This may take several days. If both parents work, they may be able to arrange to come to work late on the first days of the program. If not, they may be able to send another family member, so they will have some personal contact with the program from the start. Parents who have difficulty knowing when to leave after several days can be eased out by the staff. Let parents know from the beginning that they should plan to stay a shorter time every day, as their child becomes more involved in classroom activities. In the meantime, a staff member needs to make sure the child does become busily engaged so she can signal the parent when it is a good time to leave.

Home Visits

This may be the time to arrange home visits. You can mention to parents that you want to drop by in a few weeks to let them know how their child has adjusted to the center, and that you plan to visit all the parents to give them this information. Plan for a mutually agreeable time.

It is important to mention your intention at the beginning of the program, otherwise parents may feel threatened by a home visit, fearing their child has done something wrong. You must of course follow up with the visit. Some teachers like to take an instant print camera with them and, if the parents allow it, take a picture of the child and his parents at their front door. Take two pictures—one for the parents and one for a scrapbook in the center. The picture makes a marvelous contact point when you want to talk with the children about where they live.

Or, you might bring the parents a photo showing their child busy with a classroom activity. This also establishes a good relationship. Have the parents ask the child to tell about what she is doing in the photo. Before you leave, invite the parents to participate in some other aspect of the program. Perhaps you have a list of activities they can select from. If they seem shy, ask them to come with another parent they know, or arrange to introduce them to another parent they can ride with.

Parent Observation of Children

What should parents do at the center? They will want to watch what their child is doing. To help them focus on important child development aspects, invite them to use a checklist such as the Child Involvement Checklist in Chapter 12. Be sure to discuss the results with them afterwards, focusing on the child's positive accomplishments. Help them understand how you use such a checklist to plan for individual children.

After completing a checklist, they have raw data; the data are meaningless until they are summarized and interpreted. It is up to you, the professional, to help them do this. Suggest that they leave the checklist in their child's folder so they can compare it with their next observation.

Visitor's Role in the Classroom

Parents need to be aware that some children act up when their parents are in the classroom. Perhaps you can give that child a special role to play, an errand to do, or something to be in charge of, to take his mind off his parent. Or you might give the parents a teacher's role, inviting them to read a story to several children. Grandparents and other family members should also be invited to the center.

You can post signs in the activity areas to tell visitors what the children are doing and what the visitor's role can be. For example, in the book area, the sign might say: Children are free to choose any book to read during free choice period. Visitors and volunteers may want to read a book to a child. Or in the art area, the sign might say: Children are encouraged to try out art materials on their own. Visitors and volunteers may want to observe the children and encourage them, but let them do art activities without adult help.

Parents as Classroom Volunteers

Parents should be encouraged to volunteer in your classroom on a regular basis. If they are successful in interacting with the children when they come for a visit, they may want to work out a schedule of visits. You will need to talk with them about program goals, your goals for individual children, and what they themselves would feel comfortable doing during their stay in the classroom. It is important to stress teamwork and how they will be able to be a part of the team. The roles of the various team members also need to be discussed, so that parents understand what their own role will be and how they should carry it out.

You may want them to observe both children and teachers in the beginning, focusing on certain areas of the Teacher Skills Checklist, so that they have a better understanding of how staff members carry out program goals. The area of guidance is one that often needs an explanation. Let each parent volunteer spend a day observing and recording how staff members "Use a variety of positive guidance methods to help children control their negative behavior," "Help children establish limits for their behavior," and "Help children handle negative feelings through acceptable outlets."

Then you and your staff need to sit down with the volunteer at the end of the day and go over the Checklist together. Not only should you discuss the methods for guiding children, but also why certain methods are used. Ask the parent how he or she handles the same problems at home.

At first you may want volunteers to work in only one or two curriculum areas of the classroom until they become used to the children and the program. You or one of your team members need to give your help and support as well as intervene with sensitivity if things do not go well. Have how-to books available to lend to volunteers or suggest that they view a filmstrip or videotape about the curriculum area or guidance method they are working with. Invite the volunteers to planning sessions and inservice training programs. When they have acquired enough contact hours in your program, they may want to prepare for CDA (Child Development Associate) assessment.

COMMUNICATES FREQUENTLY WITH PARENTS

For parents to feel part of the preschool program, they need to be in close touch with what is going on. Communication can take any of the following forms:

1. Phone calls
2. Notes carried by children
3. Center newsletter
4. Parent handbook
5. Letters through the mail
6. Parent conferences in the center
7. Home visit by teaching staff
8. Program, club, or parent activity in center
9. Bulletin board in center
10. Circulating children's books

Circulating Children's Books

Some teachers communicate almost daily with parents by means of children's books that circulate into the home. These classrooms have duplicate sets of children's paperback picture books: one to read in the classroom, the other for children to take home one at a time for their parents to read to them. To communicate through this means, the teacher dittos a message such as:

> Your child chose this book to borrow overnight. We hope you have a chance to read it to him/her. He/she has been doing some interesting things in the classroom today such as ——————————————————————————
>
> ———————————————————————————————————————
>
> Please feel free to write a note on the back of this one and place it in the book for your child to return in the morning, if you want to tell us anything about your child.

You may want to invite parents to a meeting, at which you could show the filmstrip, "Preschool Book Experience" (Mediapak F), to explain about the kinds of books children enjoy based on their interests and needs and to give them ideas for using the books with children. Parents who enjoy reading books to their children might want to come to the classroom at a scheduled time to read the same books to the rest of the class. Parents who have made book puppets or constructed other activities could visit the class to share these with the other children or other parents at a parent meeting.

Newsletter

Dittoed newsletters help keep parents informed about center happenings. Some of the best are compiled weekly or monthly by parent volunteers, who collect information from each classroom, the center nurse, parent workers, and the center director, and have it typed by the office secretary. Other items of interest are the week's menu, favorite recipes from different parents, tips on activities children and parents can do together at home, the words of songs or finger plays the children are learning at the center, games parents can make for a handicapped child, and titles of books children and parents can enjoy together.

The newsletters can be sent home with the children, with a space on each inviting parents to make comments or ask questions—yet another method for two-way communication.

Parent Handbook

The center may want to print its own handbook to give parents when their child enters the program. It may contain information about:

>Goals of the center
>Class schedule
>Transportation schedule
>Holidays
>When the child is sick
>Emergency procedures
>Health information
>What the child should wear
>Lunch and snack
>Parties and treats
>Classroom activities
>Field trips
>How parents can help
>How grandparents or other family members can be involved
>Child's progress
>Visiting the classroom
>Child Involvement Checklist

Ask parents what other information the handbook should contain to make it more helpful to them, and let a parent committee be responsible for putting it together. Things are more meaningful to people if they are involved in creating them.

Face-to-Face Communication

Make it a point to talk to parents at every opportunity. The indirect methods mentioned above should not be a substitute for face-to-face communication. When you talk directly to parents, conduct yourself in a normal pleasant manner. Be yourself. Establish rapport as you would with any new acquaintance. Put the parent at ease. Don't use educational jargon, just talk normally. Accentuate the positive about their child. They already know their child very well and hope you will like him or her. Show that you do.

Communication should be a two-way process. You will not always originate it. Be sure you respond promptly to parents' requests, ideas, or questions as well.

RESPECTS PARENTS' VIEWS WHEN PROGRAM GOALS DIFFER FROM PARENTS' GOALS

We often pay lip service to the notion that the child's parent is his first and most important teacher. How do we respond in the classroom when a parent's goals are different from our own? Do we even bother to find out if this is the case? A truly effective parent-involvement program component is an interactive one. This means we will share with a parent our goals for his or her child, but also that we will listen to the parent's goals.

If we find that the two sets of goals are different, we need to find ways to communicate to parents about why we are doing what we are doing, as well as eliciting the same information from them. Then we need to come to some common understanding or agreement as to how each of us will proceed.

Sometimes the differences focus on behavioral goals. A parent may expect his child to play quietly, to sit still and listen to the teacher, or to keep her clothes clean. The program, on the other hand, may expect the same child to become involved with all the activities—both quiet and boisterous ones—to become independent of the teacher and make her own choices, or not to be so concerned about keeping clean when it is more important to experience the activities available.

Teachers and parents need to talk about these goals and their differences. If parents are unaware that young children learn best by becoming involved in activities, you might want to suggest that they view a filmstrip or read a book such as Alice S. Honig's *Playtime Learning Games for Young Children*. Or they might try using the Child Involvement Checklist (see Chapter 12) and then discussing the results.

On the other hand, if you learn from a parent how important it is that the child keep clean because of the limited clothing resources at home, you will need to find ways to make sure the child's clothing is not damaged.

There are many good, readable child development books to be shared with parents, such as Karen Miller's *Ages and Stages: Developmental Descriptions & Activities Birth Through Eight Years*. If parents read them, you will want to invite them back to talk about what they have found out. In like manner you should try to learn from parents the particular points of view they hold regarding their goals for children. If it is their cultural, ethnic, or religious background that is causing the difference of opinion, you may want to borrow a book from them or the library about their culture or religion.

Educational goals for children are sometimes the focus of home-school differences. Invite parents to training sessions on your program's curriculum or its teaching strategies if this seems appropriate. If parents are more concerned with academic learning than child development, you may want to lend them a book such as

Sydney Clemens's *The Sun's Not Broken, A Cloud's Just in the Way: On Child-Centered Teaching* that discusses both development and learning.

Parents should have the final say. They of course need to realize that your program serves many children and not just theirs, but if their goals and yours are so far apart that a resolution seems doubtful, you may want to help them find another program for their child more in line with their goals.

SUMMARY

Families can be involved in center activities in a variety of ways. They can visit the classroom to assist the staff in daily activities, field trips, or in making of materials. They can share with the children a song, a story, or a cultural practice. They can serve on committees, policy councils, or as a CDA Parent-Community Representative. But usually it is up to the classroom staff to make the initial contact with families and arrange for them to visit or participate. The focus should be on the child and should be a positive one. Parents should be encouraged to volunteer their services in the classroom, but then they need to be assisted and supported by the teacher through discussion, training, and being given specific tasks.

Communication with families should be an ongoing activity with both sides happily involved through phone calls, notes, visits, conferences, and even the use of children's circulating books. Parents' views and goals regarding their children need to be respected by the classroom staff. When differences surface, they need to be addressed by parents and staff members until a resolution is found.

LEARNING ACTIVITIES

1. Read Chapter 11, "Promoting Family Involvement," and answer Question Sheet 11-A.
2. View Mediapak F, "Preschool Book Experience," and answer Question Sheet 11-B.
3. Read one or more of the Suggested Readings or view one or more of the Sound Filmstrips. Add ten cards to your file with specific ideas for helping parents become involved in the preschool classroom. Include a reference source on each card.
4. Communicate with a parent using an idea from this chapter, and record the results.
5. Begin or work on a newsletter or parent handbook. Record your results.
6. Meet one of the parents and help him or her become involved in observing their child in the classroom. Record the results.
7. Arrange an activity to encourage family involvement. Record the results. (The trainer can visit.)

8. Continue your Portfolio of evidence of your skills. Add one piece of evidence for each of the following Teacher Skills Checklist items:
   a. Involves parents in planning and participating in children's program.
   b. Communicates frequently with parents.
   c. Respects parents' views when program goals differ from parents' goals.
   Evidence should reflect what you, not another staff member, have done.
9. Complete the Chapter 11 Evaluation Sheet and return it and the answers to Question Sheets 11-A and 11-B to the appropriate college or program official.

QUESTION SHEET 11-A

(Based on Chapter 11, "Promoting Family Involvement")

1. Why do preschool programs with strong parent involvement have the longest lasting positive effects on children?
2. What are some ways a parent can become involved in a preschool classroom?
3. How can the teacher help get parents involved?
4. Why should you have a staggered entrance process at the beginning of the year?
5. How can you set up home visits without seeming threatening to parents?
6. How can parents' classroom observations of their children become meaningful?
7. How can classroom visitors become involved?
8. How can children's books help you communicate with families?
9. Give an example of a parent's goal for her child that may differ from a program goal for the child. Who is right?
10. What should you do when a parent disagrees with the program's goals for his child?

QUESTION SHEET 11-B

(Based on Mediapak F, "Preschool Book Experience")

1. How early in a child's life should a parent begin reading to the child?
2. What difference does it make whether parents begin at this time?
3. What do parents need to know about children to choose good books for them?
4. What books might appeal to young children on the basis of their self-centeredness?
5. Name several books with fun words and phrases that children enjoy repeating.
6. Since young children like to pretend, what types of books appeal to them?
7. Why do young children respond so well to family stories?
8. Name several books that are short enough to hold your children's attention.
9. What could parents do with books besides read them to their children?
10. If parents wanted to convert book characters to a flannel board activity but cannot draw well, how could they do it?

SUGGESTED EVIDENCE FOR PORTFOLIO

1. Keep a journal of parent conferences or contacts you have had, and explain how this shows your competence in parent involvement.
2. Write about and include photos of a parent activity in your center that you planned or were in charge of.
3. Include a parent observation checklist of a child and explain how you worked with this parent and child to help the child improve in some way. Include any letters from the parent.
4. Include some parent communication form and tell how you used it with a parent or family member.
5. Write about a successful bilingual-bicultural activity you have done in your classroom to promote good home-school relations.

Each piece of evidence should be accompanied by a write-up explaining how this shows your competence in the area of **Families** and how the activity is developmentally appropriate for your children.

SUGGESTED READINGS

Berger, Eugenia Hepworth. *Parents as Partners in Education: The School and Home Working Together*, 2nd ed. Columbus, Ohio: Merrill Publishing Co., 1987

Clemens, Sydney Gurewitz. *The Sun's Not Broken, A Cloud's Just In The Way: On Child-Centered Teaching*. Mt. Rainier, Md.: Gryphon House, 1983.

Endsley, Richard C., and Marilyn R. Bradbard. *Quality Day Care, A Handbook of Choices for Parents and Caregivers*. Englewood Cliffs, N.J.: Prentice-Hall, 1981.

Hewes, Dorothy W., ed. *Administration: Making Programs Work for Children and Families*. Washington, D.C.: National Association for the Education of Young Children, 1979.

Honig, Alice S. *Parent Involvement In Early Childhood Education*. Washington, D.C.: National Association for the Education of Young Children, 1979.

———. *Playtime Learning Games For Young Children*. Syracuse, N.Y.: Syracuse University Press, 1982.

Larrick, Nancy. *A Parent's Guide to Children's Reading*. New York: Bantam, 1982.

Maples, Mary Klein. *Steps to C.D.A. for Home Visitors*. Elmira, N.Y.: McGraw Bookstore, Elmira College, 1985.

Miller, Karen. *Ages And Stages: Developmental Descriptions & Activities Birth Through Eight Years*. Marshfield, Mass.: Telshare Publishing Co., 1985.

Morrison, George S. *Parent Involvement in the Home, School, and Community*. Columbus, Ohio: Merrill Publishing Co., 1978.

Murphy, Albert T. *Special Children, Special Parents*. Englewood Cliffs, N.J.: Prentice-Hall, 1981.

Taylor, Denny, and Dorothy S. Strickland. *Family Storybook Reading*. Portsmouth, N.H.: Heinemann, 1986.

CHILDREN'S BOOKS

DePaola, Tomie. *Watch Out for the Chicken Feet in Your Soup*. Englewood Cliffs, N.J.: Prentice-Hall, 1974.

Gomi, Taro. *Coco Can't Wait*. New York: Viking Penguin, 1985.

Greenfield, Eloise. *First Pink Light*. New York: Scholastic, 1976.

Flourney, Valerie. *The Best Time of Day*. New York: Random House, 1978.

Hines, Anna Grossnickle. *Don't Worry, I'll Find You*. New York: E. P. Dutton, 1986.

Johnston, Tony. *The Quilt Story*. New York: G. P. Putnam's Sons, 1985.

Levinson, Riki. *I Go with My Family to Grandma's*. New York: E. P. Dutton, 1986.

Miles, Betty. *A House for Everyone*. New York: Knopf/Pantheon, 1958.

Ormerod, Jan. *Sunshine*. New York: Lothrop, Lee and Shepard, 1981.

Polushkin, Maria. *Mother, Mother, I Want Another*. New York: Scholastic, 1978.

Udry, Janice May. *Mary Jo's Grandmother*. Chicago: Albert Whitman, 1970.

Walter, Mildred Pitts. *My Mama Needs Me*. New York: Lothrop, Lee & Shepard, 1983.

Wells, Rosemary. *Stanley and Rhoda*. New York: Dial Press, 1978.

SOUND FILMSTRIPS

Beaty, Janice J. "Preschool Book Experience," Mediapak F, *Skills for Preschool Teachers*. Elmira, N.Y.: McGraw Bookstore, Elmira College, 1979.

Introduction for Parents. Ypsilanti, Mich.: High/Scope Foundation.

Observing in the Classroom. Ypsilanti, Mich.: High/Scope Foundation.

Parents. Tuckahoe, N.Y.: Campus Film Distributors.

Parents As Classroom Volunteers. Ypsilanti, Mich.: High/Scope Foundation.

Staying Involved. Ypsilanti, Mich.: High/Scope Foundation.

CHAPTER 11 EVALUATION SHEET
PROMOTING FAMILY INVOLVEMENT

1. Student_____

2. Trainer_____

3. Center where training occurred_____

4. Beginning date_____ Ending date_____

5. Describe what student did to accomplish General Objective

   _____

   _____

6. Describe what student did to accomplish Specific Objectives

   Objective 1_____

   _____

   Objective 2_____

   _____

   Objective 3_____

   _____

7. Evaluation of student's Learning Activities
   (Trainer Check One)   (Student Check One)

   _____ Highly superior performance   _____

   _____ Superior performance   _____

   _____ Good performance   _____

   _____ Less than adequate performance _____

Signature of Trainer: Signature of Student:

_____   _____

Comments:

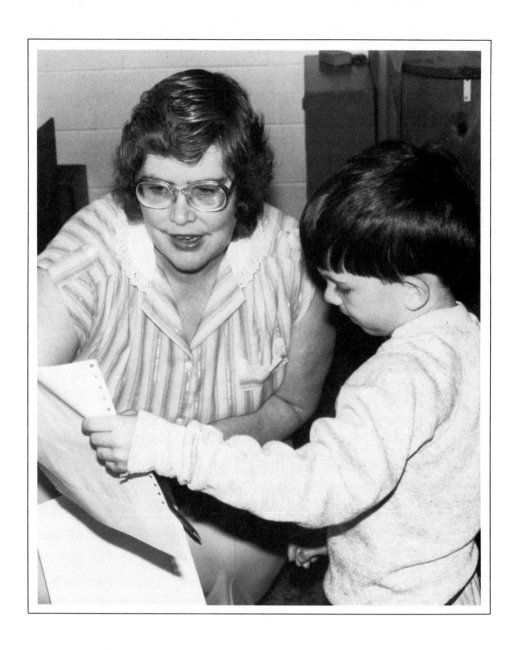

12 Providing Program Management

General Objective

To develop an effective program based on the needs of individuals and groups.

Specific Objectives

- ☐ Uses a team approach to plan a flexible classroom schedule.
- ☐ Uses transitions and small group activities to accomplish the goals of the program.
- ☐ Plans for individual needs based on child observation and interpretation of data obtained.

M anaging any program calls, first of all, for planning on the part of those who will carry it out. The keynote of daily planning in early childhood programs is balance. You need to make plans to accommodate a group of fifteen to twenty lively youngsters, at the same time meeting particular individual needs. Children need time to let off steam as well as periods of quiet relaxation. They need to develop large motor abilities but also the fine skill of eye-hand coordination. They should be exposed to total group doings, but not at the neglect of small group activities. They may be indoors for most of the day, but outdoor needs must still be met. And all activities should flow smoothly from one to the other so the children will feel the satisfying rhythm of a well-planned day.

How do you do it? If you have arranged your classroom according to the ideas in Chapter 3, you have already begun. The physical arrangement of the room already indicates what activities are available and how many children can participate in each.

Then is planning merely a matter of scheduling time? That, of course, is part of it, but it is so much more. First, it is knowing your children, knowing what they are like as a group and how they differ as individuals. It is getting a feeling for how they feel at different times of the day.

Take the first thing in the morning, for instance. Do your children walk to the center or ride? Do they come bursting in from a bus in a mob, or straggling in one by one with mothers in tow? Are they sleepy, cranky, hungry, or happy? What happens during the first half hour in the morning? What would you like to have happen?

Goals

What goals do you have for your entire group of children for a single day? For part of the day? What special goals do you have for individuals?

Your group goal may be something such as helping the children learn to work and play together in harmony, and a goal for a certain part of the day, to improve nap time so that nonsleepers don't disturb sleepers. Your individual goals may be many and varied; for example, helping Trish come out of her shell and respond to the other children and activities around her.

At the moment these are merely ideas. You need to express them concretely to act on and accomplish them. Others on your classroom team need to become aware of them. You need to know what others have in mind. All goals need to be converted into specific plans for the day or the year.

USES A TEAM APPROACH TO PLAN A FLEXIBLE CLASSROOM SCHEDULE

It is essential that everyone on the classroom team be aware of how daily plans are made, when they are made, and who is involved. If you are the teacher, you realize that in order for daily plans to be carried out, everyone on the team must participate. Participation is much more effective if the participants take part in the planning. If you are an aide or volunteer, you realize that the effectiveness of your contribution to the program depends partly on your input in planning the activities you are responsible for.

No one person in an early childhood classroom can or should do everything. Successful management of the program depends as much on staff interpersonal relations and cooperation as on any other single element. Balance is the key here, too, as the entire staff becomes involved in daily planning.

The teacher is, of necessity, the leader, and therefore needs to take the lead in encouraging expression of ideas and concerns of other team members. The head teacher must not dominate nor allow others to dominate. She should ask for suggestions from the others and give them responsibility to carry out activities without interference from her. The assistants, on the other hand, must be willing to offer suggestions and take on responsibility.

Assistants as well as the head teacher should be responsible for observing individual children and recording pertinent information. Assistants should be involved in ordering equipment and supplies. They should attend parent conferences and make home visits. They should be in charge of small groups. Teachers and assistants should both participate in setup and cleanup. This should not be relegated to an assistant while the teacher occupies herself with more "important" activities.

Good interpersonal communication makes teamwork possible. The team recognizes that the leader has overall responsibility, but is willing to work together toward a common goal. Each member trusts and respects the others, so that when things go wrong, team members are able to communicate problems and resolve them in a friendly atmosphere.

Scheduling Planning Sessions

Some staffs spend the last fifteen minutes before they leave for the day to plan for the next day. It is unusual for a staff to schedule an early morning planning period, because they need to set up activities for the day and greet early arrivers. The most frequent time for planning seems to be Friday afternoon, at which time the staff puts together daily plans for a week at a time.

In many programs, planning is more informal. A teacher may say, "We just do not have time to get together as a team, so I make up the ideas for things as I go along. I tell the others what they should do."

This teacher needs to listen to the comments of the "manager" of an especially well-run day care center: "My staff does not have the time either, but we feel so strongly about the importance of planning together that we take the time. We ask a mother to come in once a week and sit with the napping children while we plan, or we arrange for a senior citizen volunteer to come in and read the children a story. We feel that if we do not plan for something to happen, then nothing will happen in our classroom. Since we started team planning, everyone is so much happier. The staff understands their responsibilites so much better. They are much more eager to carry out activities with the children, because they have contributed to the planning. Even the children are happier because of the staff's enthusiasm. We've never accomplished so much with children as we have since we started regular staff planning sessions."

Using Time Blocks

A simple but effective way many programs schedule activities is in the form of *time blocks*. Time blocks are labeled periods of time of unspecified length that occur at approximately the same time every day, but within which there is flexibility for many things to happen. The time blocks used in many programs include:

arrival	lunchtime
work/play period (A.M.)	nap time (P.M.)
playground period (A.M.)	snack time (P.M.)
snack time (A.M.)	work/play period (P.M.)
rest time (A.M.)	circle time (P.M.)
circle time (A.M.)	departure

If yours is a half-day program, your departure would occur, of course, just after circle time (A.M.) or lunchtime.

The length of each time block as well as the order in which you schedule them depends upon your goals, your children's needs, and daily circumstances.

Advantages for using time blocks include, first, flexibility. Although the order of the time blocks remains about the same every day, their length can vary according to circumstances. For example, arrival may usually take about thirty minutes every morning. But occasionally the bus will be late, so arrival time may stretch to forty-five minutes or even an hour. You may decide to omit the work/play period entirely that morning and go immediately into the playground period, because the children have been on the bus so long they need to get out in the open where they can release their pent-up energy.

Another day, you may find the children are just too restless for circle time. What they really need is a run around the playground or outside the building.

In other words, time blocks do not tie you to specific times. Rather, they refer to activities and the order in which they occur. Their flexibility frees you and your staff to plan for a variety of activities within a certain block. It does not lock you into the kind of schedule that dictates: "Snack Time, 10 A.M." All you know about your snack time is that it follows playground period (however long that should last)—

and they might occur simultaneously, if you decide to serve the juice outside on a hot day.

A second advantage of time blocks is their built-in balance. You can easily alternate contrasting kinds of activities simply by the order in which you schedule the particular time blocks.

Just as important is the stability your program acquires through use of time blocks. The same periods tend to occur in about the same order every day. This promotes a sense of security among the children. Young children need some sort of structure that they understand and within which they feel comfortable in order to enjoy a variety of activities.

Finally, time blocks provide a simple system of program management for classroom workers. Part-time volunteers, especially, are much more at ease if they too can readily understand a daily schedule and become comfortable with it.

Let us look at the various time blocks one by one, as we would use them to plan a daily program according to our goals.

Arrival

"Helping the children learn to work and play together in harmony" was one program's daily goal. To accomplish it, the staff first looked at the various time blocks to see if they could identify any elements that were promoting this goal, any that were preventing it from happening, and what changes needed to be made. The teacher, aide, and volunteer began reconstructing the morning arrival period in their minds, realizing how important a good beginning is to the success of the rest of the day.

Their seventeen children came from two separate neighborhoods. About half of them walked to the center or were driven by their parents. The others came by bus from across the river. The arrival period lasted from about 8:30 A.M. to 9:00 or 9:15. The walkers arrived anytime during the first half hour, while the bus children came in a group between 8:55 and 9:15, accompanied by the aide.

The classroom was large, with many activity areas in which the children could become involved until everyone had arrived. The teacher was on hand to greet each child individually, although she found this difficult when all the bus children came swarming in together.

As the staff reviewed the arrival period, they decided the most helpful element was greeting children individually and having a brief conversation. The obvious negative element was the crowd of bus children arriving all at once. What began harmoniously with the walkers soon dissolved into bedlam. The staff decided to try having some individual activities on hand that would separate the crowd as they burst into the room.

Their most successful activity along this line was two-part, involving "tickets and crowns." The "tickets" sorted out the children and the "crowns" made the center a fun place to come to every morning. The staff made a cardboard name "ticket" for each child with the child's picture and name covered with clear contact paper. This was placed in some part of the room, usually on one of the tables, every morning. Each child had to find his ticket and take it to one of the staff members, who presented him with a cutout paper crown to wear, as well as an individual, "Hello, it's nice to see you this morning." The children wanted to repeat this activity every morning until the crowns were in tatters. This, of course, led to making new crowns, with the children participating, making their own hats for "morning hello time": Indian hats, paper soldier hats, and headbands the children colored to look like those that basketball and tennis players wear.

Another teacher resolved her morning mass arrival "woes" by taking a photograph of each child, fastening a tab hook at the top, covering the picture with clear contact paper, and hanging it on a pegboard. When the child arrived, he found the photo and took it to the "Job for the Day" chart, where he hung it under the labeled picture of the job he wanted for the day. Jobs included mail deliverer, secretary, zoo keeper, bookkeeper, garbage collector, delivery person, nurse, doctor, teacher, laundry person, grocer, telephone repair person, shoe clerk, barber, beautician, and so forth. These were all jobs the children had become familiar with through field trips and classroom visitors. New jobs were added to the chart from time to time, and old ones removed.

After the child selected a job, he went to the teacher, aide, or volunteer, who then bestowed the morning greeting and told the child what chore needed to be done. Zoo keeper might mean feeding the guinea pig or weighing the rabbit. Mail deliverer might mean taking a letter down the hall to the director's office. Bookkeeper might mean counting all the children (with help) and recording the number in the teacher's record book. The children loved the "Job for the Day" idea and kept the staff jumping to come up with new ideas for chores.

Occasionally, an arrival time block can be disrupted by children with particular needs that are not always obvious at the outset. Robert, for instance, frequently acted cross and belligerent when he entered the classroom in the morning, pushing and hitting anyone near him. Later on he would settle down and act friendly.

The staff discussed various possibilities. Did he stay up too late at night? Did something happen at home to get him off to a bad start? Was he a child who always had trouble getting himself together early in the morning? Talking with the mother shed no light on the behavior. He seemed to be all right at home.

Then, one day a box of crackers was left overnight on a table near the children's cubbies. Next morning, Robert made a beeline for the box, stuffing his mouth full. He soon settled down. He had simply been hungry. The teacher discovered he seldom ate breakfast before he came to the center. After that, she put out crackers and juice on a table in one corner for anyone who wanted a snack early. Some programs, of course, serve breakfast to everyone.

Sometimes, arrival problems occur only at certain times of the year. The first days and weeks of September are often a difficult time for youngsters (and their parents) who have never been separated before. Separation anxiety means tears and troubles in many preschool classrooms. Classroom staffs who are aware of this possibility can often avoid it in several ways. They may invite parents to stay in the classroom for a number of mornings until their children become involved with other children and activities. They may encourage new children to bring a toy from home, such as a car or doll, to make them feel more secure. These so-called clutchers often work like security blankets in helping children bridge the awesome gap between their comfortable homes and the completely new world of the early childhood center.

There are other ways the classroom staff can help bridge the gap. They can visit the children's homes during the weeks before school starts and get acquainted with the children, so they will not feel they are being left with strangers. They can arrange for "staggered admissions" during the first days, so that all the youngsters do not enter on the same day or at the same time, as discussed in Chapter 11. This gives the staff a chance to help a few children at a time become used to their new environment, and gives children an opportunity to become acquainted with a new world without being overwhelmed by all its inhabitants at once.

Some teachers use books to make the connection between home and center, as discussed in Chapter 11. They purchase a number of good paperback picture books to lend to the children. All are encouraged to take a book home at the end of the day for their parents to read to them, and bring back the next day. The morning activity of "book check in" with the teacher or aide is another individualized ritual the children soon catch on to, and become eager participants in. Because they can't take another book until they return the first one, most children remember to bring their books. For variety, small toys can be substituted for books if you have a large enough collection.

Once you assess your arrival time's strengths and weaknesses in light of daily goals, you should be able to institute changes that will make your center an exciting place to enter every day of the year.

Work/Play Period (A.M.)

Many programs schedule a work/play period immediately after arrival. This is a natural follow-up because so many of the children are already involved in block building, dramatic play, making puzzles, and the other permanent activities. It is different from arrival time free play only in the expanded activities available. Each classroom staff member is usually responsible for a different planned activity such as a table of dough, rolling pins, and cookie cutters; a table of yarn and uncooked macaroni for stringing necklaces; a portable climber and mats for jumping; a table of vegetable scrapers, carrots, celery, mayonnaise, and ketchup for making dips for snacks; a table of torn paper, buttons, paper clips, and glue for collages; story reading for a small group; or any one of a hundred other special activities the adult staff may set up for the children.

In light of the goal "helping children learn to work and play together in harmony," the staff needs to identify elements in the work/play period that promote this goal and those that prevent its accomplishment.

You may decide your work/play period's most important strength is the number of good activities available daily, while its principal weakness lies in getting the children involved in favorite ones without a fuss. In other words, too many children may insist on participating in the favorite activity at the same time, making it difficult for you to manage.

First, you need to know which are the favorite activities. The staff may agree that on the days they put out the water table, everyone wants to use it at once. They also dread setting up a cooking activity because of the difficulty with children not being able to wait their turns. One solution may be to have two or more of the same favorites going at one time. You might try different cooking experiences at separate tables with four chairs for each. The same can be done with water play. Use your regular water table for one, and bring in plastic dish pans or washtubs for the others, and regulate the number of children by the chairs you set up in each area.

It is no more difficult for a staff to set up three of the same activity than three different ones, but it seldom seems to happen. It is really an excellent way to extend learning experiences. One water activity could be to explore which things float and which sink; another could be to dissolve different food colors and pour the water through funnels into plastic bottles. A third activity might be to put detergent in a dishpan and whip it into suds with an eggbeater. If you set up for four children, don't forget you'll need four eggbeaters.

Children's movement from one activity to another within this same work/play period can be accomplished smoothly by the children themselves in a number of ways: (1) when one child leaves his chair another can take it; (2) you can give out color-coded tickets for each activity which the children can trade when ready; or (3) four hooks, card pockets, or pegs can be fastened in each area for children to hang name tags on; when a hook is empty another child may hang his tag on it to join in. Children can easily regulate themselves this way while teachers are busy supporting individuals with special needs. If no one wants to change, it is a sign you have truly succeeded in your planning. You may want to set up these same activities for several days running until all have had their fill, before going on to three cooking activities, or whatever.

How long should the work/play period last? It may vary from day to day, depending on the children's involvement or restlessness. If children are working and playing in harmony and contentment, it may last most of the morning. You and your staff must decide daily.

Playground Period (A.M.)

Scheduling this time block depends primarily on the children and their circumstances. Are they city children who seldom get a chance to play outside? Do they come every day from long distances on a bus? If so, you may want to schedule a playground period after arrival. This gives bus children a chance to let off steam, and restless children an opportunity to expend their energy in a positive way. Some teachers like to schedule playground period first because the children already have on their outside clothing, making it easier and less time consuming for the dressing-undressing ritual.

Snack Time (A.M./P.M.)

Snacks in the early childhood classroom may be a group or individual activity, depending on the feelings of teacher, staff, and children. Most programs have snacks as a total group experience some time in the middle of the morning. Many teachers feel young children need the nourishment and that it is good to come together at some point after working individually or in small groups. Others believe the children themselves should determine when to snack and how much snack they need. Instead of setting up tables for a total group snack, they keep a "snack bar" going on a single table for much of the morning, encouraging children to use it whenever and as much as they want. Their rationale is often a reluctance to pull children away from activities they are enjoying.

If the work/play period has been a long one, many programs schedule snack time before playground so it will not interfere with lunch. Others prefer that the children have their nourishment after a hardy physical workout. You must make your own decision after evaluating your program's circumstances.

The same considerations apply to afternoon snack time. If the children take a long nap, 1:00 to 3:00 P.M. for example, you may want to have a snack ready for them as they awaken. It gives them a chance to become reoriented to their surroundings after a deep sleep.

Whatever you do, you would be wise to involve the children. Not only do they enjoy participating in the setup and cleanup of snack time, but they also enjoy counting and sorting cups and napkins and pouring juice or milk.

Rest Time (A.M.)

The decision to have a rest time in the morning depends upon how early the children arrive and how active they are during the morning. Some programs have a quiet time just after juice, when lights are turned off and the children put their heads down on the tables. Do your children need this? They may if they have been outside playing for a half hour or more. Without a physical workout, however, rest period can be a waste. If the teacher or aide must spend the whole rest period trying to make the children rest, it hardly seems they need it. What they may need, instead, is a quick run around the outside of the building to burn up energy. You may want to decide daily about resting according to the circumstances.

Some programs choose to have a mat time, instead, just after the most active time block. Rather than put their heads down, the children sit quietly on single rugs or mats they themselves place somewhere in the room while they read a book, work on a puzzle, or play with a toy by themselves. Books and toys for mat time are often kept on a special shelf, box, or tray, and brought out especially for this period.

Circle Time (A.M./P.M.)

Sometime during the day, most programs schedule a total group time. It may be at the beginning of the day during arrival, when the children gather on a rug in the book corner to tell the teachers what has been going on in their lives since they were last together. This is the opportunity for the teacher to let the children know about any new activities or people they will be encountering that day, a time to discuss birthdays, talk about current events, or sing a favorite song.

Half-day programs sometimes schedule circle time just before lunch or just before the children leave. Other full-day programs schedule theirs at the conclusion of the day in the afternoon. The purpose for both is to pull together the daily happenings and help the children make sense of them. "What did you do this morning, Karen, that you liked best of all?" If teachers and aides listen carefully to children's answers, they can gain valuable insights about the activities that made the greatest or least impression on the children and why.

For programs that like to conduct music or story reading in a total group situation, this may be the appropriate time. Parents or special visitors can be invited to take part. Guitar players or storytellers might put in an appearance, or the teacher might demonstrate a new toy, or introduce a game or a puppet character who wants to talk with the children.

Circle time tends to be shorter than some other time blocks because of preschool children's short attention span and restlessness in large group situations. Aides and volunteers can act as "listening models" for the children around them, when they're not taking a turn as leader; in other words, they will model the behavior of a good listener for children to imitate.

Lunchtime

Does your lunchtime arrangement fulfill the daily goal of "helping children learn to work and play together in harmony"? What are its strong points? Its weaknesses? Most programs consider eating together family style in the classroom one of the most beneficial aspects of lunchtime. Teachers, aides, volunteers, and visitors sit at the tables with the children, sharing the food and conversation. It is a time of enjoyment and relaxation.

Most children love to eat, and even reluctant eaters find it hard to resist when everyone around them is so totally involved. The wise classroom staff keeps rules to a minimum, discourages nagging and pressure, and promotes a happy atmosphere at the table. Dessert is a nutritious part of the meal, not a reward or bribe to "clean up your plate."

Children feel good when adults sit next to them at the table and eat the same food they do. They feel even better when adults converse with them as equals. Fascinating information about children's understandings of themselves and their world comes out of lunchtime conversations.

Early childhood programs housed in public schools are sometimes required to use the school cafeteria. Their staffs should be aware of some of the difficulties of this situation. A noisy cafeteria full of older youngsters presents an intimidating atmosphere for three- and four-year-olds, not at all conducive to relaxed eating. If the children must go through the regular cafeteria line, they are often given portions much too large for them to handle and, as a result, end up eating very little. Furthermore, the time pressure to finish up and move out quickly achieves the opposite result with young children. Some programs in these circumstances have been able to arrange with the cafeteria staff to have the food sent to their rooms for family-style eating. School officials usually cooperate, once they are made aware of the situation.

Nap Time (A.M.)

Another of our goals for a particular part of the day concerned "improving nap time so nonsleepers don't disturb sleepers."

If yours is an all-day program, you will need to schedule a nap period in the afternoon after lunch. Not all the children must be forced to take a nap—some three- and four-year-olds can hardly function without an afternoon nap; others have outgrown it. For the latter, lying quietly for an hour or two in the same room with the sleepers is nearly impossible. Some provision needs to be made for them.

If your center has more than one early childhood classroom, you may be able to arrange to use one as the sleeping room and the other for nonsleepers. Depending on the number of nonsleepers, at least one adult should supervise this area. The focus, even for nonsleepers, should be on quiet activities, with other portions of the room sectioned off.

If you have only one room, you can reserve a section for nonsleepers where they can play quietly without disturbing the sleepers. Perhaps the block corner can serve this purpose, if it is well sectioned off. You may want the children to use small toys or books rather than blocks, because of the noise. Have a box, tray, or special shelf available to children in this area. If you talk in a low voice or whisper, you will soon find the children imitating you.

Individual mats serve the same purpose as during mat time: keeping children apart from one another while they involve themselves in quiet activities. Other classroom workers prefer to read a quiet story or two to the nonsleepers in the book corner. If you have no other means of separating sleepers from nonsleepers, cut apart a large cardboard packing carton and unfold it for a divider.

How do you get children to go to sleep successfully? Some are ready without any effort on your part, while others need help. Dimming the lights or pulling the shades is a signal many respond to. If you have no shades, use pieces of cardboard to block the windows. A drowsy song on the record player may help. Your reading a story in a low, monotonous voice adds its effect.

Some children are afraid to let themselves fall asleep in a place other than their bedroom. They may need individual reassurance, such as a gentle rub on the back.

Work/Play Period (P.M.)

How much time is available in your program between wake up from nap time until departure? A half hour? An hour? Some activities should be available to children during this late afternoon time block. Most programs rely on their regular room setups, but some insist that children not get out all the blocks or dress-up clothes. These regulations tend to be more for the adult's convenience than the children's. This is justifiable as long as there are other substitute activities the children can become involved in.

A table with a different kind of painting from that available in the morning may be the answer, or a table of different puzzles or manipulative games. If you have not used your water or sand table in the morning, this can be an excellent time for it.

Week: October 10
Goal: Better harmony in children's work/play

Theme: Animal pets
Follow up: Apples (last week's theme)

	Monday	*Tuesday*
Arrival	*Betty:* headbands with animal ears for "check-in" *Pat:* large motor at loft *Karen:* help at cubbies	*Betty:* check in books *Pat:* large motor at loft *Karen:* help at cubbies
Work/Play Table 1 Table 2	(no water table today) *Pat:* cooking—cut apples from field trip; make applesauce *Karen:* collage—from torn paper	*Pat:* sand table with animal toys *Betty:* art—coloring with crayons on sandpaper animals *Karen:* sorting squares of materials into boxes
Snack	Cut apples from cooking Milk, crackers	Apple cider and doughnuts
Playground	*Pat:* outside with children *Betty:* checklist observation of Trish	*Karen:* outside with children *Betty:* checklist
Circle	*Karen:* on top of loft with box of kittens from home	*Betty:* under loft with guitar and songs about animals
Lunch	applesauce from cooking for dessert	Cal's birthday cupcakes
Nap	*Karen:* on loft; read *Pet Show, Curious George* to nonsleepers	*Karen:* on loft; read *Harry, the Dirty Dog,* more *Curious George*
Work/Play Table 1 Table 2	*Betty:* checklist Snack *Pat:* magazines; cut out animal pictures	*Betty:* turtle and books on science table Snack *Karen:* sand table
Departure	*Betty:* check out books	*Betty:* check out books
Special Needs	Trish needs support	Trish needs support
Remember	Bring sand, sandpaper, cupcakes	Check on lunches for field trip to animal shelter

You can make this time block convenient for you yet enticing for the children if you and your staff use your imaginations and plan carefully.

Some programs prefer to take their children out on the playground for this time block. Not only do the children have the additional opportunity to exercise large muscles but they are also already dressed and ready to go home. Others prefer quieter activities, such as reading stories to individuals or small groups, or putting out special paperback books for children to look at on their own and later take home.

Departure

A good ending is as essential as a good beginning. Children need to feel satisfied about the day they have just finished in order to look forward with pleasure to the next. The staff should be on hand to help the children prepare to go home. Helping children dress and supporting them in their own efforts, conversing about what they have done during the day, checking out a book or a toy, greeting parents who pick up their children, saying a final farewell and a "See you tomorrow"—these should be pleasurable activities for all involved. If you have planned well, they signal the end of a happy, satisfying day.

Recording Daily Schedule

You need to write down your daily plans, not as an exercise to please an administrator, but for you and your staff to use: to keep you on target, to help you remember what you planned to do, to help staff members keep track of their own roles.

For programs that have a room arrangement similar to the plan in Chapter 3, a time-block schedule might look like the one on page 261. In such a room, available activities for the morning work/play period would include blocks, dramatic play, books, manipulative, woodworking, art, and sand/water play. The three staff members are Betty, the teacher, Karen, the aide, and Pat, the volunteer. The tables referred to are those in the art and manipulative areas, theme refers to the curriculum idea the staff intends to cover during the week, end checklist refers to an individual assessment and planning tool we will discuss later.

This schedule shows two days of the week as planned by the staff the preceding Friday afternoon.

USES TRANSITIONS AND SMALL GROUP ACTIVITIES TO ACCOMPLISH THE GOALS OF THE PROGRAM

Management also involves helping children move from one activity to another with ease. Ordering young children around does not work, nor should it. If we allow the children to choose their own small group activity, we need to get them involved in changing from one activity to the next as well. Transition games, songs, and stories allow this to happen. Every preschool teacher needs a repertoire of such activities to use when she wants the children to move from free play to pickup, from playtime to juice or lunch, or to get ready to go outside.

Transitional Activities

Transitional activities might include any of the following, some of which can be made up on the spot and others learned from books. Every preschool teacher should collect a card file of them:

> Name games
> Concept games
> Songs
> Finger plays
> Body action chants
> Stories
> Pickup games
> Follow-the-leader

Name Games

Name games are always popular with children because they love anything that focuses attention on them. While children are waiting for lunch to begin, to go outside, or for the bus to come, the teacher can start a name game. One is "Do What the Rhyme Says," in which the teacher says a rhyme about a child's name, telling him to perform an action. First the named child does it, then everyone does it. For example:

> Billy, Billy,
> Dressed in blue,
> See if you can
> Touch your shoe.
>
> Chris, Chris,
> Dressed in brown,
> See if you can,
> Turn around.

> Sheila, Sheila,
> With long hair,
> Raise your hand
> High in the air.
>
> Larry, Larry,
> Act like a clown,
> Jump very quickly
> Up and down.

If the named child doesn't respond, name another child and mention the same action. Make three-by-five cards with enough rhymes for everyone in your class.

Concept Games

Concept games also involve individual children. Teachers use them to send one child at a time to the next activity, which helps spur the others to get ready for that activity. For instance:

> The boy with the red shirt
> May go to lunch.
>
> The girl with the blue dress
> May get on the bus.

The children who can hold up three fingers
May take a seat.

The children who can make a triangle with their fingers
May sit down for juice.

Transition Songs

Presumably you are using songs throughout the day, not just during music period. While the children stand in line or in a group waiting for something to begin, a song makes an excellent transition. You can make up one about what will happen next, or use any of the children's favorites.

Here we stand
In a line,
Waiting for
The sun to shine
With a clap, clap,
Stamp, stamp,

Throw the dog a bone,
Soon we will be going home.
Here we stand
Getting numb,
Waiting for
The bus to come . . . (Tune: "This Old Man")

Finger Plays

You will also want in invest in a song book and finger play book to give you more ideas. Tom Glazer's *Eye Winker Tom Tinker Chin Chopper* features musical finger plays with guitar chords and finger directions. Old favorites include "The Wheels on the Bus," "Bingo," "On Top of Spaghetti," "This Old Man," and "Where is Thumbkin?" Finger plays without music are featured in the excellent book *Finger Frolics*, or, you can make up your own:

Caterpillar

Crawl, crawl, caterpillar,
Munch, munch, munch;
Chew, chew, caterpillar,
What's for lunch?
Spin, spin, caterpillar,
Sway, sway, sway,
Stretch, stretch, butterfly,
Fly away!

(fingers crawl in air)
(fingers chew like mouth)

(turn over hands in question)
(hands make winding motion)
(hands sway)
(arms over head)
(arms flap)

Body action chants are finger plays done in place with the whole body. Again, you can make up your own to suit the occasion.

Lunch time

Lunch time,
Munch time,
Can you wait?

(Jump up and down)

Brunch time,
Crunch time,
Don't be late!   (Shake head)

Here's your table,
Take a seat,   (Squat down)
Clap your hands,
It's time to eat!   (Jump up and clap)

Stories

While you wait for the children to assemble, you might consider telling a story as a transitional activity to those who have already gathered around you. It is sure to speed up the others. You could start with a spooky "tale without an end" done in a deep whisper:

> It was a dark and stormy night. Three robbers sat around the fire. The captain said, "Shorty, tell us a story," So Shorty began: "It was a dark and stormy night. . . . "

It's fun to make up stories as you go along. Start with a sentence like: "On my way to school this morning I was walking along the street when all of a sudden, what do you think I saw?" You can make up strange, funny, or exciting happenings, or let each child add his or her own idea to the story. If you can't think of something to say, describe the things you really saw that morning, but have them all moving backwards, or upside down, or flying.

Pickup Games

Pickup games are the best way to involve children in picking up blocks, toys on the floor, clothes in the housekeeping corner, etc. No one needs to be scolded about not helping with pickup when you do it as a game. In the block corner, you can pretend a large block is a bulldozer that shoves all the other blocks over to the shelves. The block shelves can be a hungry monster that must be fed with blocks. Or, you can start an assembly line of children across the room to the shelves and pass the blocks from one to the other until the floor is cleared.

There are many other pickup activities. Put on a favorite record and see if the children can finish before the music stops. Have the children pretend to be dump trucks or creatures from outer space who like to eat toys. Use your imagination to make cleanup seem like a game.

Follow-the-Leader Games

Follow-the-leader games can also help with pickup. Have the children follow you around the room, picking up as they weave in and out, putting toys in their proper places. This activity is a great way to gather up children on the playground when it is time to go in, too.

Transitions from one activity to the next will never be difficult in your classroom if you use some of these ideas.

Importance of Small Groups

Because our primary concern in the preschool classroom is for the individual child, we need to structure the organization in groups of a size that will not overpower a child. The total group of fifteen or more is too large for children three to five years old. These highly self-centered beings with their demands for exclusive attention are really lost in a group of that size. As a result, they often resort to negative attention-getting devices, or they withdraw.

To help them learn the social skills of taking turns and waiting their turns discussed in Chapter 9, the group size needs to be small enough so they do not have to wait an inordinate amount of time. Individual needs can also be accommodated much more easily in a small group.

In addition, the role of the adult in managing the class becomes easier when small groups rather than the total group are involved. Because preschool classrooms have at least two and possibly three or more adults, one person can easily be in charge of each of the groups.

Number of Groups

How many groups should you have? That will depend upon your particular circumstances. An ideal size is four or five children to a group, so you may decide to have three or possibly four groups. If you want an adult in charge of each, the number of classroom staff will have a bearing as well. So does the amount of space. Three groups may fit well into your classroom size, but four may be too many.

Size of Groups

Each group need not be the same size as the others. Groups can be formed for a variety of reasons, and should not be considered permanent. You may have room for six children to work in a cooking activity one day, while three work with play dough, and five in the block corner. At another time, you may take five children on a field trip to the store, while your staff stays behind with two groups of five each.

Forming Groups

How are the groups formed? If we sincerely want children to become self-confident and self-directed in their learning, we should allow them to choose the group they prefer. This can be done in various ways. Your room can be set up with a certain number of chairs at a table where puzzles or play dough are used. You can use a symbol such as a stick figure for the number of children each activity area can accommodate. You might have four stick figures pasted in the block area, the book corner, and at the water table, for example. This not only means that children can choose their own groups, but also that they can change when they wish. This self-regulation adds another steppingstone to the path of independence your children are building for themselves.

A slightly more structured method for choosing groups, as previously mentioned, involves name tags. Each child finds his own tag when he arrives and hangs it on a hook in the activity area where he wishes to go. The number of hooks in each area regulates the number of children in the groups. Children can move to another group if they can find someone to exchange hooks with them.

Teacher's Role

The classroom team not only sets up the areas ahead of time, but also decides who will be in charge of each activity, if they feel this is necessary. This does not mean a teacher should hover over children at the water table during the entire play period; instead, an adult should play an active role where necessary and act as an observer or supporter at other times.

For instance, one teacher might read a book to a small group in the book area. Another might supervise a cooking activity, while a third observes or helps a shy child become involved in dramatic play. On another day, all the activity groups might operate on their own while staff members work with individuals who need help or support. Someone could work on a one-to-one basis with a bilingual child who needs help learning words in a second language, or help a physically handicapped child with a small motor game. Another teacher might keep track of overall supervision to make sure the children's self-regulation is working and assist if things get out of hand.

Total Group

Is there no place for a total group activity within the daily schedule? Not necessarily. Many teachers find it valuable to have the total group together in a "circle time" when they first come in or just before they leave. As mentioned earlier, children have a chance to talk about things that interest them, listen to others, hear what activities are planned for the day, or summarize some of the things they have learned that day.

PLANS FOR INDIVIDUAL NEEDS BASED ON CHILD OBSERVATION AND THE INTERPRETATION OF DATA OBTAINED

The program we are talking about had as one of its individual goals, "Helping Trish to come out of her shell and respond to the other children and the activities around her." Many programs have a Trish, or someone like her, who needs individual assistance. To help such children, it is first necessary to find out more about them. Is Trish always withdrawn, or only at certain times? Does she respond to any of the children? Which ones? Any staff? Does she get involved in any activities? Which ones? When?

To find the answers, someone on the staff must step back unobtrusively and observe the child, giving special attention to the identified needs.

Someone on the staff needs to step back and observe a child, giving special attention to identified needs.

Some programs use a checklist to focus on particular behavior. The Child Involvement Checklist is arranged according to the activity areas found in most early childhood programs. The items are stated in positive terms. The observer checks any item she sees, and places an ''N'' before any item for which there is no opportunity to observe. The blanks thus indicate areas of possible need.

Child involvement checklist

Child's Name _Trish B._

Time _9-10, 11:30-12:30, 2-3_ Date _10/10-10/13_

Observer _Betty_

(Check items you see the child performing. Use "N" for "no opportunity to observe.")

1. Child in classroom
   _____ Chooses activity area without a fuss
   _____ Stays with one activity long enough to complete it
   _____ Changes from one activity to another without a fuss
   _____ Plays with other children peacefully
   __✔__ Handles bathroom routine by himself/herself
   _____ Retreats to private area only infrequently
2. Child in block building area
   _____ Carries blocks, fills and dumps, doesn't build
   _____ Builds in flat rows on floor or stacks vertically
   _____ Makes "bridges" (two blocks with space between connected by third block)
   _____ Makes "enclosures" (at least four blocks enclosing a space)
   _____ Makes representations, names buildings, role plays
   _____ Builds in solitary manner
   _____ Builds parallel to other child(ren)
   _____ Builds cooperatively with other child(ren)
   _____ Follows block building rules/limits without a fuss
3. Child in book area
   __✔__ Shows interest in the pictures in a book
   _____ Talks about the pictures
   _____ Pretends to read
   __✔__ Recognizes some words at sight
   __✔__ Handles books carefully
   _____ Asks adults to read to him/her
   _____ Uses books in dramatic play
4. Child in dramatic play area
   _____ Plays a role (pretends to be someone else)
   __✔__ Makes believe in regard to objects (pretends about a thing)
   _____ Makes believe in regard to situations and actions (pretends to do something or go somewhere)

_____ Stays with role for at least ten minutes

_____ Interacts with others in his/her role

_____ Uses verbal communication during the role play

5. Child in large motor area

__N__ Balances on a board

__✓__ Goes up and down steps easily

__✓__ Runs without falling

__✓__ Climbs easily

__✓__ Gets down from high places easily

__✓__ Jumps with both feet over an object

__✓__ Rides wheeled equipment with ease

__N__ Throws a ball/bean bag

__N__ Catches a ball/bean bag

6. Child in manipulative area

__✓__ Stacks objects with ease

__N__ Fastens and unfastens buttons

__N__ Fastens and unfastens zippers

__N__ Threads objects on a string

__N__ Laces shoes or a lacing frame

__✓__ Makes puzzles easily

__✓__ Traces around an object

__✓__ Crayons inside a space fairly well

__✓__ Stays with activity until finished

7. Child in art area

__✓__ Handles materials without adult help

__✓__ Paints with brushes

__N__ Does fingerpainting

__N__ Plays with dough/clay

__N__ Cuts well with scissors

__N__ Uses paste or glue appropriately

__N__ Mixes colors with understanding

__N__ Uses materials creatively

8. Child in music area

_____ Plays record player without adult help

_____ Sings songs by himself/herself

_____ Sings songs with others

__N__ Participates in movement activities

__N__ Plays rhythm instrument

_____ Shows enjoyment of musical activities

9. Child in science/math area

_____ Explores materials in area

_____ Asks questions about materials

__N__ Brings in new materials for area

_____ Uses senses to examine things

_____ Counts materials accurately up to _____

_____ Sorts materials accurately by size, shape, color

_____ Shows understanding of likeness and difference

_**N**_ Participates in recording/record keeping

_____ Takes care of classroom plants, animals

10. Child in sand/water area

_____ Becomes absorbed in sand/water play

_____ Respects established rules or limits

_____ Helps regulate number of children playing

_____ Can share or take turns with materials without too much fuss

_____ Uses sand/water in imaginative ways

_____ Talks about what he/she is doing

11. Child in woodworking area

_____ Handles tools with confidence

_____ Pounds in nails

_____ Saws wood

_____ Makes things out of wood

_____ Uses vise without help

_____ Respects rules or limits

12. Child in cooking area

_**N**_ Peels or slices fruit or vegetables with knife

_**N**_ Uses utensils with minimum adult help

_**N**_ Uses names of utensils and foods

_**N**_ Understands recipe chart

_**N**_ Talks with others about what he/she is doing

13. Child in outdoor playground

_✔_ Uses swings without adult help

_✔_ Uses slides with confidence

_✔_ Climbs to top of monkey bars

_✔_ Gets down from high places without help

_✔_ Runs without falling

_____ Participates with others in play

14. Child's health condition

_✔_ Has good attendance

_✔_ Is seldom ill

_✔_ Looks generally healthy

_✔_ Seldom complains about feeling sick

_✔_ Goes to sleep at nap time

_✔_ Eats most of lunch

_✔_ Does not get tired easily

15. Child's visual and auditory skills

_____ Makes comments or notices new pictures or materials

_✔_ Recognizes his/her written name

_____ Plays lotto or visual matching games easily

_____ Matches things of similar color

_____ Matches things of similar shape

_____ Identifies sounds in sound games

_✔_ Listens to directions

_✔_ Listens to stories

16. Child's communication skills

_____ Talks with adults

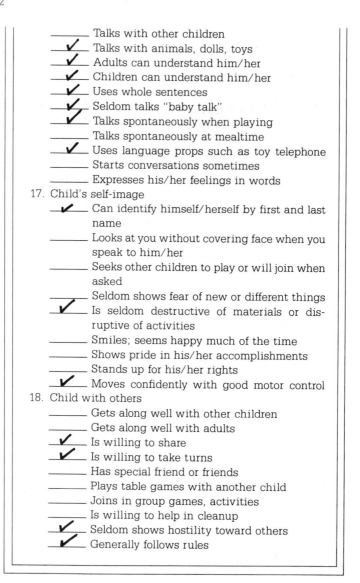

_____ Talks with other children
___✔___ Talks with animals, dolls, toys
___✔___ Adults can understand him/her
___✔___ Children can understand him/her
___✔___ Uses whole sentences
___✔___ Seldom talks "baby talk"
___✔___ Talks spontaneously when playing
_____ Talks spontaneously at mealtime
___✔___ Uses language props such as toy telephone
_____ Starts conversations sometimes
_____ Expresses his/her feelings in words

17. Child's self-image
    ___✔___ Can identify himself/herself by first and last name
    _____ Looks at you without covering face when you speak to him/her
    _____ Seeks other children to play or will join when asked
    _____ Seldom shows fear of new or different things
    ___✔___ Is seldom destructive of materials or disruptive of activities
    _____ Smiles; seems happy much of the time
    _____ Shows pride in his/her accomplishments
    _____ Stands up for his/her rights
    ___✔___ Moves confidently with good motor control

18. Child with others
    _____ Gets along well with other children
    _____ Gets along well with adults
    ___✔___ Is willing to share
    ___✔___ Is willing to take turns
    _____ Has special friend or friends
    _____ Plays table games with another child
    _____ Joins in group games, activities
    _____ Is willing to help in cleanup
    ___✔___ Seldom shows hostility toward others
    ___✔___ Generally follows rules

Betty, the teacher in the program described earlier, scheduled time in her daily activities to observe Trish. Using the preceding checklist over a period of several days, she recorded the results.

Using Information from the Observation

As she reviewed the results. Betty was surprised to realize how much better Trish seemed to get along on the playground than in the classroom. She decided to concentrate on Trish's strong points to help her overcome what seemed to be a lack of confidence, a shyness, or the fact that she was still not at ease inside the classroom.

The staff considered several alternatives, and finally decided on the activities listed on the Learning Prescription that follows.

Since Trish showed confidence on the climber, they felt she might be able to help Helen, a newcomer, learn how to use it. They also decided to let her take some of the dramatic play materials outside, where she seemed to feel more comfortable. They hoped she might let some of the other children get involved in her play with the dolls or the phones, which might lead her to play with the others inside in the dramatic play corner. Because Trish talked well with dolls, Betty thought she might feel comfortable talking to someone else through a puppet. Perhaps Trish could tell Helen a story through one of the puppets.

These ideas were also recorded under "special needs" on the daily schedule, so they would not be forgotten. At the next planning session, the staff could de-

---

Learning Prescription for _Trish B._ Date _Oct. 14_

Areas of Strength and Confidence

1. _Large motor activities (especially outside)_
2. _Language (talks mostly to inanimate objects)_
3. _Seems to like books, some art, some manipulative_

Areas Needing Strengthening

1. _Involvement with other children_
2. _Self-image_
3. _Involvement in classroom activities_

Activities to Help

1. _Ask Trish to help Helen on climber_
2. _Give Trish dolls and telephone to take outside_
3. _Give Trish puppets. Could one of her puppets tell Helen a story?_

cide how successful they had been and whether to continue to expand activities. In this way, individual needs can be incorporated into daily plans for the total group.

The final step is to apply the results of the interpretation by setting up a special activity to help the child, giving him special support, making a particular effort, or whatever is called for. Remember that the child needing help should not be singled out from the others. Rather, the activity you set up can be used for all of the children with special benefits for particular individuals, as discussed previously.

If this process seems too complex and time-consuming, remember that you are only looking at one child at a time, and that this is the kind of information you need to be able to help that child. Start by observing children with special needs. Later as you involve them in activities to improve their skills, you can begin to observe the other children, one at a time, as well.

Don't forget, though, that the raw data (e.g., checklist results, running records) should not be shared with anyone other than the classroom team. It is the interpretation you have recorded that should be used for your planning and can be shared with others such as parents.

Almost every person who has taken time to observe and record in this manner has been pleasantly surprised about how many new things they learned about a child they thought they already knew. You need to step back from the ordinary classroom activities in order to see with the clear eye of the observer. It is truly worth your while.

SUMMARY

In developing a professional program based on the needs of individuals and groups, you should assess the needs of individual children by using a focused observing and recording technique such as the Child Involvement Checklist. Then you and your staff will need to interpret the results (the raw data) and from your interpretation make an individual educational plan. This plan can be incorporated into your weekly plans for your entire class, so that the child will not feel singled out and embarrassed by your attention.

In making plans for your program, you and your staff will also need to keep in mind the goals you have set both for the group and individuals. Daily goals can be carried out by a program that uses time blocks, since these flexible periods can accommodate activities of varying lengths for individuals as well as a more stable schedule for the entire class. Moving children through a daily schedule works more effectively when you use transitional activities in between time blocks.

All members of your classroom team, including volunteers, should be involved in the planning process. Then they will be more committed and willing to carry out the plans.

LEARNING ACTIVITIES

1. Read Chapter 12, "Providing Program Management," and answer Question Sheet 12-A.
2. View Mediapak B, "Managing the Daily Program," and answer Question Sheet 12-B.
3. Read one or more of the Suggested Readings or view one or more of the Sound Filmstrips. Add ten cards to your file with specific ideas for managing your program more effectively. Include a reference source on each card.
4. Participate in a team planning session to discuss using time blocks in planning the daily schedule, according to group interests and needs. Record the results and work out a schedule for three days.
5. Make file cards for five new transitional activities. Discuss when and how you would use them, and implement one of them. (The trainer can observe.)
6. Divide the class into small groups with activities for each, using ideas from the chapter and based on previous planning with the classroom staff. (The trainer can observe.)
7. Observe a child, using the Child Involvement Checklist. Summarize and interpret the results and make up a Learning Prescription for the child.
8. Continue your Portfolio of evidence of your skills. Add one piece of evidence for each of the following Teacher Skills Checklist items:
   a. Uses a team approach to plan a flexible classroom schedule.
   b. Uses transitions and small group activities to accomplish the goals of the program.
   c. Plans for individual needs based on child observation and interpretation of data obtained.
   Evidence should reflect what you, not another staff member, have done.
9. Complete the Chapter 12 Evaluation Sheet and return it and the answers to Question Sheets 12-A and 12-B to the appropriate college or program official.

QUESTION SHEET 12-A

(Based on Chapter 12, "Providing Program Management")

1. What do you need to know to plan your daily program effectively?
2. What should be the roles of the various staff members during the planning process?
3. What do you need to know about your children to plan for their arrival?
4. What are time blocks and for what purpose are they used?
5. Should you have a rest time in the morning? How can you decide?
6. What is the purpose of a total group activity such as "circle time"?
7. What are transitions and how can they be used?
8. Why should small groups be set up for most classroom activities?
9. How should the staff members work with the groups they have set up?
10. How can you plan for an individual child with special needs?

QUESTION SHEET 12-B

(Based on Mediapak B, "Managing the Daily Program")

1. Why is balance important in planning the daily program?
2. What kinds of balance are apparent in this particular classroom?
3. How does the room setup facilitate managing the children?
4. How is the work/play time block in this particular program different from arrival?
5. How is the length of the work/play time block determined?
6. How is the transition from work/play to snack handled in this classroom?
7. How is the transition from wash up to lunch handled?
8. What happens to nonsleeping children during nap time?
9. How is the afternoon work/play time different from work/play in the morning?
10. How can you tell if you have planned your daily program successfully?

SUGGESTED EVIDENCE FOR PORTFOLIO

1. Describe how you organize the groups of children in your center and how this shows your competence in program management.
2. Describe the responsibilities that team members have in your center, how these are decided, and how this contributes to your competence in program management.
3. Photograph a transitional activity you have led and describe how this helps children move effectively from one activity to another.
4. Make an audiotape of a planning session and write a description of your participation and its results.
5. Include a Child Involvement Checklist and Learning Prescription you have done with a child and write up the results.

Each piece of evidence should be accompanied by a write-up explaining how this shows your competence in the area of **Program Management** and how the activity is developmentally appropriate for your children.

SUGGESTED READINGS

Beaty, Janice J. *Observing Development of the Young Child.* Columbus, Ohio: Merrill Publishing Co., 1986.

Brown, Janet F., ed. *Administering Programs for Young Children.* Washington, D.C.: National Association for the Education of Young Children, 1984.

Caruso, Joseph J., and M. Temple Fawcett. *Supervision in Early Childhood Education.* New York: Teachers College Press, 1986.

Cromwell, Liz, and Dixie Hibner. *Finger Frolics.* Livonia, Mich.: Partner Press, 1976.

Glazer, Tom. *Eye Winker Tom Tinker Chin Chopper.* Garden City, N.Y.: Doubleday, 1973.

Hewes, Dorothy W., ed. *Administration: Making Programs Work for Children and Families.* Washington, D.C.: National Association for the Education of Young Children, 1979.

Strom, Sherry. *The Human Side of Child Care Administration.* Washington, D.C.: National Association for the Education of Young Children, 1985.

SOUND FILMSTRIPS

Beaty, Janice J. "Managing the Daily Program," Mediapak B, *Skills for Preschool Teachers.* Elmira, N.Y.: McGraw Bookstore, Elmira College, 1979.

CHAPTER 12 EVALUATION SHEET
PROVIDING PROGRAM MANAGEMENT

1. Student_____

2. Trainer_____

3. Center where training occurred_____

4. Beginning date_____ Ending date_____

5. Describe what student did to accomplish General Objective

   _____

   _____

6. Describe what student did to accomplish Specific Objectives

   Objective 1_____

   _____

   Objective 2_____

   _____

   Objective 3_____

   _____

7. Evaluation of student's Learning Activities
   (Trainer Check One)   (Student Check One)

   _____ Highly superior performance   _____

   _____ Superior performance   _____

   _____ Good performance   _____

   _____ Less than adequate performance _____

Signature of Trainer: Signature of Student:

_____   _____

Comments:

13 Promoting Professionalism

General Objective

To continue professional growth as a teacher of young children.

Specific Objectives

- ☐ Puts children and families first.
- ☐ Treats information about children and families confidentially.
- ☐ Takes every opportunity to improve professional growth.

W hat is a "professional" in the early childhood field, and what behaviors are exhibited that make a person a professional? Whether you are a college student, a teacher's aide, a parent volunteer, a CDA candidate, or a teacher, this is an important question for you to consider carefully. What *does* make one a professional in this particular field? What will be expected of you that is different from what you are already doing? Although there may be several answers to this question, most "early childhood professionals" themselves agree that to be a professional in the field of early childhood you must:

1. Make a commitment to the field
2. Behave in an ethical manner
3. Have a knowledge base in the field
4. Have completed some type of training
5. Have completed some type of service

PUTS CHILDREN AND FAMILIES FIRST

The commitment an early childhood professional makes is an important one. Ours is a helping profession, which means that we must put our clients, the children and families we serve, first in our professional lives. Translated into practical terms, it means that we may have to come in early and stay late to make sure that classes are covered and children are served; that we may have to take children home if the bus breaks down or a parent fails to come; that we may miss coffee breaks or even lunch if there is a classroom problem that needs our attention; that we may have to spend many hours at home preparing activities for the following day.

In other words, we must put ourselves and our own needs second when it comes to our professional lives. A professional commitment in any of the helping professions requires us to give of ourselves without expecting to be paid for every hour we contribute. It is also a commitment of time and energy. We may have to work extra hours or even come in when we are not feeling up to par because a particular situation demands it of us.

This behavior is often quite different from that of the paraprofessional or nonprofessional. Often people paid on an hourly basis look at their work on the basis of the hours they put in. They are often reluctant to respond to demands made on them outside of their normal working hours. The professional, on the other hand, must take a broader view of program demands, and be willing to sacrifice time and energy if the need arises. It is a giving of oneself without expecting a particular reward that marks the true professional in fields such as early childhood.

In addition to putting children and their families first, a professional also demonstrates a positive attitude toward them at all times. No matter what the family background, no matter how serious the problems faced by the family, no matter what the past behavior of the child and family, a true professional retains an objective view of the situation and treats the child and family in a positive manner.

TREATS INFORMATION ABOUT CHILDREN AND FAMILIES CONFIDENTIALLY

A second important area of professionalism in early childhood education is that of ethical behavior, including treating information about children and families confidentially.

As a preschool teacher, you are probably very much a "people person." You are probably interested in every aspect of the children and their families. Your position allows you to find out all kinds of information about them. You'll know good things and bad: health problems, family problems, promotions, firings, new babies, new husbands, gossip.

But your position as a professional child care worker requires that you not discuss any of this information with anyone other than the person involved or another professional who might give help. You do not, for instance, talk about children or their families with another parent. You do not even discuss your children or their families among other teachers in your center as an item of gossip.

If you hear other teachers doing this, you should not join in, but remind them as tactfully as possible that this kind of information is confidential. If parents ply you with gossip about other parents or children, let them know in a diplomatic way that you cannot listen to such information.

You should not talk with parents about their children when the children are present. These conversations are confidential and can be damaging to a child's self-concept. If parents start talking to you about their child while the child is standing there, tell them you prefer to talk at another time or that perhaps the child can play in another room while you chat.

Parents who understand how professionally you treat information about them and others are bound to respect both you and your program.

TAKES EVERY OPPORTUNITY TO IMPROVE PROFESSIONAL GROWTH

The true professional strives to improve his or her performance and therefore seeks out growth and learning opportunities by reading new books and journal articles about children, viewing films, attending workshops, conferences, inservice training, and college courses. He or she joins professional organizations such as the National Association for the Education of Young Children (NAEYC), 1834 Connecticut Ave., N.W., Washington, D.C. 20009, or its local chapter, or other early childhood organizations and participates in their activities.

The National Association for the Education of Young Children sponsors a large national conference held annually in a major U.S. city. The conference offers the early childhood professional a wide variety of workshop topics and speakers who discuss everything from the latest early childhood research to the most effective curriculum materials. It is an unparalleled opportunity to meet other professionals in the field as well as authors of early childhood textbooks and respected persons in the field.

Membership in the organization includes a subscription to an early childhood journal, with articles that discuss the latest ideas, findings, and issues in the field.

Knowledge Base in the Field of Early Childhood

Professionals in every field must have a familiarity and understanding of the knowledge upon which the field is founded. In early childhood this includes familiarity with the principal contributors to early childhood education such as Rousseau, Pestalozzi, and Froebel from the eighteenth and nineteenth centuries, Montessori from the early twentieth century; the contributions from the field of psychology of Freud, Gesell, Erikson, Piaget, Skinner; the kindergarten and nursery school movement in the United States at the turn of the century; the day care movement given impetus during World War II; and Head Start and the compensatory education movement born during the War on Poverty of the 1960s.

In addition, professionals in the field must have a knowledge of child development; need an understanding of conflicting development theories such as the maturationist, the behaviorist, and the cognitive/interactionist points of view; should be familiar with learning theories as applied to young children so that they can help to design a developmentally appropriate curriculum for their own children; should be aware of various curriculum models of early childhood as well as the ongoing research supporting them. It is a never-ending task to keep up with developments in this new and growing field. A true professional makes the effort to acquire this knowledge by taking college courses and workshops, reading textbooks and journal articles about the field, inviting knowledgeable guest speakers to their programs, attending conferences where such knowledge is disseminated, and visiting early childhood programs that feature particular curriculum models.

Training Opportunities

To keep up with the latest information in the early childhood field, you should make training an ongoing part of your life. Like Head Start, many programs have inservice training built into their schedules. The year begins with a preservice workshop for all teachers and aides and continues with on-site or regional workshops in the various component areas such as curriculum, nutrition, health, mental health, and parent involvement.

Two-year and four-year colleges also offer courses and workshops in early childhood education. If your local college does not, you might approach someone at the college with the idea of offering workshops in early childhood education. Hospitals are often willing to sponsor early childhood parent training programs, as are agencies such as Cooperative Extension.

Becoming a CDA (Child Development Associate)

In addition to the traditional modes of training for early childhood educators there is another increasingly popular method for developing the necessary competence in the field: Child Development Associate (CDA) training, assessment, and credentialing. CDA training is competency-based and performance-based, which means that a certain percentage of the training must occur in the early childhood classroom (this often varies from 50 percent to 100 percent) and that the trainee must demonstrate competence with children in such a setting.

It is tailored to the individual based on an initial assessment of the trainee's needs (see "Initial Assessment"). Once an initial assessment is completed, an individualized training prescription is developed by the trainee and the trainer based on the needs that surfaced during the initial assessment and conference. Then the trainee proceeds through the training, eventually demonstrating by his or her performance in the early childhood classroom that competence has been achieved in the thirteen prescribed CDA Functional Areas.

In the CDA training provided by colleges and universities, successful trainees receive college credit in addition to the CDA Credential. On the other hand, some CDA training is carried out by early childhood program educational coordinators who work with their own teachers and aides. Once trainees have successfully completed training and final assessment they are awarded just the CDA Credential.

This textbook is designed to be used in CDA training programs either by individuals who prefer the self-taught module approach (see "Introduction"), or by colleges or training programs who prefer the group or class approach. The Teacher Skills Checklist can be used by any CDA trainee and trainer as an initial assessment tool. Then a Training Prescription can be developed for the trainee to follow as he or she proceeds through CDA training. Each chapter of this book represents one of the thirteen CDA Functional Areas:

Safe
Healthy
Learning Environment
Physical
Cognitive
Communication
Creative
Self

Social
Guidance
Families
Program Management
Professionalism

A CDA is defined as "a person who is able to meet the specific needs of children and who, with parents and other adults, works to nurture children's physical, social, emotional, and intellectual growth in a child development framework. The CDA Credential is awarded to child care providers and home visitors who have demonstrated their skill in working with young children and their families by successfully completing the CDA assessment process" (CDA National Credentialing Program, 1986, p. 2).

The CDA approach is a threefold one, involving training, assessment, and credentialing. The training is based on the CDA Competency Standards developed and refined by the CDA National Credentialing Program which is operated by the Council for Early Childhood Professional Recognition of the National Association for the Education of Young Children. Training is "conducted by more than 300 colleges and universities around the country as well as many day care programs, independent consultants and Head Start centers. Funding and administration of these programs is independent of the CDA National Credentialing Program" (CDA National Credentialing Program, 1986, p. 1).

CDA training is not a requirement for final assessment. Those candidates who feel they are already competent, and who have completed the required number of hours working in an early childhood classroom, may apply for CDA final assessment. Just as all candidates for final assessment, they must collect evidence of their competence by assembling a CDA Portfolio with at least three pieces of evidence for each of the thirteen CDA Functional Areas. (See Suggested Evidence for Portfolio at the end of each chapter.)

They must have a trainer/advisor who has observed and recorded evidence of their competence in the thirteen Functional Areas as well as a Parent-Community Representative who has not only observed and recorded but has also distributed and collected parent questionnaires evaluating the candidate's classroom skills. Then, like all candidates for CDA final assessment, they must send in their Readiness Form along with the appropriate fee. They will then be assigned a CDA Representative who will assemble the Local Assessment Team (LAT) and conduct the assessment. Upon successful completion of this process and payment of all fees, the candidate will be issued a CDA Credential from the National Credentialing Program.

According to the National Credentialing Program, "assessment is available to caregivers working in several settings—center-based programs serving infants, toddlers, and preschool children; family day care programs; and home visitor programs. An optional bilingual specialization is available to candidates working in Spanish/English programs. A CDA Credential is awarded to a person who demonstrates competence in caring for young children by successfully completing the CDA assessment process" (CDA National Credentialing Program, 1986, p. 1).

Why Become a CDA?

Why should you become a CDA? First, it will help you in your work as a classroom teacher or aide. It will help you improve your skills in working with young children and their families; in setting up an appropriate physical environment; in keeping your children safe and healthy; in providing opportunities for them to improve their physical, cognitive, language, and creative development; and in planning activities and managing individuals and groups.

It will also help you assess your strengths and the areas that need strengthening, so you will be able to make the necessary improvements. You will do this not only through your self-evaluation, but also through the eyes of a CDA Advisor whom you will come to know as a friend, a Parent-Community Representative who will become another staunch supporter, and a CDA Representative assigned by the National Credentialing Program.

Receiving the CDA Credential will elevate your status in your program. In some instances, you may receive a promotion or a raise. This credential may be worth college credit at certain institutions. Since the CDA is a national credential, your talents will also be more marketable in other states if you move.

Finally, it will induct you as a professional into the field of early childhood education. Some professions require a bachelor's or master's degree for entry; the early childhood field is coming more and more to recognize the CDA as the first professional step in an ever expanding career.

The CDA Credential is not a certificate based on courses or credits. Instead, it certifies that you are competent in the skill areas mentioned and that you have demonstrated this competence with children in a classroom.

Because the CDA training, assessment, and credentialing system is at present going through a transitional period of changes and refinements, interested persons should write to the Council for Early Childhood Professional Recognition (1718 Connecticut Avenue N.W., Washington, D.C. 20009) for the latest information regarding CDA. Upon making application and submitting the application fee, you will receive a packet of information regarding competency standards for your choice of setting as well as information on how to assemble the CDA Portfolio.

Local Clubs

Many communities have a local branch of the Association for the Education of Young Children. If yours does not, consider starting such a group and inviting local specialists to speak or show films on topics of interest to the participants. You might be surprised at the extent of your resources. Most state and local library systems have free films available for use by clubs. They may be able to supply you with a projector and films on child development, health, parenting, or children's books to get you started. You could personally present a program to such a club about your experience of going through the CDA assessment or your training program. Other programs might feature a pediatrician, a nutritionist, a children's librarian, or a school psychologist discussing such topics as children with handicapping conditions, child abuse, health and nutrition, discipline, children's books, or whatever the membership decides.

If you or your program cannot afford to subscribe to early childhood journals, try to interest your local library in subscribing. They may be willing if they feel the general public will benefit.

Club members might be private nursery school teachers and aides, family day care mothers, Head Start personnel, kindergarten teachers, classroom personnel from programs such as United Cerebral Palsy and the Association for Retarded Children, and community day care and health care personnel.

Your imagination is the only limit to the professional growth opportunities you can find or make for yourself.

SUMMARY

In order to become a professional in the early childhood field you must first make a commitment to the field by putting children and families first in your professional life. This often means sacrificing time and energy to make sure children and families are served by your program as they should be. It may mean coming in to the program early and leaving late. It also means providing services yourself when no one else is available.

A professional also treats information about children and families confidentially. When parents or staff members begin gossiping about children, a professional should not participate and should help others to understand why this behavior cannot be condoned.

To continue your professional growth as a teacher of young children you should also take every opportunity to gain knowledge and skills in the field. One of the best methods for acquiring competence in the field is by becoming a CDA (Child Development Associate). This training, assessment, and credentialing program requires trainees to perform competently in an early childhood classroom setting in thirteen Functional Areas. The trainee must assemble a Portfolio of competence in these areas, must be observed by a trainer/advisor selected by the trainee, must have a Parent-Community Representative to collect data from parents on his or her competence, and finally must go through a final assessment process led by a CDA Representative who has been assigned by the National Credentialing Program.

LEARNING ACTIVITIES

1. Read Chapter 13, "Promoting Professionalism," and answer Question Sheet 13-A.
2. Read one or more of the Suggested Readings. Add ten cards to your file with specific ideas for improving your professional outlook or that of others. Include a reference source on each card.
3. Make an assessment of another early childhood teacher or aide using the Teacher Skills Checklist. Summarize the results and discuss them with him or her.

4. Make a self-assessment using the Teacher Skills Checklist; discuss the results with your trainer after you complete Activity #5.
5. Have your trainer assess you using the Teacher Skills Checklist. Discuss the results after you complete the self-assessment.
6. Make a list of organizations or agencies in your community (or county) that are concerned with young children. Attend one of their meetings and write a summary of it.
7. Subscribe to or obtain a copy of an early childhood journal, magazine, or newsletter and write a summary of interesting ideas from the first issue you receive.
8. Continue your Portfolio of evidence of your skills. Add one piece of evidence for each of the following Teacher Skills Checklist items:
   a. Puts children and families first.
   b. Treats information about children and families confidentially.
   c. Takes every opportunity to continue own professional growth.
9. Complete the Chapter 13 Evaluation Sheet and return it and the answers to Question Sheet 13-A to the appropriate college or program official.

QUESTION SHEET 13-A

(Based on Chapter 13, "Promoting Professionalism")

1. What does it mean to be a professional in the early childhood field?
2. What is the difference between a professional and a nonprofessional in the early childhood field?
3. What kinds of information about children and families must you treat confidentially? Why?
4. What should you do if a parent begins to talk to you about her child while the child is present?
5. What kinds of knowledge should a professional be familiar with in the early childhood field?
6. How is CDA training different from traditional early childhood training?
7. How is CDA training tailored to the individual trainee?
8. What must a trainee do to be ready for the final CDA assessment?
9. Why should you become a CDA?
10. What professional growth opportunities can a local early childhood club offer?

SUGGESTED EVIDENCE FOR PORTFOLIO

1. Include one of the Teacher Skills Checklists you have used along with a written explanation of the results and suggestions for future training for the teacher you observed.
2. Include a self-evaluation of your skills using this Checklist or another means and summarize the results and recommendations.
3. Make a list of the training activities you have participated in during the last two years and mention ideas you have gained for use with young children.

4. Make a list of early childhood books and journals you have read in the past year and discuss some of the useful ideas you gained from them.
5. Put on a program for parents or co-workers using a professional film or speaker, and write about the results.

Each piece of evidence should be accompanied by a write-up explaining how this shows your competence in the area of **Professionalism** and how the activity is developmentally appropriate for your children.

SUGGESTED READINGS

Berger, Eugenia Hepworth. *Parents as Partners in Education: The School and Home Working Together*, 2nd ed. Columbus, Ohio: Merrill Publishing Co., 1987.

CDA National Credentialing Program. *Child Development Associate Assessment System and Competency Standards*. Washington, D.C.: author, 1986.

Cleverley, John, and D.C. Phillips. *Visions of Childhood: Influential Models from Locke to Spock*. New York: Teachers College Press, 1986.

Feeney, Stephanie, Doris Christensen, and Eva Moravcik. *Who Am I in the Lives of Young Children? An Introduction to Teaching Young Children*, 3rd ed. Columbus, Ohio: Merrill Publishing Co., 1987.

Gordon, Ann Miles, and Kathryn Williams Browne. *Beginnings and Beyond: Foundations in Early Childhood Education*. Albany, N.Y.: Delmar, 1985.

Maples, Mary Klein. *Steps to C.D.A. for Home Visitors*. Elmira, N.Y.: McGraw Bookstore, Elmira College, 1985.

Roopnarine, Jaipaul, and James E. Johnson, eds. *Approaches to Early Childhood Education*. Columbus, Ohio: Merrill Publishing Co., 1987.

Spodek, Bernard, Olivia N. Saracho, and Michael D. Davis. *Foundations of Early Childhood Education*. Englewood Cliffs, N.J.: Prentice-Hall, 1987.

SOUND FILMSTRIPS

Beaty, Janice J. *CDA Portfolio*. Elmira, N.Y.: 3 to 5, P.O. Box 3213, 14905. (slides/tape) 1983.

CHAPTER 13 EVALUATION SHEET
PROMOTING PROFESSIONALISM

1. Student_____

2. Trainer_____

3. Center where training occurred_____

4. Beginning date_____ Ending date_____

5. Describe what student did to accomplish General Objective

   _____

   _____

6. Describe what student did to accomplish Specific Objectives

   Objective 1_____

   _____

   Objective 2_____

   _____

   Objective 3_____

   _____

7. Evaluation of student's Learning Activities
   (Trainer Check One)   (Student Check One)

   _____ Highly superior performance   _____

   _____ Superior performance   _____

   _____ Good performance   _____

   _____ Less than adequate performance _____

Signature of Trainer: Signature of Student:

_____   _____

Comments:

INDEX